LAND OWNERSHIP MAPS

A Checklist of Nineteenth Century United States County Maps
in the Library of Congress

Compiled by Richard W. Stephenson
Geography and Map Division, Reference Department

THE ODOMETER.

Library of Congress • Washington : 1967

Heritage Books
2023

HERITAGE BOOKS
AN IMPRINT OF HERITAGE BOOKS, INC.

Books, CDs, and more—Worldwide

For our listing of thousands of titles see our website
at
www.HeritageBooks.com

Published 2023 by
HERITAGE BOOKS, INC.
Publishing Division
5810 Ruatan Street
Berwyn Heights, MD 20740

Originally published by the Library of Congress 1967

L.C. Card: 67-60091

All rights reserved. No part of this book may be reproduced or transmitted in any form or by any means, electronic or mechanical, including photocopying, recording or by any information storage and retrieval system without written permission from the author, except for the inclusion of brief quotations in a review.

International Standard Book Number
Paperbound: 978-0-7884-3788-5

PREFACE

This checklist records 1,449 United States county land ownership maps in the Geography and Map Division, Library of Congress. Included are manuscript and printed maps, as well as photocopies of originals in other repositories. The list is accompanied by an essay tracing the historical development of the county land ownership map and a general index to county names, cartographers, surveyors, and publishers.

Most of the maps cover an entire county or a major part of one; a few embrace several counties. The arrangement is alphabetical-chronological within each State. As maps that include more than one county are listed only under the name of the first county mentioned in the title, users are advised to consult the general index to locate all pertinent maps of a particular county. The majority of maps described in this checklist give names of many residents, but some, especially the early county maps of Virginia and Pennsylvania, name only a few.

The five columns of the checklist include, respectively: 1) entry number; 2) county name and date; 3) author and/or surveyor; 4) publisher and, if noted on the map, the place of publication; and 5) natural scale and map size. Authors', surveyors', and publishers' names are given as they appear on the maps, except that the words "and" and "Company" are consistently abbreviated "&" and "Co." The scale is stated as a ratio and the size in inches. The last column indicates the number of parts or sheets in the Library's file copy. Unless otherwise noted in this column, the item recorded is a printed map.

Black-and-white photoreproductions of most of the maps cited in this checklist may be purchased from the Photoduplication Service, Library of Congress, Washington, D. C., 20540. Requests for cost estimates or purchase orders should refer to this publication by title and give the entry numbers of desired maps.

The Library of Congress has a very large but not entirely complete collection of 19th-century county land ownership maps. The nucleus of the collection consists of maps received by copyright deposit, but the files have also been enriched by transfers from other Federal agencies, purchases, donations, and photocopies of originals in other libraries. The Geography and Map Division is interested in securing originals or photocopies of maps not already in its collection and will welcome information which may lead to such acquisitions.

                                            Richard W. Stephenson

March 1967

TABLE OF CONTENTS

Preface iii

Introduction vii

Checklist 1

Index 75

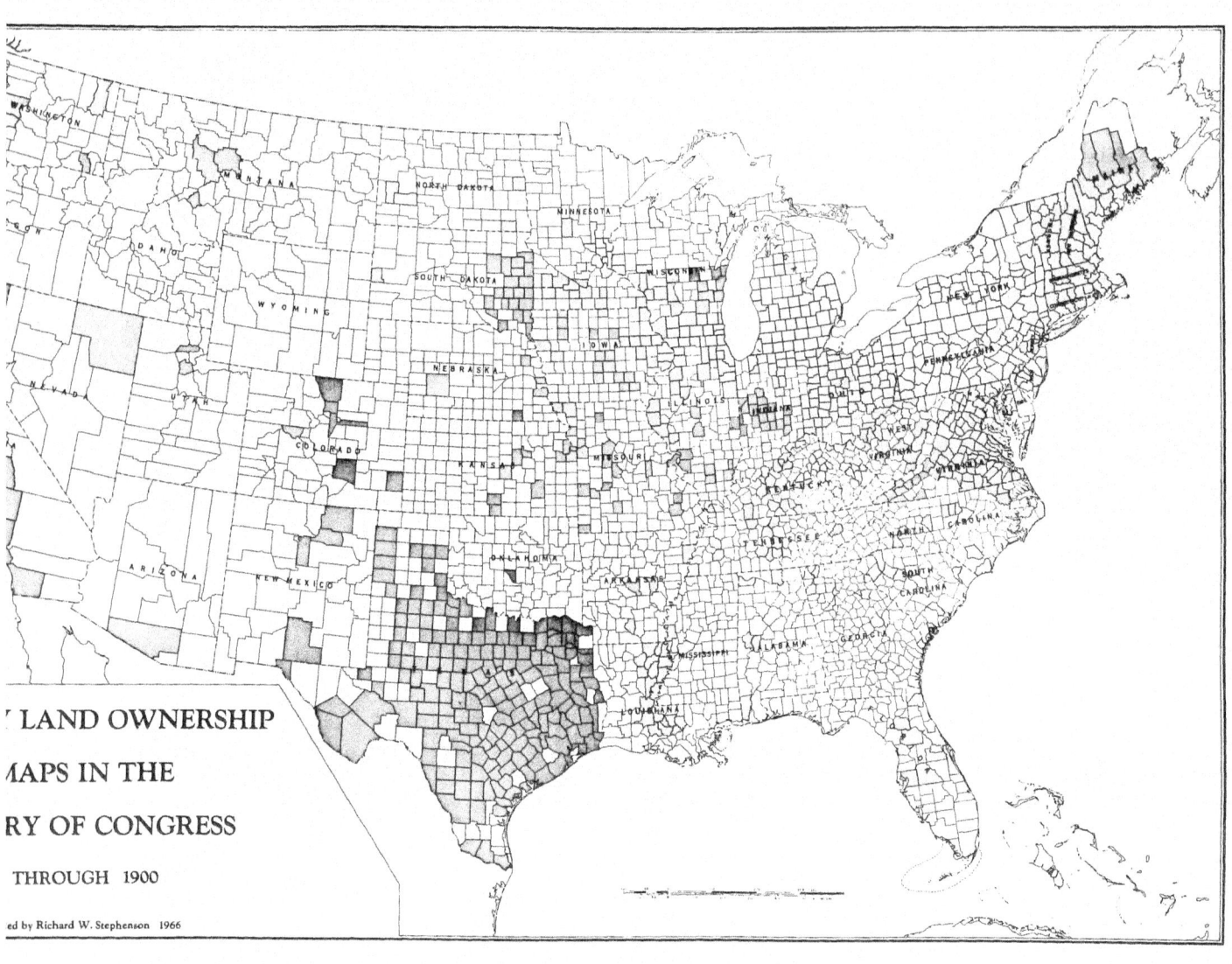

Plate 1. Counties covered by land ownership maps are shaded gray.

INTRODUCTION

Nineteenth-century land ownership maps of United States counties are among the more significant groups of Americana in the map collections of the Library of Congress. These maps are especially important because they predate the more publicized county platbook and the topographic surveys of the U.S. Geological Survey. Today, county land ownership maps are invaluable to the genealogist in tracing family backgrounds, to the geographer for studying the rural landscape of a century ago, and to the local historian in reconstructing the cultural life of the mid-eighteen hundreds.

County maps were included in A List of Maps of America in the Library of Congress, published in 1901. This out-of-print bibliography provides an inadequate approach to county maps because of the large number that have been added to the Library's collections during the past half century. The Library's holdings of pre-20th-century land ownership maps include 1,449 county maps relating to 1,041 counties concentrated mainly in the Northeast and North Central States, and in Virginia, California, and Texas. Approximately one-third of all United States counties are represented in the collection.

Of the county maps in the Library, only 7 percent were made by 1840. Most of these are of counties in Pennsylvania and Virginia, where legislative acts in both States in 1816 stimulated county map preparation.

About 24 percent of the county maps in the checklist were published between 1841 and 1860. Virtually all counties in the Northeastern States, parts of Ohio and southern Michigan, as well as scattered counties in Indiana, Illinois, Wisconsin, and Iowa, were mapped before 1860. In the South, maps showing plantations were made of counties along the Mississippi River. Some 327 maps were produced between 1851 and 1860, more than in any other single decade of the 19th century.

Maps prepared between 1861 and 1880 are primarily of counties in Virginia, Texas, Pennsylvania, and the North Central States. Few are of counties in New England. Although 38 percent of the maps on file were issued during these two decades, the period is characterized by the decline of the commercially published map. Nearly half of the county mapping in this period was of an official nature carried out by Confederate engineers during the Civil War, and by the Texas General Land Office, which initiated an extensive mapping program in 1879.

Maps made between 1881 and 1900, approximately 30 percent of the Library's holdings, are of widely dispersed counties, except for some concentration in California, eastern South Dakota, and Texas. The Texas General Land Office, which continued its cadastral surveys, accounted for about 27 percent of all county maps made during this period.

County maps vary in scale from 1:3,960 to 1:600,000. Of the 1,373 maps which have determinable scales, 1,050, or 76 percent, were published at scales larger than 1:100,000. Commercial publishers preferred scales ranging from 1:31,680 to approximately 1:65,000 with the most popular being 1:42,240 (1-1/2 inches per mile) and 1:63,360 (1 inch per mile). Government-issued county maps were on smaller and more uniform scales. Maps of Virginia counties prepared by Confederate engineers, for example, are at the scale of 1:80,000 while those prepared by the Texas General Land Office in the 1870's and 1880's are at 1:133,320 (1 inch per 4,000 varas) and in the 1890's at 1:66,660 (1 inch per 2,000 varas).

Cadastral maps represent one of the earliest forms of cartographic expression. Babylonians, more than 2,000 years before Christ, mapped individual land holdings on clay tablets, and the ancient Egyptians made cadastral maps of the Nile Valley. It has been reported that Ramses II began a cadastral survey of Egypt in the 13th century B.C., and it is reasonable to assume that the surveys were recorded on maps. The Egyptians drew their maps on papyrus and, unfortunately, few have survived the ravages of time.

Cadastral surveys of small parcels of land made in Europe in the Middle Ages were usually recorded in descriptive text rather than on maps. Not until the Renaissance were surveys of individual European estates frequently depicted cartographically. By the 18th century, English mapmakers were publishing maps of entire counties locating houses and naming residents.

Some of the earliest American maps were small land plats based on cadastral surveys. Land surveying was an honorable and reasonably profitable occupation in the colonies in the 18th century. Surveyors were in demand to delineate boundaries of newly settled tracts of land, and many prominent individuals actively engaged in this profession. George Washington, a licensed surveyor in Virginia, "surveyed in the course of his life more than 200 tracts, containing upwards of 66,000 acres of land."[1]

Lt. John Hills' maps of Somerset and Middlesex Counties, N. J., may be the earliest cadastral maps covering entire counties in the North American Colonies. Hills, a British Army officer, based his maps on surveys made in 1766 of Somerset County by Benjamin Morgan and Middlesex County by Az. Dunham. Drawn in pen and ink, the maps are among the Sir Henry Clinton papers in the William L. Clements Library, Ann Arbor, Mich.[2] They are somewhat distinctive, for few 18th-century county maps show land ownership. Sketch maps of the principal routes of travel, prepared by military engineers during the Revolutionary and French and Indian Wars, however, frequently locate rural dwellings and give names of residents.

Published county land ownership maps were not introduced in America until the first decade of the 19th century when Charles Varlé, a geographer and engineer, produced two printed maps of counties in Maryland and Virginia. Varlé's "A Map of Frederick and Washington Counties, State of Maryland" was published in 1808, and his "Map of Frederick, Berkeley, & Jefferson Counties in the State of Virginia" (see plate 2) appeared in the following year.[3] Both were engraved in Philadelphia, the first by Francis Shallus and the second by Benjamin Jones. The maps are similar in content and execution, both denoting county boundaries, roads, towns, churches, taverns, saw and grist mills, rural residents, and drainage. Principal mountain ridges and gaps are indicated by hachures. Varlé used stylized drawings of double-chimneyed, two-story houses for rural residences. This is reminiscent of 18th-century English county maps on which "Gentlemen's seats" were sometimes identified by illustrations of houses. A geographical discourse, published by Varlé in 1810, supplements his map of the Virginia counties.[4]

By the beginning of the 19th century, it was evident that existing State maps were inadequate for the needs of a rapidly developing young country, and that commercial publishers alone could not meet the demands. Various States, therefore, enacted legislation calling for the preparation of official State maps based on new county surveys. This trend did much to stimulate the compilation and publication of county maps.

One of the early proponents of State-subsidized maps was the Philadelphia geographer and mapmaker John Melish,[5] who recommended to a committee of the Pennsylvania Legislature that the Commonwealth sponsor a scientifically constructed map. "After a short interview, the plan of the map was matured and brought before the legislature. With some slight modifications, it passed both houses by great majorities, and, receiving the governor's assent, became a law [on March 19, 1816]."[6] The act directed the Secretary of the Commonwealth and the Surveyor General to "contract with the deputy surveyors respectively, or with any other suitable person, or persons ... for the formation of a map of each of the counties within this commonwealth; which maps shall be on a scale of two miles and a half to an inch."[7] The information thus obtained was to be used in constructing a map of the entire State at 5 miles to the inch. County surveyors provided the maps as ordered, and in 1822 the official map of the State was published under the direction of John Melish. It was well received, and revised editions were published in 1824, 1826, and 1832.

To assist persons interested in preparing county maps, Melish published the following "Directions for Constructing the County Maps, in Terms of the Act of Assembly."[8]

> 1st. Ascertain, as near as possible, the latitude of the seat of justice, and its longitude from Washington; and run a true meridian line, and an east and west line through it, as in the specimen.
> 2d. Set off from these lines the limits of the county, on a scale of two miles and a half to an inch: taking care to ascertain the proportion that the latitude bears to the longitude in the county to be exhibited.
> 3d. Delineate the border exactly on the model exhibited in the specimen, and graduate the scale on the inner margin in miles of latitude and longitude.
> 4th. Having made these preparations, insert with geographical accuracy, the following particulars:
> 1. The county and township lines.
> 2. The rivers, lakes, and principal water courses; locate exactly the sources of the navigable waters, and designate by appropriate marks the head of boat and canoe navigation.
> 3. The mountains and valleys.
> 4. The minerals and mineral springs.
> 5. The cities, towns, villages, and post-offices.
> 6. The state roads, post roads, and principal county roads. The distances to be marked in miles along the principal roads.
> 7. The most remarkable public buildings, churches, mills, and manufactories.
> 8. The principal bridges and canals.

Although the specifications did not call for the inclusion of cadastral information, 23 of the 44 original manuscript county maps now preserved in the Pennsylvania Department of Internal Affairs at Harrisburg do include names of some residents.

As early as 1816, Melish noted his desire to publish the individual county maps "on the large scale on which they are originally delineated, provided there be a sufficient number of subscribers to

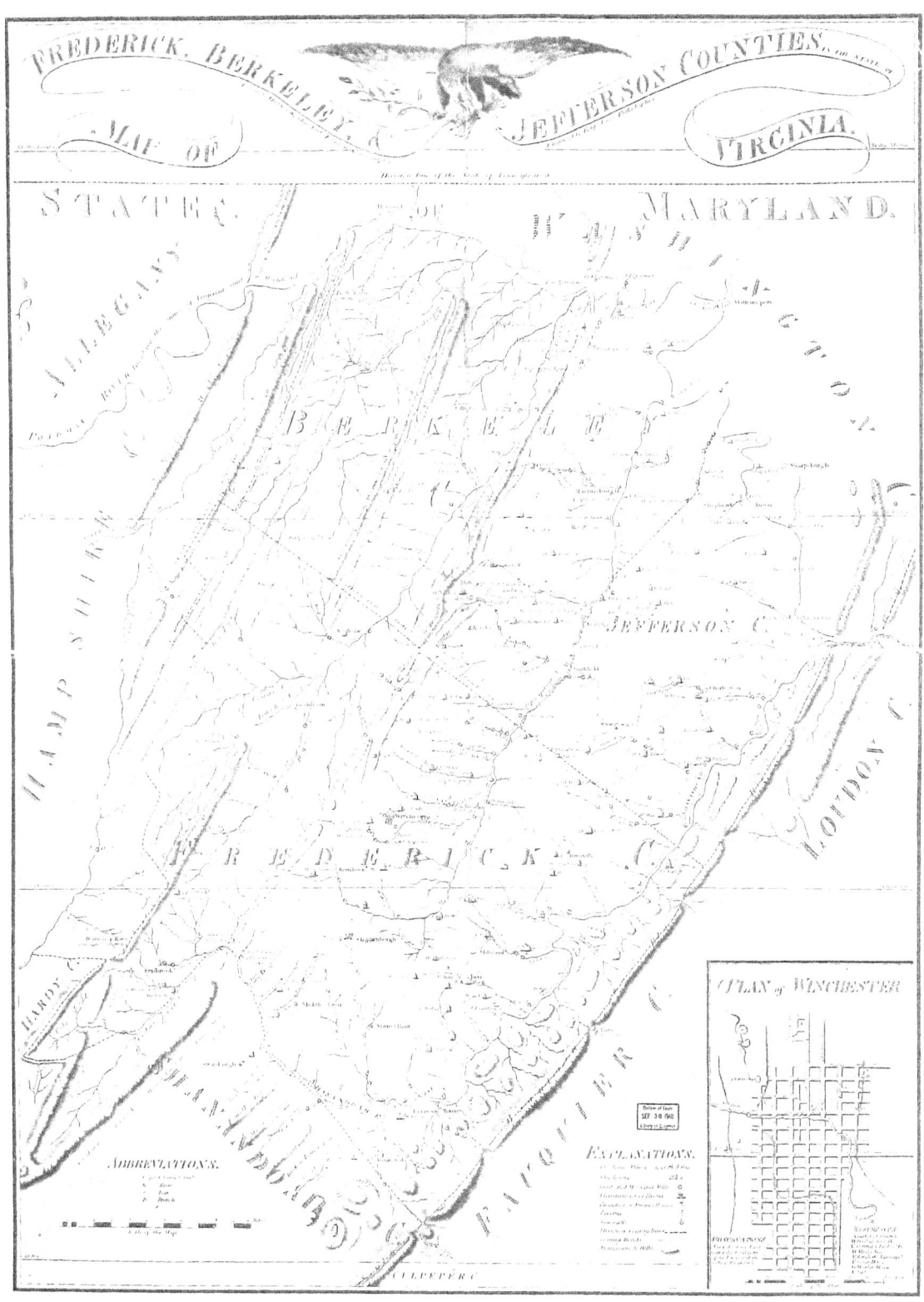

Plate 2. One of the first printed U.S. county maps to show land ownership.

defray the expense."[9] Unfortunately, only a few of these maps were issued before his death on December 30, 1822.

In Virginia, as in Pennsylvania, legislative action stimulated the preparation of county maps. The Virginia Legislature passed an act on February 27, 1816, which authorized compilation of a State-subsidized map. This law required each county "within twelve months after the passage of this Act to contract with some fit person or persons for making an accurate chart of their respective counties."[10] One copy of the county map "shall be delivered ... to the Clerk of the Court of the county, to be by him carefully preserved for the use of his county, and the other [copy] forwarded to the executive, to be deposited among the archives of the Commonwealth."[11] Many of the county maps authorized by this legislation were prepared by the schoolteacher and mathematician, John Wood. After Wood's death in May 1822, Herman Böÿe was hired to complete the remaining county surveys and to prepare for publication the map of the entire State. Böÿe's manuscript map, at the scale of 5 miles to 1 inch, was sent to Philadelphia for engraving by Henry S. Tanner. John Tyler, Governor of Virginia, copyrighted it on April 14, 1826, and in August 1827 the finished map, engraved on 9 plates, was placed on public sale for $20 a copy. The separate county maps were never published, but at least 42 manuscripts have survived; 37 are in the Virginia State Library, Richmond, and 5 are in the National Archives, Washington, D. C. The names of a few residents are included on 39 of these maps.[12]

Philadelphia, a leading center for printing and publishing from colonial days, became a major county map publishing center in the 19th century. The accompanying checklist testifies to this dominance. Two hundred and forty-two maps, 38 percent of those which indicate the place of publication, were published in Philadelphia, while New York, its closest rival, produced only 92 maps in the same period. Approximately 50 percent of the maps produced in both cities were issued in the decade of the 1850's.

The first county land ownership map published in Philadelphia is probably Jason Torrey's "Map of Wayne & Pike Counties, Pennsylvania," copyrighted April 7, 1814. Torrey had intended to publish a map of Wayne County, but before the engraving was completed, Pike County was formed from Wayne on March 26, 1814. Fortunately, he was able to revise the engraving plate to show the change and in an advertisement dated March 30, 1814, announced that "He is now enabled to render the map complete for both counties."[13]

Torrey's method for depicting land ownership differs from that used by most 19th-century map publishers. He did not inscribe the names of land owners on the face of the map, but gave instead the boundaries of the tracts with the official number of each as recorded in the Office of the Wayne County Commissioner of Taxes. Torrey's map was accompanied by a 78-page pamphlet containing the names of land owners, property numbers corresponding with those found on the map, and the size of each tract.[14] The map was engraved by Henry S. Tanner of Philadelphia, who later became one of America's foremost publishers of commercial maps.[15]

In 1816 John Melish advertised Jason Torrey's map and pamphlet on page 168 of his <u>A Geographical Description of the United States</u> and commented that "This work is of peculiar importance to those holding lands in these counties, or who may want it as a model for a similar work." The map did not, however, set a pattern, because other publishers found it more convenient and less expensive to increase the map scale and record the names directly on the face of the map. Torrey's map apparently was not a bestseller, for in 1816 Melish offered it for $10;[16] in 1818, for $5;[17] and in 1822, for $3.[18]

A few commercial publishers did find Torrey's technique useful for avoiding clutter on small-scale maps. Forty-two years later, his system was used again in Pike County when John T. Cross compiled a new county map. Cross commented, in the preface to the pamphlet that accompanied his map, that "Torrey's Map of Wayne and Pike Counties, published as early as 1814, is the only map extant professing to show the location of the original surveys embraced within the present limits of the County of Pike," and added that "The numbers upon Torrey's map ... have been preserved in every instance."[19]

A few cadastral maps were published in the early decades of the 19th century, but most county surveys remained in manuscript form in State archives or in official records in county courthouses. Not until the decade immediately before the Civil War did a market develop among the affluent rural residents in the Northeastern States and Ohio for published maps with sufficient detail to indicate locations of individual dwellings and names of occupants. The rapid growth of county map publishing between 1851 and 1860 is apparent in the cartographic collections of the Library of Congress, which include 327 county maps published during these years, but only 28 in the preceding decade. One man who contributed greatly to the mapping boom and helped make Philadelphia the center of the industry was Robert Pearsall Smith, son of the distinguished Librarian of the Library Company of Philadelphia, John Jay Smith. Robert Smith was involved in the preparation of county maps from about 1846 to 1864. His name, however, appears as publisher on only 7 of the county maps in the Library of Congress,[20] but behind the scenes he was instrumental in the manufacture of 100 or more land ownership maps issued under the names of other publishers. Evidence that Smith was involved in the preparation of these maps is found in the often obscure notes, on at least 82 maps, which identify him as copyright claimant.[21]

Perhaps the most skillful, and certainly one of the most

prolific, county mapmakers of the mid-19th century was Henry Francis Walling (1825-1888).[22] He began his mapmaking career in Providence, R. I., in partnership with the civil engineer Samuel Barrett Cushing. His first cadastral map, of the town of Northbridge, Mass., was published in 1848. Within the next several years he made some 30 maps of other towns and cities in that State. In 1850, in conjunction with O. Harkness and J. Hanson, Walling made his first cadastral map of an entire county, that of Newport County, R. I. The following year he compiled maps of the counties of Bristol and Providence, R. I., which were published by G. C. Brown of Providence. His initial success in the cadastral map field led him, in 1852, to establish his own business in Boston. He published maps of every county in Massachusetts, as well as of scattered counties in Alabama, Connecticut, Illinois, Indiana, Maine, New Hampshire, New Jersey, New York, Ohio, Pennsylvania, Rhode Island, Vermont, and Wisconsin. It was reported that in addition to "maps of over twenty states and provinces" and "one hundred cities and special localities," Walling produced maps of "two hundred and eighty counties."[23] The accompanying checklist records 68 of these county maps.

After the Civil War Walling abandoned county map publishing and concentrated for a time on the publication of State atlases. In 1870, after a long and successful career as a commercial mapmaker, he accepted a Government appointment with the U.S. Coast and Geodetic Survey. Subsequently, he was employed by the U.S. Geological Survey and served with that agency until his death in 1888.

In 1900 the Library of Congress obtained, by transfer from the U.S. Coast and Geodetic Survey, a unique collection of county maps by Walling and other 19th-century publishers. Many years before being transferred to the Library, the maps had been cut and mounted on sheets of paper measuring approximately 17 by 13 inches and bound into 44 volumes. The checklist describes 39 maps from this collection not found elsewhere in the Library's map files. This group of material is identified in the Geography and Map Division as the "Coast Survey Collection."

By the decade preceding the Civil War, the county map had begun to lose some of its cartographic individuality. The format had become somewhat stylized and invariably showed political boundaries, roads, railroads, villages, mills, manufactories, churches, schools, houses and names of residents, as well as rivers, streams, hills, and mountains. Each map usually had several enlarged inset plans of the principal villages, views of important public buildings, factories and farms, and occasionally, a portrait of a leading citizen. An elaborate title embellished the map, and the entire product was enclosed within an ornate border. Most maps were so large (between 5 and 6 feet square) that they were lithographed in about four parts and then mounted in one piece on cloth. Some were hand colored, with the map surface protected by a coat

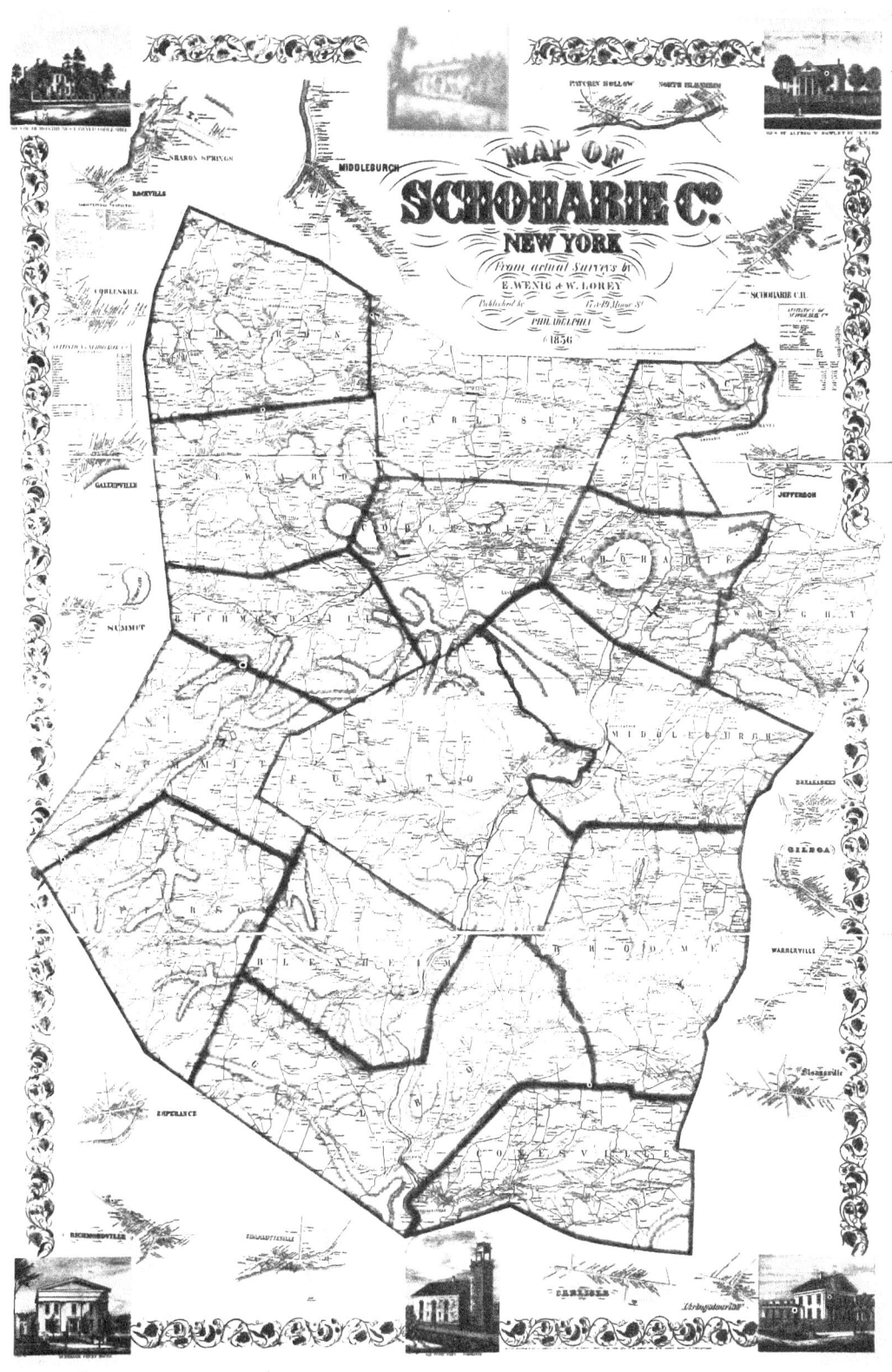

Plate 3. Typical county land ownership map of the mid-19th century.

Plate 4. A county mapper using an odometer. Reproduced from Bates Harrington, How 'Tis Done (Chicago, 1879).

of varnish. Wenig and Lorey's 1856 map of Schoharie County, N. Y. (plate 3), is representative of the commercial county map of that time. Although the mid-19th-century maps lost some of their distinctiveness, each contained a wealth of information not previously available in cartographic form. Before the Federal topographic mapping program was established under the direction of the U.S. Geological Survey, the county cadastral maps filled a real cartographic need.

Insets, containing enlarged plans of villages and views of important buildings, were introduced very early on American county maps. Charles Varlé included insets of "Hagers Town" and "Frederick Town" on his 1808 map of Frederick and Washington Counties, Md., and a street plan of Winchester is an inset on his map of Frederick, Berkeley, and Jefferson Counties, Va., which was published the following year (see plate 2). The first oblique or panoramic view on a published county map may be "South West View of the Bridge over the Schuylkill at Reading," which appears on Henry M. Richards' Map of Berks County, Pa., printed about 1820.

The inclusion of such a variety and quantity of information on wall maps made them somewhat unwieldy to use and store. Because of their large size and the publisher's desire to present even more information, the multisheet atlas was developed. The first county atlases were published in 1864,[24] and within a few years this cartographic form outstripped the wall map as the principal means of depicting cadastral information.[25] For a short time, however, the single-sheet wall map was supreme.

In compiling a county map, the surveyor gathered whatever

information he could from the tax records and maps on file in the county courthouse. A rough survey of the county roads was then made. Distances were measured by odometer (see plate 4), and directions were determined with the magnetic compass. The mapmaker then drew the road network on a map and added information obtained from the courthouse and from personal observations of the cultural and physical landscapes. Within a relatively short period of time, a reasonably accurate map of the county could thus be compiled.

The importance of the odometer to county mappers in determining distances cannot be overemphasized. In a letter read to the American Philosophical Society in 1864, Robert Pearsall Smith noted that 300 counties had been covered by odometer surveys and "They have formed the basis of the recently published and very correct State maps of New York, Pennsylvania, and New Jersey."[26] Smith accompanied his letter to the society with a map colored to show the counties covered by these surveys, a reduced uncolored version of which is published in the Proceedings.[27] Bates Harrington, in his contemporary but not altogether factual account of the county map and atlas business, describes the odometer as consisting "of an apparatus resembling a wheelbarrow, upon which is perched a clocklike piece of mechanism. The instrument is wheeled over the roads, and, by the revolution of the wheel, which is mathematically constructed, a record of the distance traversed is made by the 'clock,' and shown on the dial."[28]

In Midwestern States, the process of mapping some of the counties could be accelerated by obtaining accurate township plats from the U.S. General Land Office. The plats served as excellent bases for the cadastral information gathered by the surveyors. Unfortunately, in some cases the cadastral information was hastily obtained and the resulting map was of poor quality. Bates Harrington comments as follows on the field methods of some of the less scrupulous midwestern mapmakers:

> It is a fact that a great many of the subscribers expected a regular surveyor, with chain and compass, making an actual survey of his entire farm. How must he have felt when he saw or heard a man riding along in a buggy in fine style, stop a moment in front of his house, make a dot on his plat, and drive on, and would make the entire surveys of an average township in three days?[29]

Before beginning a new county map, the typical midwestern publisher sought the support of county officials, lawyers, bankers, real estate dealers, and other prominent men of the community. Generally, their endorsement appeared in the local newspapers along with an appeal for financial assistance from every citizen. Canvassers were then sent to every farmstead to solicit subscriptions for the proposed map. Actual work on it did not begin until the canvassers had obtained enough signatures to assure the financial success of the enterprise.

About 1,000 copies of each map, which sold for about $5, were printed. The lithographic stones were then cleaned and reused for a new map of another county. Midwestern publishers quickly discovered that the lithographic view, which had been a popular feature from the very beginning of the published county map, could be developed into a major source of revenue. Thus, through skillful canvassing, the mapmakers increased their profits by charging the owner of each business or residence depicted in the views between $36 and $60.

Little is known about the profits realized by publishers of county maps in the Northeast, but more than likely they were quite small. The average publisher of a county map in the Midwest, however, cleared about $5,000 on each venture. The table quoted below gives some indication of the gross profits, production costs, and net profits to be expected from the publication of a typical midwestern county map in the decade following the Civil War.[30]

COST AND SALES OF A COUNTY MAP

Such as Published by Thompson & Everts

Estimate being on an ordinary County of Sixteen Townships, with sales of 1,200 copies, which is an average

SALES

1,200 Maps, at $6 each	$7,200	
50 Views, at $40 each	2,000	
		$9,200

COST

Commissions on Maps, 50 cents each	$ 600
Commissions on Views, 10 per cent	200
Copying Township Plats from Tax Lists, $3.50 each	56
Making Township Maps from observation and copying, $28 each	448
Making City and Township Plats	25
Engraving 16 Townships, $15 each	240
Engraving Plats	20
Printing 1,200	140
Lithographing 50 Views, $5.50 each	275
Heading and Extras	20
Sketching Views, 10 per cent	200
Mounting and Coloring 1,200 Maps, 90 cents each	1,080

Paper	$ 200	
Freight and incidental expenses	300	
Commissions for collecting on Maps, 40 cts. each	480	
Commissions for collecting Views, 3 per cent	60	
		$4,344
Profits		$4,856

Not all cadastral maps of the 19th century were produced by commercial firms. About 22 percent of all county land ownership maps for this period, in the Library of Congress, were made by two government groups, the Confederate Army Engineers and the Texas General Land Office.

The outbreak of war between North and South immediately produced a need for large-scale maps of anticipated battle areas. Field commanders on both sides relentlessly pressed their superiors for more and better maps. The few maps of counties in Virginia and southern Pennsylvania, published by commercial firms before the war, were in great demand by both armies. In his communication to the American Philosophical Society, in March 1864, Robert Pearsall Smith told how on the eve of the invasion of Pennsylvania in 1863, Confederate soldiers in advance of the main army captured all the maps of Franklin, Cumberland, and Adams Counties that they could find.

> For a day or two, not a map of the seat of war was to be obtained at Harrisburg for the use of the Governor and his staff. General Couch had but a single copy at his headquarters. An order on Philadelphia could only be filled by sending out a special agent, who succeeded, at great personal risk, in procuring one or two of each county. Judge Watts, of Carlisle, informed me that the maps were torn hastily from the walls of the farmers' houses, and sent with the horses and other valuables for safety, over the North Mountain, into the Juniata Valley. The rebel visitation was very complete; he thought it likely that not a single house had been overlooked....
> A rebel general is understood to have made a reconnoissance of these counties previous to the invasion under the guise of a map-peddler, and while selling some of a more general character, no doubt bought up county maps to be used in the invasion.[31]

The Federal Government, through the established mapping and

reproduction facilities of the Corps of Topographical Engineers, the Corps of Engineers, and the U.S. Coast Survey, eventually was able to produce reasonably detailed maps of the theater of war. The Confederate Army, however, had difficulty throughout the war in supplying its field officers with adequate maps. The situation in the South was acute from the beginning of hostilities because of the lack of established government mapping agencies capable of preparing large-scale maps, and the inadequacy of printing facilities for producing them. The situation was further complicated by the almost total absence of surveying and drafting equipment, and the lack of trained military engineers and mapmakers to use the equipment that was available.

To alleviate the critical shortage of large-scale maps, the Confederate Army began a program to survey and map the Virginia counties in which fighting was likely to occur. Most of these maps were made under the direction of Maj. Gen. Jeremy F. Gilmer, Chief of Engineers, and Maj. Albert H. Campbell, Chief of the Topographical Department of the Army of Northern Virginia. In later years, the maps produced under their direction became known as the "Gilmer-Campbell maps."

Between 1862 and 1864, Confederate engineers prepared detailed maps of most counties in eastern and central Virginia. The maps were drawn in ink on tracing linen and filed in the Topographical Department. Initially, when requests were received for maps of a particular area, a draftsman was assigned to make a tracing of the file copy. By 1864, the department was capable of supplying field officers with photoreproductions and thereby avoided making a time-consuming tracing or a costly lithographic print. The photocopies were quite legible and were frequently cut and mounted in sections on cloth to fold to a convenient size to fit an officer's pocket or saddle bag.

County maps drawn by the Confederates were most often on a scale of 1:80,000, with a few at 1:40,000. Each generally indicated county boundaries, villages, roads, railroads, relief (by hachures), mountain passes, woodland, drainage, fords, ferries, bridges, mills, houses, and names of residents (see plate 5). Except for the slightly smaller scale and the lack of insets, these maps closely resemble the commercial county maps of the preceding decade.

The Gilmer-Campbell county maps provide an invaluable record of rural residents in Virginia during the Civil War. Fortunately, many of the original manuscript county maps are extant today. A few are preserved in the Library of Congress, while others are in the Virginia Historical Society at Richmond and the U.S. Military Academy at West Point. The manuscripts in the Library of Congress, plus photocopies or blue prints of the copies in the other institutions, are recorded in the accompanying checklist.

Plate 5. A county land ownership map made by Confederate Army Engineers during the Civil War.

Maps of other Virginia counties were prepared, during and after the Civil War, by Maj. Jed. Hotchkiss, who served with distinction as a topographic engineer with the Army of Northern Virginia. Hotchkiss was perhaps the finest cartographer to serve on either side during the war. Wherever his travels with the army took him, he carefully recorded, on scraps of paper or in notebooks, roads and distances, topographic features, and the location of dwellings and names of occupants. Hotchkiss eventually placed much of this information on detailed county and regional maps. The accompanying checklist records only the county maps by Hotchkiss which contain cadastral information. His entire map collection, including his sketch books, battle plans, and regional maps, is described at length in Clara Egli LeGear's The Hotchkiss Map Collection (Washington, Library of Congress, 1951).

Relatively few land ownership maps have been made of counties in western United States except in Texas, for which the Library of Congress has 298 county cadastral maps, all issued in the last three decades of the 19th century. A few were published by the Land Department of the Texas and Pacific Railway Company and by the Texas Land and Immigration Company of New York, but the vast majority were produced by the Texas General Land Office. Commissioner W. C. Walsh reported in 1880 that "Under authority of the Act of March 20, 1879, I contracted with Messrs. August Gast & Co., of St. Louis, Mo., for the lithographic printing of the maps of the various counties of the State."[32] He noted in this same report that his office had completed only 57 counties "owing to pressure of work in the drafting department, and the necessity of recompiling many of the maps."[33] Apparently the maps did not sell well "at 50 cents and $1.00 each," for he commented that "The sales would be much more rapid if the names of counties printed were advertised," and he further suggested that "The price authorized by law to be charged for these maps might be reduced and the sales largely increased."[34]

In a later report Commissioner W. L. McGaughey reported that many of the original maps on file in his office were in bad condition and needed to be reconstructed. He commented that "The recompilation of many old maps is a work of so much importance that it should be kept up and carried on as fast as possible."[35] This apparently was done, for Texas county maps on file in the Library of Congress include the earlier lithographic maps as well as blue prints made from the later tracings.

Production of cadastral maps in the United States did not stop abruptly at the end of the 19th century. A few maps of this type are still published, and some closely resemble the maps of that bygone era. Large-scale maps of counties in the Southwest and South Central States showing the location of oil and gas wells, plus property ownership, are a modern adaptation of the 19th-century cadastral map. For the most part, however, the golden age of the county land ownership map has passed.

Footnotes

1 Lawrence Martin, ed., The George Washington Atlas (Washington, United States George Washington Bicentennial Commission, 1932), preface. A map showing the "Localities Where George Washington Did Surveying" is reproduced as plate 18.

2 The maps are described as items 497 and 501 in Christian Brun, Guide to the Manuscript Maps in the William L. Clements Library (Ann Arbor, University of Michigan, 1959).

3 An original of the 1808 map is in the Maryland Historical Society, Baltimore, and the 1809 map is in the Geography and Map Division, Library of Congress.

4 Charles Varlé, Topographical Description of the Counties of Frederick, Berkeley & Jefferson, Situated in the State of Virginia, in Which the Author Has Described the Natural Curiosities of Those Counties, Their Minerology [sic] and Lithology: Also, the Quality of the Soil, the Manufactories, Mills, &c. the Number of Inhabitants, Towns, Villages, &c. to Which is Added a Beautiful Map of Those Counties (Winchester, Printed by W. Heiskell, 1810), 34 p. The Library of Congress' copy of the map is lacking the pamphlet. There is a copy of it without the map in the University of West Virginia Library, Morgantown.

5 For a description of his life and works, see Walter W. Ristow, "John Melish and His Map of the United States," The Library of Congress Quarterly Journal of Current Acquisitions, v. 19, Sept. 1962, p. 159-178.

6 John Melish, A Geographical Description of the United States, With the Contiguous British and Spanish Possessions, Intended as an Accompaniment to Melish's Map of These Countries (Philadelphia, 1816), p. 175.

7 From "An Act Directing the Formation of a Map of Pennsylvania," as quoted in Melish, Ibid., p. 176.

8 Ibid., p. [179].

9 Ibid., p. 182.

10 "An Act to Provide an Accurate Chart of Each County and a General Map of the Territory of this Commonwealth," as quoted in Earl G. Swem, "Maps Relating to Virginia..." Virginia State Library Bulletin, v. 7, no. 2-3, 1914, p. 102.

11 Ibid.

[12] John Wood's county maps of Sussex (1819) and Culpeper (1821) in the National Archives, and Fluvanna (1820) in the Virginia State Library, do not include the names of residents.

[13] Jason Torrey, *An Index to the Map of Wayne and Pike Counties, Pennsylvania* (Philadelphia, Printed by Joseph Rakestraw, 1814), p. 5.

[14] *Ibid*.

[15] As noted earlier, Tanner was also the engraver of the Wood-Böye map of Virginia.

[16] Melish, *op. cit.*, p. 168.

[17] John Melish, *A Geographical Description of the United States* (Philadelphia, 1818), p. 178.

[18] John Melish, *A Catalogue of Maps and Geographical Works, Published and for Sale* (Philadelphia, 1822), p. 22.

[19] John T. Cross, *An Index to the Map of the County of Pike, Pennsylvania* (New York, Printed by Charles Vinten, 1856), p. [3].

[20] The seven counties are Delaware (1848) and Bucks (1850), Pa.; Montgomery (1853), Tompkins (1853), Washington (1853), and Erie (1854), N. Y.; and Henrico (1853), Va.

[21] Smith's name as copyright claimant was noted on 51 New York county maps; 16 in Ohio; 5 in New Jersey; 3 in Virginia; 2 in Maine; and 1 each in Connecticut, Delaware, Maryland, Rhode Island, and Vermont.

[22] For a discussion of the life and works of Henry F. Walling, plus a general description of county land ownership maps, see Walter W. Ristow, "Nineteenth-Century Cadastral Maps in Ohio," *Papers of the Bibliographical Society of America*, v. 59, 3d quarter, 1965, p. 306-315.

[23] "Henry Francis Walling, M. Am. Soc. C. E.," *American Society of Civil Engineers Proceedings*, v. 15, Sept.-Oct. 1889, p. 141.

[24] Clara E. LeGear, *United States Atlases; A List of National, State, County, City, and Regional Atlases in the Library of Congress* (Washington, Library of Congress, 1950), v. 1, p. iii.

[25] For an interesting and informative article on the American county atlas business, see Norman J. W. Thrower, "The County Atlas of the United States," *Surveying and Mapping*, v. 21, Sept. 1961, p. 365-373.

[26] Robert Pearsall Smith, "Communication ... Respecting the Published County Maps of the United States," American Philosophical Society. *Proceedings*, v. 9, Mar. 1864, p. 351.

[27] *Ibid.* The manuscript map collections of the Library of Congress include an undated map signed by Smith, entitled "Sketch Showing by Color the Counties Embraced in the Local Surveys, Made by Measurement of Course & Distance of the Roads, - and Published in the Form of County Maps."

[28] Bates Harrington, *How 'Tis Done. A Thorough Ventilation of the Numerous Schemes Conducted by Wandering Canvassers* ... (Chicago, Fidelity Pub. Co., 1879), p. 19-20.

[29] *Ibid.*, p. 37.

[30] *Ibid.*, p. 49.

[31] Smith, *op. cit.*, p. 350.

[32] *Report of the Commissioner of the General Land Office of the State of Texas, for the Fiscal Year ending August 31, 1880* (Galveston, 1880), p. 6.

[33] *Ibid.*

[34] *Ibid.*

[35] *Report of the Commissioner of the General Land Office, State of Texas. September 1, 1890, to August 31, 1892* (Austin, 1892), p. 4.

CHECKLIST

ALABAMA

No.	County and Date	Author or Surveyor	Publisher and Place	Scale and Size (Inches)
1	Colbert, 1896	Delos H. Bacon	Colbert County Abstract Co., Tuscumbia, Ala.	1:65,000 25 x 43
2	Greene, 1856	V. Gayle Snedecor	. . .	1:42,000 2 parts, 28 x 60 ea.
3	Hale, 1870	V. Gayle Snedecor	Walling & Gray, Boston	1:43,000 6 parts, 20 x 21 ea.
4	Madison, 1875	James H. Mayhew	. . .	1:63,360 40-1/2 x 30
5	Mobile, 1895	Henry Fondé	. . .	1:126,720 36 x 26

ARIZONA

No.	County and Date	Author or Surveyor	Publisher and Place	Scale and Size (Inches)
6	Pima, 1893	George J. Roskruge	Pima County Board of Supervisors	1:210,000 28-1/2 x 54-1/2

ARKANSAS

No.	County and Date	Author or Surveyor	Publisher and Place	Scale and Size (Inches)
7	Calhoun, 1865	Topographical Bureau, Dist. Arks.	. . .	1:63,360 41-1/2 x 30
8	Mississippi, 1898	James Anthony	. . .	1:63,360 46 x 38-1/2
9	Prairie, 1892	J. G. Thweatt	. . .	1:42,500 2 parts, 32-1/2 x 40 ea.
10	Pulaski, 1898	George A. Merrick & G. P. C. Rumbough	. . .	1:63,360 4 parts, 20 x 23-1/2 ea.

CALIFORNIA

No.	County and Date	Author or Surveyor	Publisher and Place	Scale and Size (Inches)
11	Alameda & Contra Costa (portions), 1894	Theodore Wagner & George Sandow	. . .	1:42,240 4 parts, 20 x 26-1/2 ea.

CALIFORNIA (Cont.)

No.	County and Date	Author or Surveyor	Publisher and Place	Scale and Size (Inches)
12	Amador, 1866	J. M. Griffith	. . .	1:84,480 26 x 40-1/2
13	Amador, 1881	J. A. Brown	. . .	1:47,520 2 parts, 49 x 36 ea.
14	Butte, 1877	. . .	James McGann	1:63,360 2 parts, 31-1/2 x 55-1/2 ea.
15	Butte, 1886	James McGann	. . .	1:63,360 8 parts, 16 x 28 ea.
16	Colusa, 1885	De Jarnatt & Crane	. . .	1:79,200 6 parts, 25-1/2 x 17-1/2 ea.
17	El Dorado, 1895	Punnett Bros.	Shelley Inch, Placerville, Calif.	1:66,000 3 sheets, 2 are 39-1/2 x 27 ea. & 1 is 39-1/2 x 24-1/2
18	Kern, 1875	Ferd. Von Leicht & Chas. Kaufman	Board of Supervisors of Kern County	1:190,080 2 parts, 25 x 26 ea.
19	Kern (portion), 1888	. . .	Britton & Rey, San Francisco	1:230,000 14 x 19-1/2
20	Kern (portion), 1897	Kern County Land Company	. . .	1:126,720 22 x 27
21	Lake, 1892	S. H. Rice	. . .	1:80,000 2 parts, 25 x 32 & 29-1/2 x 32
22	Los Angeles, 1877	J. H. Wildy & A. J. Stahlberg	. . .	1:126,720 2 sheets, 25-1/2 x 47 ea.
23	Los Angeles, 1888	V. J. Rowan	. . .	1:95,040 8 parts, 6 are 18 x 30 ea. & 2 are 20 x 30 ea.
24	Los Angeles, 1898	E. T. Wright & C. N. Perry	. . .	1:95,000 4 parts, 28 x 26 ea.
25	Los Angeles & parts of Orange & Ventura, 1900	A. L. George & N. B. Blunt	Stoll & Thayer Co., Los Angeles	1:185,000 28-1/2 x 26
26	Marin, 1892	Geo. M. Dodge	. . .	1:47,520 54 x 53
27	Modoc, 1887	A. A. Smith & D. W. Jenks	. . .	1:63,360 64 x 77
28	Monterey (portion), 1898	. . .	. . .	1:97,000 48 x 35-1/2
29	Napa, 1876	Geo. G. Lyman & S. R. Throckmorton, Jr.	David L. Haas, Napa & St. Helena, Calif.	1:63,360 4 parts, 25-1/2 x 22 ea.
30	Napa, 1895	O. H. Buckman	Punnett Bros.	1:51,000 2 parts, 33 x 46 & 34 x 46
31	Nevada, 1880	J. G. Hartwell	. . .	1:79,200 4 parts, 2 are 19 x 31 ea. & 2 are 19 x 28-1/2 ea.
32	Orange, 1889	S. H. Finley	. . .	1:47,520 2 parts, 25-1/2 x 56 & 27 x 56

CALIFORNIA (Cont.)

No.	County and Date	Author or Surveyor	Publisher and Place	Scale and Size (Inches)
33	Plumas, 1892	Arthur W. Keddie	Arthur W. Keddie, Quincy, Calif.	1:95,040 2 sheets, 25-1/2 x 68 ea.
34	Sacramento, 1885	Fred. A. Shepherd	. . .	1:47,520 6 parts, 4 are 20 x 25-1/2 ea. & 2 are 22 x 25-1/2 ea.
35	San Diego, 1889-90	T. D. Beasley & Jas D. Schuyler	. . .	1:190,080 3 parts, 37 x 21, 37 x 21-1/2 & 37 x 23
36	San Joaquin, 1895	H. T. Compton & R. T. Andrews	. . .	1:48,000 8 parts, 4 are 18 x 25 ea., 2 are 19-1/2 x 25 ea. & 2 are 20 x 25 ea.
37	San Mateo, 1894	Davenport Bromfield	. . .	1:31,680 8 parts, 4 are 21 x 27 ea. & 4 are 22 x 27 ea.
38	Santa Barbara, 1889	Paul Riecker	Riecker, Huber & Mench	1:77,000 2 sheets, 49 x 35-1/2 ea.
39	Santa Clara, 1890	A. T. Herrmann, Chas. Herrmann & S. Wislocki	[Santa Clara Co.] Board of Supervisors	1:39,000 8 sheets, 35-1/2 x 24-1/2 ea.
40	Santa Cruz, 1889	A. J. Hatch	A. J. Hatch, San Francisco	1:39,600 2 sheets, 47-1/2 x 32-1/2 ea.
41	Shasta, 1862	[William Magee]	. . .	1:555,000 Photograph, 8-1/2 x 13
42	Siskiyou, 1887	J. M. Davidson	. . .	1:120,000 44-1/2 x 70-1/2
43	Solano, 1890	E. N. Eager	. . .	1:47,520 8 parts, 4 are 25 x 15 ea. & 4 are 25 x 16 ea.
44	Sonoma, 1900	L. E. Ricksecker	W. B. Walkup	1:63,360 2 parts, 55-1/2 x 33 ea.
45	Sutter, 1873	J. T. Pennington	. . .	1:63,360 41-1/2 x 30
46	Sutter, 1895	Punnett Bros.	Punnett Bros., San Francisco	1:54,000 Photocopy (pos.) in 4 parts, 26 x 21 ea.
47	Tehama, 1878	H. B. Shackelford & F. J. Nugent	. . .	1:98,000 4 parts, 20 x 30-1/2 ea.
48	Trinity, 1894	H. L. Lowden & Jno. F. Johnson	. . .	1:126,720 2 parts, 26 x 34 ea.
49	Tulare, 1884	Alfred Bannister	Board of Supervisors	1:126,720 33-1/2 x 66
50	Yolo, 1871	J. S. Henning	. . .	1:63,360 4 parts, 22 x 26 ea.
51	Yolo, 1900	P. N. Ashley	. . .	1:47,520 4 sheets, 30 x 34 ea.
52	Yuba, 1887	J. M. Doyle	. . .	1:50,688 2 parts, 30 x 41 ea.

COLORADO

No.	County and Date	Author or Surveyor	Publisher and Place	Scale and Size (Inches)
53	Jefferson, Boulder & Arapahoe (portions), 1899	. . .	W. C. Willits, Denver	1:40,000 4 parts, 26 x 23 ea.
54	Larimer, 1883	H.P. Handy	. . .	1:170,000 21 x 25-1/2
55	Pitkin, 1884	G. C. Vickery	The Aspen [Colorado] Times	1:126,720 18 x 26-1/2
56	Prowers, 1889	George Trommlitz	George Trommlitz, Lamar, Colo.	1:63,360 4 parts, 2 are 26 x 21 ea. & 2 are 27-1/2 x 21 ea.
57	Pueblo, 1888	V. G. Hills	Z. V. Trine & V. G. Hills	1:62,000 4 parts, 2 are 31 x 32-1/2 ea. & 2 are 31 x 26-1/2 ea.

CONNECTICUT

No.	County and Date	Author or Surveyor	Publisher and Place	Scale and Size (Inches)
58	Fairfield, 1856	J. Chace, Jr. & W. J. Barker	Richard Clark, Phila.	1:49,500 52 x 60-1/2
59	Fairfield, 1858	J. Chace, Jr. & W. J. Barker	Richard Clark, Phila.	1:49,500 2 parts, 60-1/2 x 25-1/2 & 60-1/2 x 26-1/2
60	Hartford, 1855	E. M. Woodford	H. & C. T. Smith, Phila.	1:63,360 6 parts, 3 are 22-1/2 x 24 ea. & 3 are 24 x 24 ea.
61	Hartford (portion), 1884	. . .	Albert A. Hyde & Co., New York	1:50,000 41-1/2 x 40-1/2
62	Litchfield, 1859	G. M. Hopkins, Jr.	Richard Clark, Phila.	1:50,688 2 sheets, 31 x 52-1/2 ea.
63	Middlesex, 1859	H. F. Walling	H. & C. T. Smith & Co., New York	1:31,680 2 parts, 29-1/2 x 60-1/2 ea.
64	New Haven, 1852	R. Whiteford	A. Budington & R. Whiteford, New Haven	1:51,500 2 parts, 39 x 26 ea.
65	New Haven, 1856	. . .	H. & C. T. Smith, Phila.	1:51,000 6 parts, 27-1/2 x 18-1/2 ea.
66	New London, 1854	H. F. Walling	William E. Baker, Phila.	1:47,520 4 parts, 2 are 27-1/2 x 36-1/2 ea. & 2 are 27-1/2 x 38 ea.
67	Tolland, 1857	Wm. C. Eaton & H. C. Osborn	Woodford & Bartlett, Phila.	1:43,000 6 parts, 18 x 23 ea.
68	Windham, 1856	E. P. Gerrish, W. C. Eaton & D. S. & H. C. Osborn	E. M. Woodford, Phila.	1:43,000 6 parts, 2 are 18-1/2 x 23 ea., 2 are 19-1/2 x 23 ea. & 2 are 20-1/2 x 23 ea.

DELAWARE

No.	County and Date	Author or Surveyor	Publisher and Place	Scale and Size (Inches)
69	Kent, 1859	J. H. French & J. L. Skinner	A. D. Byles, Phila.	1:42,240 8 parts, 15 x 26-1/2 ea.
70	New Castle, 1849	Saml. M. Rea & Jacob Price	Smith & Wistar, Phila.	1:52,000 50 x 35
71	New Castle, 1881	. . .	G. M. Hopkins & Co., Phila.	1:36,204 8 parts, 4 are 16 x 25 ea. & 4 are 17 x 25 ea.

FLORIDA

No.	County and Date	Author or Surveyor	Publisher and Place	Scale and Size (Inches)
72	Alachua, [18-?]	. . .	Matheson & McMillan, Gainesville, Fla.	1:95,040 2 parts, 36 x 20-1/2 ea.
73	Brevard, 1885	J. Francis Le Baron	J. F. Le Baron, Jacksonville, Fla.	1:190,080 39 x 29-1/2
74	Duval, 1884	J. Francis Le Baron	. . .	1:120,000 18-1/2 x 22-1/2
75	Duval, 1898	J. Francis Le Baron	J. F. Le Baron, Jacksonville, Fla.	1:63,360 2 parts, 37 x 25 & 37 x 25-1/2
76	Hillsborough, 1882	J. J. Treveres & Florida Land & Improvement Co.	F. Bourquin, Phila.	1:63,360 38-1/2 x 51-1/2
77	Leon, 1883	LeRoy D. Ball & Jno. Bradford	. . .	1:71,000 27-1/2 x 41
78	Marion, 1883	J. W. Bushnell & A. T. Williams	F. Bourquin	1:126,720 24-1/2 x 34
79	Marion, 1885	J. W. Bushnell & A. T. Williams	F. Bourquin, Phila.	1:126,720 22 x 28
80	Marion, 1887	G. W. Bromley & Co.	Fred. Bourquin, Phila.	1:126,720 22 x 28
81	Orange, 1890	J. O. Fries	. . .	1:63,360 6 parts, 2 are 19 x 18-1/2 ea. & 4 are 19 x 17 ea.
82	Polk, 1883	J. J. Treveres	C. Benedict & W. T. Bauskett	1:63,360 50 x 59
83	Volusia, 1883	D. D. Rogers	J. L. Smith, Phila.	1:63,360 6 parts, 2 are 20-1/2 x 31-1/2 ea., 2 are 22 x 31-1/2 ea. & 2 are 23 x 31-1/2 ea.

GEORGIA

No.	County and Date	Author or Surveyor	Publisher and Place	Scale and Size (Inches)
84	Chatham, 1816	John McKinnan. Copied 1887 by W. W. Gross & C.H. Dorsetts	. . .	1:23,760 Ms., 6 parts, 4 are 30-1/2 x 16 ea. & 2 are 30-1/2 x 17 ea.
85	Chatham, 1875	Charles G. Platen	. . .	1:40,000 50-1/2 x 40

GEORGIA (Cont.)

No.	County and Date	Author or Surveyor	Publisher and Place	Scale and Size (Inches)
86	Chatham, 1875	Charles G. Platen	. . .	1:180,000 13-1/2 x 9
87	Cherokee, 1895	W. P. Bullock & A. C. Conn	Cherokee Map Co.	1:55,000 27-1/2 x 37-1/2
88	Clarke, 1893	Charles Morton Strahan	. . .	1:42,500 25 x 30
89	Coffee, [1891]	Thomas B. Marshall	Thomas B. Marshall, Willacoochee, Ga.	1:110,880 29 x 25
90	Floyd, 1895	Guy Beauman	Floyd County Commissioners of Roads and Revenues	1:56,000 27-1/2 x 37-1/2
91	Fulton, 1872	Daniel Pittman & William Phillips	J. L. Smith, Phila.	1:31,680 2 parts, 26 x 25-1/2 ea.
92	Hart, 1889	J. W. Baker	. . .	1:52,000 28 x 31-1/2
93	Jefferson, 1879	I. F. Adkins	. . .	1:63,360 2 parts, 20 x 27 ea.
94	Oglethorpe, 1894	Thos. B. Moss	. . .	1:63,360 29 x 41
95	Paulding, 1896	M. D. West	. . .	1:72,000 21-1/2 x 18
96	Walker, 1893	Sam Street	Sam Street, Dalton, Ga.	1:126,720 23-1/2 x 18
97	Washington, 1897	N. Newman & M. L. Jackson	. . .	. . . 2 parts, 18-1/2 x 33-1/2 ea.
98	Whitfield, 1879	Sam'l M. Street & Wm. P. Schultz	Smith & Stroup, Phila.	1:63,360 28-1/2 x 22

ILLINOIS

No.	County and Date	Author or Surveyor	Publisher and Place	Scale and Size (Inches)
99	Adams, 1889	John P. Edwards	John P. Edwards, Quincy, Ill.	1:36,205 6 parts, 4 are 27 x 18 ea. & 2 are 27 x 19-1/2 ea.
100	Carroll, 1869	Thompson & Everts	Thompson & Everts, Geneva, Ill.	1:43,000 2 parts, 35-1/2 x 27-1/2 & 35-1/2 x 29
101	Christian, 1872	L. M. Snyder & R. M. Powel	Snyder Brothers, Chicago	1:52,000 4 parts, 26-1/2 x 24 ea.
102	Christian, 1893	. . .	Herald Despatch, Decatur, Ill.	1:58,000 37 x 31
103	Cook & Du Page & parts of Kane, Kendall & Will, 1851	James H. Rees	. . .	1:79,200 2 parts, 21-1/2 x 40-1/2 ea.
104	Cook, 1861	W. L. Flower	S. H. Burhans & J. Van Vechten	1:52,000 3 parts, 2 are 24 x 62 ea. & 1 is 21-1/2 x 62
105	Cook, 1862	W. L. Flower	S. H. Burhans & J. Van Vechten	1:52,000 70 x 63
106	Cook, 1870	. . .	J. Van Vechten, Chicago	1:53,000 2 parts, 29-1/2 x 48 & 30-1/2 x 48

ILLINOIS (Cont.)

No.	County and Date	Author or Surveyor	Publisher and Place	Scale and Size (Inches)
107	Cook, 1886	. . .	L. M. Snyder & Co., Chicago	1:42,240 8 parts, 4 are 18 x 31 ea. & 4 are 19 x 31 ea.
108	Cook & Du Page, 1890	. . .	F. M. Snyder, Chicago	1:42,240 6 parts, 4 are 37 x 16-1/2 ea. & 2 are 37 x 15 ea.
109	Cook & Du Page, 1898	. . .	William L. Mitchell, Chicago	1:42,240 73 x 62-1/2
110	De Kalb, [1860]	Daniel W. Lamb	. . .	1:63,360 40-1/2 x 28-1/2
111	Edgar, 1870	. . .	Warner & Higgins, Phila.	1:36,205 6 parts, 4 are 27 x 20-1/2 ea. & 2 are 27 x 22 ea.
112	Edwards, 1891	. . .	Aug. Gast Bank Note & Litho. Co., St. Louis	1:32,500 4 parts, 24-1/2 x 17-1/2 ea.
113	Franklin, 1900	. . .	Guy Beauman, Vienna, Ill.	1:38,500 4 parts, 21 x 21-1/2 ea.
114	Greene, 1861	. . .	Charles R. Arnold	1:48,500 2 parts, 23 x 45 ea.
115	Hancock, 1859	. . .	Holmes & Arnold	1:45,000 2 parts, 55 x 28 & 55 x 29
116	Henry, 1860	P. Holmes	P. Holmes	1:63,360 47 x 45-1/2
117	Iroquois & Kankakee, 1860	John Wilson	. . .	1:126,720 42 x 33
118	Jefferson, 1900	. . .	Guy Beauman	1:80,000 21-1/2 x 20
119	Kane, 1860	Adin Mann	Matthews, Crane & Co., Phila.	1:42,000 2 parts, 28 x 53 ea.
120	Knox, 1861	M. H. Thompson	M. H. Thompson	1:42,000 2 sheets, 33-1/2 x 48-1/2 & 31 x 51
121	La Salle, 1895	Maierhofer & Briel	Maierhofer & Briel, Ottawa, Ill.	1:47,520 3 sheets, 2 are 22 x 42 ea. & 1 is 23-1/2 x 42
122	Lake, 1861	George Hale & J. M. Truesdell	. . .	1:48,500 4 parts, 2 are 25 x 18 ea. & 2 are 24 x 18 ea.
123	Lake, 1873	Frost & McLennan	Frost & McLennan, Chicago	1:40,000 4 sheets, 27 x 21, 27 x 17, 20-1/2 x 17 & 20-1/2 x 21
124	Logan, 1893	. . .	Herald Despatch Co., Decatur, Ill.	1:56,500 42 x 28
125	McHenry, 1862	M. H. Thompson & Brother	M. H. Thompson & Brother	1:42,240 6 parts, 23 x 20 ea.
126	Madison, 1861	. . .	Holmes & Arnold, Buffalo, N. Y.	1:47,520 6 parts, 17 x 28-1/2 ea.

ILLINOIS (Cont.)

No.	County and Date	Author or Surveyor	Publisher and Place	Scale and Size (Inches)
127	Madison, 1892	...	Robt. Hagnauer, Henry Riniker & Geo. K. Dickson	1:43,000 6 parts, 4 are 20-1/2 x 27-1/2 ea. & 2 are 22 x 27-1/2 ea.
128	Peoria, 1861	D. B. Allen	Matthews, Crane & Co., Phila.	1:42,240 52 x 49-1/2
129	Pike, 1860	...	Holmes & Arnold, Buffalo, N. Y.	1:47,520 2 parts, 27 x 62 ea.
130	St. Clair, 1863	...	J. W. Holmes	1:47,520 6 parts, 27 x 20 ea.
131	St. Clair, 1899	...	Guy Beauman, Vienna, Ill.	1:74,000 26 x 26
132	Stephenson, 1859	H. F. Walling & C. T. Dunham [Coast Survey Coll.]	C. T. Dunham, New York	1:39,600 18 parts, 17 x 13 ea.
133	White, 1871	J. B. Westbrook	J. B. Westbrook	1:42,240 4 parts, 2 are 24-1/2 x 20 ea. & 2 are 24-1/2 x 18-1/2 ea.
134	Whiteside, 1896	Edw. O. Hills	...	1:44,000 4 parts, 18 x 24-1/2 ea.
135	Will, 1862	S. H. Burhans & J. Van Vechten	S. H. Burhans & J. Van Vechten	1:51,500 2 parts, 25 x 63 ea.
136	Winnebago, 1859	T. J. L. Remington	H. F. Walling, New York	1:39,600 2 parts, 26-1/2 x 54 ea.

INDIANA

No.	County and Date	Author or Surveyor	Publisher and Place	Scale and Size (Inches)
137	Boone & Clinton, 1865	A. Warner & J. S. Higgins	Cowles & Titus, Phila.	1:50,688 6 parts, 4 are 16-1/2 x 26 ea. & 2 are 17-1/2 x 26 ea.
138	Carroll, 1897	J. D. Rauch	C. F. & O. A. McGreevy	1:32,000 2 parts, 43 x 21-1/2 ea.
139	Carroll, 1898	...	Delphi Journal	1:63,360 23 x 22
140	Clark, 1875	George W. Davis	Chas A. McCann & David S. Koons	1:32,000 8 parts, 6 are 27 x 17-1/2 ea. & 2 are 27 x 16-1/2 ea.
141	De Kalb, 1863	E. B. Gerber & C. A. O. McClellan	E. B. Gerber & C. A. O. McClellan, Phila.	1:37,000 45 x 51
142	Dearborn, 1860	Thomas Pattison	...	1:32,000 4 parts, 27 x 19 ea.
143	Elkhart, 1861	Geil, Harley & Joseph D. Nash	Samuel Geil, Phila.	1:50,688 4 parts, 20 x 23-1/2 ea.
144	Floyd, 1859	...	P. O'Beirne & Co., New York & Jersey City, N. J.	1:31,680 2 sheets, 33 x 23 ea.
145	Floyd, 1882	George M. Smith	...	1:32,000 32 x 40

INDIANA (Cont.)

No.	County and Date	Author or Surveyor	Publisher and Place	Scale and Size (Inches)
146	Fountain & Warren, 1865	D. J. Lake & A. Warner	Stone & Titus, Phila.	1:50,688 6 parts, 4 are 17 x 26-1/2 ea. & 2 are 18-1/2 x 26-1/2 ea.
147	Grant, [186-]	Wm. Neal & A. C. Overman	. . .	1:32,000 6 parts, 4 are 24-1/2 x 17-1/2 ea. & 2 are 24-1/2 x 18-1/2 ea.
148	Hamilton, 1866	C. S. Warner, L. C. Warner & S. B. Hayes	C. A. O. McClellan, S. L. Yandes & T. B. Tucker, Waterloo, Ind.; C. S. Warner, J. Willard & A. Shoemaker, Newtown, Conn.	1:42,240 42-1/2 x 50-1/2
149	Hendricks, 1865	D. J. Lake & A. Warner	Stone & Titus, Phila.	1:42,240 4 parts, 22-1/2 x 24 ea.
150	Henry, 1857	Harwood & Watson	Harwood & Watson, Newcastle, Ind.	1:42,000 4 parts, 22 x 21 ea.
151	Huntington, 1866	Warner, Hayes & Warner	E. B. Gerber, Ligonier, Ind. & C. S. Warner, Newtown, Conn.	1:42,240 2 parts, 23 x 44-1/2 ea.
152	Jefferson, 1900	C. Reynolds Cosby	. . .	1:42,240 4 parts, 21 x 20 ea.
153	Kosciusko, 1866	C. S. Warner	E. B. Gerber, Ligonier, Ind. & C. S. Warner, Newtown, Conn.	1:42,240 6 parts, 4 are 18-1/2 x 23-1/2 ea. & 2 are 20 x 23-1/2 ea.
154	La Porte, 1862	Geil, Harley, Leamings, Cathcart & J. D. Nash	Geil, Leamings & Cathcart, Phila.	1:50,688 54-1/2 x 38-1/2
155	Lagrange, 1864	E. B. Gerber [Coast Survey Coll.]	E.B. Gerber, Ligonier, Ind.	1:42,240 14 parts, 17 x 13 ea.
156	Lawrence, [186-?]	W. H. Stairs & W. W. Dill [Coast Survey Coll.]	. . .	1:42,240 13 parts, 17 x 13 ea.
157	Marion, 1855	Condit, Wright & Hayden	. . .	1:32,500 4 parts, 24-1/2 x 22 ea.
158	Marion, 1866	A. Warner	C. O. Titus, Phila.	1:42,240 6 parts, 4 are 26 x 21 ea. & 2 are 26 x 22 ea.
159	Montgomery, 1864	D. J. Lake & A. Warner	Cowles & Titus, Phila.	1:42,240 6 parts, 4 are 17 x 26-1/2 ea. & 2 are 18-1/2 x 26-1/2 ea.
160	Morgan, 1875	G. H. Currie	W. W. Richie, Phila.	1:31,680 6 parts, 2 are 19-1/2 x 25-1/2 ea., 2 are 21 x 25-1/2 ea. & 2 are 20-1/2 x 25-1/2 ea.
161	Noble, [186-?]	E. B. Gerber	E. B. Gerber, Ligonier, Ind.	1:36,500 6 parts, 4 are 24-1/2 x 18-1/2 ea. & 2 are 24-1/2 x 19 ea.
162	Ohio, 1876	G. W. Morse	. . .	1:29,000 Photocopy (pos.), 21-1/2 x 39
163	Perry, 1894	George Minto	. . .	1:42,240 4 parts, 23 x 17 ea.

INDIANA (Cont.)

No.	County and Date	Author or Surveyor	Publisher and Place	Scale and Size (Inches)
164	Putnam, 1864	D. J. Lake & A. Warner	Cowles & Titus, Phila.	1:42,240 4 parts, 23 x 25-1/2 ea.
165	Randolph, 1865	C. S. Warner, L. C. Warner & S. B. Hayes	C. A. O. McClellan, Waterloo, Ind. & C. S. Warner, Newtown, Conn.	1:42,240 2 sheets, 28 x 42 & 27 x 42
166	Rush, 1856	Condit, Hayden & Wright	. . .	1:32,500 4 parts, 27 x 20 ea.
167	Rush & Decatur, 1867	A. Warner	C. O. Titus, Phila.	1:50,688 6 parts, 4 are 19 x 26-1/2 ea. & 2 are 20 x 26-1/2 ea.
168	St. Joseph, 1863	. . .	M. W. Stokes, South Bend, Ind.	1:28,160 6 parts, 3 are 25-1/2 x 23 ea. & 3 are 26-1/2 x 23 ea.
169	Shelby & Johnson, 1866	A. Warner, J. S. Higgins, G.P. Sanford & R. M. Sherman	C. O. Titus, Phila.	1:50,688 6 parts, 4 are 25 x 18-1/2 ea. & 2 are 25 x 20 ea.
170	Starke, 1898	John P. Edwards	John P. Edwards, Knox, Ind.	1:31,360 4 parts, 18-1/2 x 24-1/2 ea.
171	Steuben, 1864	C. S. Warner [Coast Survey Coll.]	C. A. O. McClellan, Phila.	1:36,205 14 parts, 17 x 13 ea.
172	Tippecanoe, 1866	A. Warner, J. S. Higgins, G. P. Sanford, R. M. Sherman & R. H. Harrison	C. O. Titus, Phila.	1:42,240 6 parts, 4 are 17-1/2 x 29-1/2 ea. & 2 are 18-1/2 x 29-1/2 ea.
173	Vermillion, 1872	Jas. Tarrance	. . .	1:42,240 3 parts, 2 are 19-1/2 x 24-1/2 ea. & 1 is 20 x 24-1/2 ea.
174	Vigo, 1858	H. F. Walling	Wm. C. Peckham, New York	1:31,680 50 x 59
175	Wabash, 1861	R. J. Skinner	R.J. Skinner, Hamilton, Ohio	1:31,680 6 parts, 18-1/2 x 26-1/2 ea.
176	Whitley, 1873	Willard, Kingman, McConahy, Ellis Kiser, W. H. Leas & A. C. Lewis	Willard, Kingman & McConahy	1:42,240 4 parts, 2 are 22 x 21 ea. & 2 are 24-1/2 x 21 ea.

IOWA

No.	County and Date	Author or Surveyor	Publisher and Place	Scale and Size (Inches)
177	Allamakee, 1872	John G. Ratcliffe	John G. Ratcliffe, Waukon, Iowa	1:42,240 4 parts, 28 x 23-1/2 ea.
178	Black Hawk, 1887	Sedgwick Brothers & Stilson	E. W. Smith & Co., Phila.	1:31,680 2 parts, 24-1/2 x 56 & 26-1/2 x 56
179	Buchanan, 1900	. . .	W. W. Hixson, Rockford, Ill.	1:42,240 38-1/2 x 37-1/2
180	Buena Vista, [1891?]	W. W. Hixson & Co.	Walpole & Smith, Storm Lake, Iowa	1:42,240 2 parts, 27 x 42 ea.

IOWA (Cont.)

No.	County and Date	Author or Surveyor	Publisher and Place	Scale and Size (Inches)
181	Butler, 1897	E. V. Franke	Gordon L. Elliott, Allison, Iowa	1:42,240 4 parts, 27-1/2 x 23 ea.
182	Cedar, [1863-65?]	Wells Spicer	. . .	1:43,000 2 parts, 24-1/2 x 39 ea.
183	Clay, 1896	. . .	Geo. Long	1:65,000 25-1/2 x 24
184	Clinton, 1865	M. H. Thompson & Bro.	M. H. Thompson & Bro., Dundee, Ill.	1:43,000 6 parts, 21 x 20 ea.
185	Crawford, 1883	. . .	Warner & Foote	1:33,792 4 sheets, 26 x 29-1/2 ea.
186	Crawford, 1898	Morris McHenry	Denison Bulletin, Denison, Iowa	1:51,000 34-1/2 x 38-1/2
187	Delaware (portion), 1869	Thompson & Everts	Thompson & Everts, Geneva, Ill.	1:42,000 42 x 37
188	Dickinson, 1883	M. B. Haynes	B. B. Van Steenburg & J. A. Smith, Spirit Lake, Iowa	1:39,600 4 parts, 17 x 25 ea.
189	Dubuque, [1900]	. . .	[W. W. Hixson, Rockford, Ill.]	1:45,000 2 parts, 41 x 23 & 41 x 25
190	Jackson, 1867	Thompson & Everts	Thompson & Everts, Anamosa, Iowa	1:43,000 6 parts, 26 x 23-1/2 ea.
191	Jasper, 1871	Geo. E. Warner	Harrison & Warner, Marshall-town, Iowa	1:47,520 2 parts, 25 x 48 ea.
192	Jefferson, 1871	Geo. E. Warner	Harrison & Warner, Fairfield, Iowa	1:42,240 4 parts, 25 x 21-1/2 ea.
193	Keokuk, 1861	S. A. James [Coast Survey Coll.]	R. L. Barnes, Phila.	1:42,500 16 parts, 17 x 13 ea.
194	Linn, 1859	McWilliams & Thompson	McWilliams & Thompson	1:38,400 Photocopy (pos.) in 2 parts, 26-1/2 x 40 & 28-1/2 x 40
195	Linn (portion), 1869	D. W. Ensign	Thompson & Everts, Geneva, Ill.	1:42,240 2 parts, 32 x 57 ea.
196	Louisa, 1858	A. B. Miller	C. R. Dugdale	1:42,500 2 parts, 23-1/2 x 39 ea.
197	Mahaska, 1871	Geo. E. Warner	Harrison & Warner, Oskaloosa, Iowa	1:39,600 6 parts, 4 are 20 x 24-1/2 ea. & 2 are 19 x 24-1/2 ea.
198	Mahaska, 1884	Byron V. Seevers	Oskaloosa Weekly Herald, Oskaloosa, Iowa	1:32,400 6 parts, 4 are 20 x 25 ea. & 2 are 19 x 25 ea.
199	Mahaska, 1895	. . .	E. H. Gibbs	1:25,344 6 parts, 22 x 31 ea.
200	Marshall, 1896	Melzar M. Dickson	Times-Republican, Marshall-town, Iowa	1:65,000 24-1/2 x 25

IOWA (Cont.)

No.	County and Date	Author or Surveyor	Publisher and Place	Scale and Size (Inches)
201	Polk, 1872	. . .	Geo. A. McVicker	1:32,000 6 parts, 4 are 21-1/2 x 29 ea. & 2 are 23 x 29 ea.
202	Polk, 1885	. . .	Warner & Foote, Minneapolis & Phila.	1:36,205 6 parts, 2 are 26-1/2 x 15 ea., 2 are 25-1/2 x 15 ea., 1 is 26 x 17-1/2 & 1 is 25-1/2 x 17-1/2
203	Polk, 1895	. . .	Iowa Engraving Co., Des Moines	1:45,000 39-1/2 x 36-1/2
204	Scott, 1860	A. Hodge	E. W. Brady & John Hale	1:42,240 37-1/2 x 49
205	Story, 1883	. . .	Warner & Foote, Minneapolis	1:31,680 4 sheets, 27-1/2 x 25-1/2 ea.
206	Wapello, 1870	Geo. E. Warner	Harrison & Warner, Ottumwa, Iowa	1:36,205 6 parts, 4 are 20 x 22-1/2 ea. & 2 are 21 x 22-1/2 ea.
207	Wapello, 1893	C. R. Allen	C. R. Allen, Ottumwa, Iowa	1:31,680 6 sheets, 2 are 14-1/2 x 29 ea., 2 are 20 x 29 ea. & 2 are 25 x 29 ea.
208	Warren, [1859?]	Dan. A. Poorman	Dan. A. Poorman	1:32,000 6 parts, 4 are 28 x 16 ea. & 2 are 28 x 17 ea.
209	Woodbury, 1884	. . .	Warner & Foote, Minneapolis	1:42,240 4 sheets, 20 x 33 ea.
210	Worth (portion), [c1894]	. . .	[E.H. Dwelle]	1:43,000 27-1/2 x 18-1/2
211	Wright, 1885	. . .	Warner & Foote, Minneapolis	1:36,205 4 sheets, 25-1/2 x 23 ea.

KANSAS

No.	County and Date	Author or Surveyor	Publisher and Place	Scale and Size (Inches)
212	Dickinson, 1885	Jno. F. Fuller	. . .	1:52,000 4 parts, 23 x 17 ea.
213	Douglas, 1887	John P. Edwards	John P. Edwards, Quincy, Ill.	1:31,680 4 parts, 2 are 22-1/2 x 25 ea. & 2 are 24-1/2 x 25 ea.
214	Geary, 1897	H. H. Mead, J. B. Callen & Geo. E. Kyner	J. B. Callen & Geo. E. Kyner	1:42,240 2 parts, 21-1/2 x 39-1/2 ea.
215	Greenwood, 1877	J. Hoenscheidt	. . .	1:126,720 22-1/2 x 33
216	Harper, 1893	. . .	Southwestern Map Co.	1:77,000 25 x 27
217	Johnson, 1886	. . .	John P. Edwards, Phila. & Quincy, Ill.	1:31,680 6 parts, 20 x 25 ea.
218	Kingman, 1887	. . .	Reynolds & Darling	1:50,000 2 parts, 32-1/2 x 24 ea.

KANSAS (Cont.)

No.	County and Date	Author or Surveyor	Publisher and Place	Scale and Size (Inches)
219	Leavenworth, 1894	F. C. Waite & Harold C. Short	. . .	1:31,680 4 parts, 33 x 23-1/2 ea.
220	McPherson, 1898	. . .	H. A. Rowland, McPherson, Kans.	1:68,000 31-1/2 x 30
221	Wyandotte, 1885	. . .	John P. Edwards, Phila. & Quincy, Ill.	1:21,120 4 parts, 22-1/2 x 26 ea.
222	Wyandotte, [c1887]	. . .	G. M. Hopkins, Phila.	1:31,680 2 parts, 27-1/2 x 18 ea.

KENTUCKY

No.	County and Date	Author or Surveyor	Publisher and Place	Scale and Size (Inches)
223	Ballard (portion), 1853	Wm. Forsyth	. . .	1:39,600 Ms., 34 x 27
224	Barren, 1879	Beers & Lanagan	Beers & Lanagan, Phila.	1:50,688 2 parts, 23-1/2 x 37 & 24-1/2 x 37-1/2
225	Bourbon, Fayette, Clark, Jessamine & Woodford, 1861	E. A. & G. W. Hewitt	Smith, Gallup & Co., New York	1:63,360 3 parts, 2 are 18-1/2 x 55-1/2 ea. & 1 is 17-1/2 x 55-1/2
226	Boyle & Mercer, 1876	D. G. Beers & Co.	D. G. Beers & Co., Phila.	1:50,688 4 parts, 25 x 21 ea.
227	Christian, 1878	D. G. Beers & Co.	D. G. Beers & Co., Phila.	1:50,688 6 parts, 4 are 16 x 24 ea. & 2 are 16-1/2 x 24 ea.
228	Clay (portion), [1883?]	A. W. Chastain, A. L. Jonas, James Helton, Dale C. Lyttle & Willis Sisemore	Van Campen & Johnson, New York	1:79,200 & larger 13 sheets, 19-1/2 x 24 ea.
229	Cumberland (portion), [187-?]	J. B. G. Rand	. . .	1:43,000 30-1/2 x 24-1/2
230	Fayette, 1891	W. R. Wallis	. . .	1:36,000 2 parts, 24-1/2 x 40-1/2 ea.
231	Hancock & parts of Ohio, Grayson & Breckinridge, [1887?]	P. N. Moore, W. B. Page, I. B. Hoeing, Eugene Underwood & M. S. Cole	Kentucky Geological Survey	1:60,000 2 sheets, 25-1/2 x 34 & 25-1/2 x 32-1/2
232	Harrison, 1877	D. G. Beers & Co.	D. G. Beers & Co., Phila.	1:42,240 42 x 37
233	Jefferson, 1784	James Carnahan & Benjamin Lodge	. . .	. . . Ms., 43 pages, 15 x 9 ea.
234	Jefferson, 1858	. . .	G. T. Bergmann, Louisville	1:42,240 4 parts, 23 x 25-1/2 ea.
235	Larue, 1899	. . .	Charles Williams & C. M. Barnes	. . . 30 x 33-1/2
236	Lewis & Greenup (portion), [1812-1855]	. . .	. . .	. . . Ms., 2 parts, 22-1/2 x 37 ea.
237	Madison, 1876	D. G. Beers & Co.	D. G. Beers & Co., Phila.	1:42,240 6 parts, 27 x 13 ea.
238	Marion & Washington, 1877	D. G. Beers & Co.	D. G. Beers & Co., Phila.	1:50,688 4 parts, 27-1/2 x 19 ea.

KENTUCKY (Cont.)

No.	County and Date	Author or Surveyor	Publisher and Place	Scale and Size (Inches)
239	Montgomery, 1879	Beers & Lanagan	Beers & Lanagan, Phila.	1:42,240 2 parts, 22-1/2 x 30-1/2 ea.
240	Morgan & Johnson & parts of Magoffin, Floyd & Martin, [1880?]	. . .	Kentucky Geological Survey	1:105,000 22 x 36-1/2
241	Scott, 1879	Beers & Lanagan	Beers & Lanagan, Phila.	1:42,240 3 parts, 2 are 16-1/2 x 30 ea. & 1 is 17 x 30
242	Warren, 1877	D. G. Beers & Co.	D. G. Beers & Co., Phila.	1:50,688 4 parts, 27-1/2 x 19-1/2 ea.
243	Woodford, 1870	. . .	[D. G. Beers & Co.]	. . . Photocopy (pos.), 29-1/2 x 22-1/2

LOUISIANA

No.	County and Date	Author or Surveyor	Publisher and Place	Scale and Size (Inches)
244	Avoyelles & part of Rapides, 1860	. . .	McCerren, Landry & Powell, New Orleans	1:70,000 2 parts, 30 x 40-1/2 & 30-1/2 x 40-1/2
245	Avoyelles, 1879	S. B. Robertson	. . .	1:52,466 2 parts, 21 x 40 ea.
246	Caldwell, 1860	. . .	McCerren, Landry & Powell, New Orleans	1:63,360 27 x 39
247	Catahoula, 1860	. . .	McCerren, Landry & Powell, New Orleans	1:80,000 44 x 40-1/2
248	Concordia, 1841	Caleb G. Forshey	. . .	1:100,000 58 x 34
249	Concordia, 1860	. . .	McCerren, Landry & Powell, New Orleans	1:85,000 41 x 30
250	East Baton Rouge, 1895	A. Kaiser & J. A. Swensson	. . .	1:43,000 2 parts, 23 x 42 & 20 x 42
251	East Carroll, West Carroll & part of Richland, 1860	. . .	McCerren, Landry & Powell, New Orleans	1:75,000 40-1/2 x 30
252	East Carroll, La. & Issaquena, Miss. (portions), [186-?]	A. McFarland	. . .	1:63,360 32-1/2 x 19-1/2
253	Franklin, 1860	. . .	McCerren, Landry & Powell, New Orleans	1:70,000 40-1/2 x 30-1/2
254	Iberville & parts of West Baton Rouge, St. Martin, Ascension & Pointe Coupee, 1883	C. H. Dickinson	. . .	1:63,360 4 parts, 20 x 25 ea.
255	Livingston (portion), 1870	K. Loew & John Lynch	. . .	1:32,000 21 x 26
256	Madison, 1860	. . .	McCerren, Landry & Powell, New Orleans	1:63,360 30-1/2 x 40
257	Madison, 1891	F.M. Dawson & W. M. Washburn	Aug. Gast Bank Note & Litho. Co., St. Louis	1:31,680 8 parts, 4 are 27-1/2 x 19 ea. & 4 are 27-1/2 x 20 ea.

LOUISIANA (Cont.)

No.	County and Date	Author or Surveyor	Publisher and Place	Scale and Size (Inches)
258	Morehouse, 1860	. . .	McCerren, Landry & Powell, New Orleans	1:75,000 30 x 40
259	Morehouse, 1896	A. E. Washburn	. . .	1:75,000 Photocopy (pos.), 29-1/2 x 33
260	Ouachita, 1858	William Everard Marshall	William Everard Marshall, Monroe, La.	1:65,000 39 x 40-1/2
261	Ouachita, 1860	. . .	McCerren, Landry & Powell, New Orleans	1:70,000 30 x 40
262	St. Martin & St. Landry (portions), 1860	. . .	McCerren, Landry & Powell, New Orleans	1:63,360 2 parts, 20 x 30 ea.
263	Tensas, 1860	. . .	McCerren, Landry & Powell, New Orleans	1:75,000 40 x 30
264	Tensas (portion), 1873	John Johnson	. . .	1:63,360 21-1/2 x 34

MAINE

No.	County and Date	Author or Surveyor	Publisher and Place	Scale and Size (Inches)
265	Androscoggin, 1858	J. Q. Page	J. Chace, Jr., Phila. & Portland, Maine	1:52,000 54 x 53
266	Cumberland, 1857	Sidney Baker	J. Chace, Phila.	1:52,000 59 x 57
267	Franklin, 1861	H. F. Walling	W. E. Baker & Co., New York	1:63,360 2 parts, 26-1/2 x 54 & 27-1/2 x 54
268	Hancock, 1860	H. F. Walling	Lee & Marsh, New York	1:70,000 62 x 60
269	Kennebec, 1856	J. Southwick, S. Baker & Baker & Co.	J. Chace, Jr. & Wm. R. Shaw, Phila. & Augusta, Maine	1:50,688 2 parts, 27-1/2 x 56 ea.
270	Lincoln, 1857	G. M. Hopkins	Lee & Marsh, Phila.	1:50,688 2 parts, 29 x 58-1/2 ea.
271	Oxford, 1858	H. F. Walling	Gillette & Huntington, New York	1:79,200 4 sheets, 2 are 29 x 38 ea. & 2 are 29 x 19 ea.
272	Penobscot, 1859	H. F. Walling & L. H. Eaton	Lee & Marsh, New York	1:80,000 2 parts, 30-1/2 x 60-1/2 ea.
273	Piscataquis, 1858	H. F. Walling & L. H. Eaton	Lee & Marsh, New York	1:63,360 2 parts, 52-1/2 x 27 ea.
274	Sagadahoc, 1858	J. Chace, Jr., Sid. Baker, Jos. Southwick & Wm. R. Shaw	J. Chace, Jr., L. J. Batchelor, Wm. R. Shaw, John Knox & G. D. Wakefield, Phila. & Portland, Maine	1:39,600 6 parts, 19 x 25 ea.
275	Somerset, 1860	J. Chace, Jr., J. L. Page, J. B. McChesney, J. J. Batchelor & A. F. Church	J. Chace, Jr. & D. S. Stinson, Portland, Maine & Phila.	1:63,360 2 parts, 68 x 27 ea.
276	Waldo, 1859	D. Kelsey, D. H. Davison & J. Chace, Jr.	J. Chace, Jr. & Co., Portland, Maine & Phila.	1:63,360 3 parts, 23 x 52 ea.
277	Washington, 1861	H. F. Walling	Lee & Marsh, New York	1:80,000 2 parts, 31-1/2 x 59-1/2 & 29-1/2 x 59-1/2

MAINE (Cont.)

No.	County and Date	Author or Surveyor	Publisher and Place	Scale and Size (Inches)
278	York, 1856	J. Chase [i.e., Chace], Jr.	J. L. Smith & Co., Phila. & Boston	1:63,360 2 sheets, 27-1/2 x 52-1/2 & 28-1/2 x 52-1/2

MARYLAND

No.	County and Date	Author or Surveyor	Publisher and Place	Scale and Size (Inches)
279	Anne Arundel (portion), [ca. 1650]	Caleb Dorsey (c1958)	. . .	1:31,680 20 x 27-1/2
280	Anne Arundel (portion), 1649-1665	James E. Moss (1949)	. . .	1:21,000 Photocopy (pos.) in 2 parts, 17-1/2 x 23 & 17-1/2 x 14-1/2
281	Anne Arundel, 1860	Geo. W. Beall, Amos R. Harman & Simon J. Martenet	Simon J. Martenet, Baltimore	1:63,360 44-1/2 x 33
282	Baltimore (portion), [1639-1705]	H. J. Berkley (1935)	. . .	. . . Blue print, 14-1/2 x 17
283	Baltimore, 1850	J. C. Sidney	James M. Stephens, Baltimore	1:63,360 2 parts, 23-1/2 x 33 & 20-1/2 x 33
284	Baltimore, 1857	Robert Taylor	Robert Taylor, Baltimore	1:43,000 2 parts, 63 x 26 ea.
285	Baltimore, 1863	W. F. Raynolds & Geo. Kaiser	Middle Department & 8th Army Corps	1:63,360 40 x 31
286	Caroline, 1875	John B. Isler	. . .	1:40,000 3 sheets, 20-1/2 x 37 ea.
287	Carroll, 1862	S. J. Martenet	Simon J. Martenet, Baltimore	1:42,240 47 x 51
288	Carroll, 1863	W. O. Shearer	. . .	1:31,680 2 parts, 27-1/2 x 56 ea.
289	Cecil, [18-?]	. . .	. . .	1:79,200 Photocopy (neg.) in 2 parts, 18 x 19 ea.
290	Cecil, 1858	Simon J. Martenet	. . .	1:42,240 4 sheets, 22 x 20-1/2 ea.
291	Frederick & Washington, 1808	Chs. Varlé	. . .	1:150,000 Photocopy (neg.), 19-1/2 x 34
292	Frederick, 1858	Isaac Bond	. . .	1:63,360 45 x 34-1/2
293	Frederick, [1860]	Isaac Bond	. . .	1:63,360 45 x 34-1/2
294	Harford, 1858	L. W. Herrick	Jennings & Herrick	1:41,000 51 x 42
295	Harford, 1878	Simon J. Martenet & J. W. McNabb		1:50,688 2 parts, 20-1/2 x 36 & 21 x 36

MARYLAND (Cont.)

No.	County and Date	Author or Surveyor	Publisher and Place	Scale and Size (Inches)
296	Howard, 1860	Simon J. Martenet	John Schofield, Ellicotts Mills, Md.	1:42,240 2 parts, 35 x 27-1/2 ea.
297	Kent, 1860	C. H. Baker & Simon J. Martenet	Simon J. Martenet, Baltimore	1:63,360 34-1/2 x 33
298	Montgomery, 1863	Bureau of Topographical Engineers	. . .	1:126,720 18 x 21
299	Montgomery, 1865	S. J. Martenet	Simon J. Martenet, Baltimore	1:63,360 30-1/2 x 36
300	Prince Georges, before Apr. 23, 1696	Louise Joyner Hienton	. . .	1:135,000 21-1/2 x 25
301	Prince Georges, 1860	G. W. Beal[1] & Simon J. Martenet	Simon J. Martenet, Baltimore	1:63,360 41 x 29
302	Prince Georges, 1861	G. W. Beall & Simon J. Martenet	Simon J. Martenet, Baltimore	1:63,360 43-1/2 x 30-1/2
303	Talbot, 1858	William H. Dilworth	. . .	1:40,000 2 parts, 45-1/2 x 23 ea.
304	Washington, 1859	Thomas Taggart & S. S. Downin	L. McKee & C. G. Robertson	1:32,500 2 parts, 29-1/2 x 68 ea.
305	Worcester, [ca. 1800]	James B. Robins	. . .	1:180,000 Photocopy (pos.), 13-1/2 x 18

MASSACHUSETTS

No.	County and Date	Author or Surveyor	Publisher and Place	Scale and Size (Inches)
306	Barnstable, Dukes & Nantucket, 1858	Henry F. Walling	D. R. Smith & Co., Boston & New York	1:63,360 2 sheets, 61-1/2 x 28-1/2 ea.
307	Berkshire, 1858	Henry F. Walling	Smith, Gallup & Co., Boston & New York	1:50,688 2 sheets, 31 x 62-1/2 ea.
308	Bristol, 1852	H. F. Walling	C. & A. Taber, New Bedford, Mass.	1:50,688 4 parts, 2 are 26-1/2 x 20 ea. & 2 are 27 x 20 ea.
309	Bristol, 1858	Henry F. Walling	John L. Smith & Co., New York	1:47,520 59 x 61-1/2
310	Essex, 1856	H. F. Walling	Smith & Morley, Boston	1:45,257 59-1/2 x 61
311	Franklin, 1858	H. F. Walling	Smith & Ingraham, Boston & New York	1:47,520 2 parts, 25-1/2 x 61 ea.
312	Hampden, 1855	Henry F. Walling, T. W. Baker, T. B. Mann, S. D. Kendall, A. S. Mowry, Wm. Short & J. Howe	H. A. Haley, Boston	1:47,520 2 parts, 22 x 68 & 22-1/2 x 68
313	Hampden, 1857	Henry F. Walling, T. W. Baker, T. B. Mann, S. D. Kendall, A. S. Mowry, Wm. Short & J. Howe	H.A. Haley, Boston	1:47,520 6 parts, 4 are 22-1/2 x 22-1/2 ea. & 2 are 22-1/2 x 24 ea.
314	Hampshire, 1856	H. F. Walling	. . .	1:47,520 4 parts, 2 are 20 x 29 ea. & 2 are 20 x 30 ea.
315	Hampshire, 1860	Henry F. Walling	H. & C. T. Smith & Co., New York	1:47,520 2 parts, 30 x 59-1/2 ea.

MASSACHUSETTS (Cont.)

No.	County and Date	Author or Surveyor	Publisher and Place	Scale and Size (Inches)
316	Middlesex, 1856	Henry F. Walling & Thos. W. Baker	Smith & Bumstead, Boston	1:50,417 59-1/2 x 61
317	Norfolk, 1853	Henry F. Walling	. . .	1:65,000 27-1/2 x 38-1/2
318	Norfolk, 1858	Henry F. Walling	Smith & Bumstead, Boston & New York	1:40,000 2 sheets, 31 x 58-1/2 ea.
319	Plymouth, 1857	Henry F. Walling	D. R. Smith & Co., Boston & New York	1:47,520 2 sheets, 30-1/2 x 59 ea.
320	Worcester, 1857	Henry F. Walling & T. W. Baker	Wm. E. Baker & Co., Boston & New York	1:63,360 63 x 63

MICHIGAN

No.	County and Date	Author or Surveyor	Publisher and Place	Scale and Size (Inches)
321	Allegan, 1864	I. M. Gross, Geil & Harley	Samuel Geil, Phila.	1:63,360 43-1/2 x 48
322	Branch, 1858	Geil & Jones	Geil & Jones, Phila.	1:37,000 2 parts, 52 x 26 ea.
323	Calhoun, 1858	Bechler & Wenig	Geil, Harley & Siverd, Phila.	1:50,688 2 parts, 28-1/2 x 53-1/2 ea.
324	Cass, Van Buren & Berrien, 1860	Geil & Jones [Coast Survey Coll.]	Geil, Harley & Siverd, Phila.	1:63,360 24 parts, 17 x 13 ea.
325	Cass, 1897	. . .	Home Publishing Co., Battle Creek, Mich.	1:42,000 40 x 37-1/2
326	Clinton & Gratiot, 1864	D.S. Harley, J. P. Harley, J. D. Nash, H. G. Brigham & M. C. Wagner	Samuel Geil, Phila.	1:63,360 2 parts, 25 x 42 ea.
327	Eaton & Barry, 1860	Joseph D. Nash, Geil & Jones	Geil, Harley & Siverd, Phila.	1:63,360 6 parts, 4 are 23 x 18 ea. & 2 are 23 x 18-1/2 ea.
328	Genessee & Shawassee, 1859	Geil, Jones, J. W. Stout, J. D. Nash & C. Wilson	Geil & Jones, Phila.	1:50,688 2 parts, 58 x 30-1/2 & 58 x 31-1/2
329	Gratiot, 1876	F. W. Beers	F.W. Beers & Co., New York	1:50,688 6 parts, 4 are 20 x 22-1/2 ea. & 2 are 21-1/2 x 22-1/2 ea.
330	Hillsdale, 1857	S. Geil & S. L. Jones [Coast Survey Coll.]	Daniel Kellogg, Phila.	1:36,500 18 parts, 17 x 13 ea.
331	Hillsdale, 1857	S. Geil & S. L. Jones	Kellogg & Randall, Phila.	1:36,500 2 parts, 27-1/2 x 51-1/2 ea.
332	Huron, 1875	F. W. Beers	F. W. Beers & Co., New York	1:51,000 2 parts, 25 x 57-1/2 ea.
333	Ingham & Livingston, 1859	Geil & Co., A. Jackson, I. G. Freed, J. D. Nash, C. Wilson, S. Geil & S. L. Jones	Geil, Harley & Siverd, Phila.	1:50,688 8 parts, 4 are 28 x 18 ea., 2 are 28 x 19-1/2 ea. & 2 are 28 x 17 ea.
334	Ionia, 1861	Geo. W. Wilson	. . .	1:31,680 2 parts, 32-1/2 x 59-1/2 ea.

MICHIGAN (Cont.)

No.	County and Date	Author or Surveyor	Publisher and Place	Scale and Size (Inches)
335	Jackson, 1858	S. Geil & S. L. Jones	Jos. M. Alexander, Phila.	1:39,600 2 parts, 57-1/2 x 30-1/2 ea.
336	Kalamazoo, 1861	I. Gross, S. L. Jones, & Geil & Harley	Geil & Harley, Phila.	1:47,520 2 parts, 47 x 24 ea.
337	Kalkaska, 1878	H. J. Frost	. . .	1:126,720 15-1/2 x 15-1/2
338	Kalkaska, 1898	J. R. Jenkins	J. R. Jenkins, Mancelona, Mich.	1:42,240 4 parts, 2 are 19-1/2 x 18-1/2 ea. & 2 are 21-1/2 x 18-1/2 ea.
339	Kent, [1871]	Sheldon Leavitt [Coast Survey Coll.]	Sheldon Leavitt, Grand Rapids, Mich.	1:63,360 11 parts, 17 x 13 ea.
340	Lake, 1900	. . .	The Consolidated Publishing Co., Minneapolis	1:31,680 6 parts, 4 are 17-1/2 x 25 ea. & 2 are 20 x 25 ea.
341	Lapeer, 1863	W. E. Doughty, I. Gross, & Geil & Harley	Samuel Geil, Phila.	1:47,520 2 parts, 23 x 42 ea.
342	Lenawee, 1857	G. R. Bechler & E. Wenig	Bechler, Wenig & Co., Phila.	1:50,688 2 parts, 39-1/2 x 29-1/2 ea.
343	Livingston, 1859	Geil & Co. & A. Jackson, I. G. Freed, J. D. Nash, C. Wilson, S. Geil & S. L. Jones	Geil, Harley & Siverd, Phila.	1:50,688 2 parts, 28 x 36 ea.
344	Macomb & St. Clair, 1859	Geil & Jones	Geil, Harley & Siverd, Phila.	1:63,360 2 parts, 26-1/2 x 62-1/2 ea.
345	Menominee, 1898	Albert Hass	. . .	1:63,360 62-1/2 x 33
346	Missaukee, 1878	H. J. Frost	. . .	1:126,720 15-1/2 x 15-1/2
347	Monroe & Wayne (portions), [18-?]	. . .	. . .	1:253,440 25 x 35
348	Monroe, 1859	Geil & Jones	Geil, Harley & Siverd, Phila.	1:39,600 2 parts, 45 x 31-1/2 ea.
349	Montcalm, 1875	F. W. Beers	F. W. Beers & Co., New York	1:43,000 8 parts, 17 x 28 ea.
350	Oakland, [186-?]	F. Hess [Coast Survey Coll.]	S. H. Burhans	1:42,240 30 parts, 17 x 13 ea.
351	Oceana, 1876	F. W. Beers	F. W. Beers & Co., New York	1:50,000 52 x 34-1/2
352	Ottawa & Muskegon & part of Allegan, 1864	I. M. Gross, Geil & Harley [Coast Survey Coll.]	Samuel Geil, Phila.	1:63,360 17 parts, 17 x 13 ea.
353	Saginaw & Tuscola & parts of Genesee, Lapeer, Huron & Midland, 1858	D. A. Pettibone	D. A. Pettibone, Bridgeport Center, Mich.	1:100,000 38 x 49
354	Saginaw & Tuscola & parts of Genesee, Lapeer, Huron & Midland, 1859	D. A. Pettibone [Coast Survey Coll.]	. . .	1:100,000 11 parts, 17 x 13 ea.

MICHIGAN (Cont.)

No.	County and Date	Author or Surveyor	Publisher and Place	Scale and Size (Inches)
355	Saginaw, 1890	Charles Holmes	. . .	1:42,240 2 parts, 47 x 26-1/2 ea.
356	St. Joseph, 1858	Geil & Jones, & M. Lampen	Geil, Harley & Siverd, Phila.	1:36,205 2 parts, 31 x 60 ea.
357	St. Joseph, 1897	. . .	Home Publishing Co., Battle Creek, Mich.	1:42,240 2 parts, 20 x 37-1/2 ea.
358	Sanilac, 1876	F. W. Beers	F. W. Beers & Co., New York	1:53,000 2 parts, 63-1/2 x 24-1/2 ea.
359	Tuscola, 1875	F. W. Beers	F. W. Beers & Co., New York	1:50,000 2 parts, 61 x 25-1/2 ea.
360	Washtenaw, 1856	G. R. Bechler & E. Wenig	Bechler, Wenig & Co., Phila.	1:50,688 43 x 48
361	Washtenaw & Lenawee, 1864	G. R. Bechler & E. Wenig	Samuel Geil, Phila.	1:63,360 4 sheets, 2 are 28-1/2 x 38 ea. & 2 are 28-1/2 x 19 ea.
362	Washtenaw, [c1896]	. . .	M. M. Dickson & Co., Ann Arbor, Mich.	1:63,360 24-1/2 x 31
363	Wayne, 1812	McNiff, Robt. King & Wm. Tatham	. . .	1:135,000 Ms., 27-1/2 x 44-1/2
363a	Wayne, 1855	John Farmer	. . .	1:67,000 29-1/2 x 35
364	Wayne, 1860	Geil & Jones, Geil & Harley, & I. G. Freed	Geil, Harley & Siverd, Phila.	1:42,240 6 parts, 4 are 26 x 18-1/2 ea. & 2 are 26 x 19-1/2 ea.
365	Wayne & part of Oakland & Macomb, 1894	Mason L. Brown	Silas Farmer & Co., Detroit	1:42,240 67-1/2 x 56-1/2

MINNESOTA

No.	County and Date	Author or Surveyor	Publisher and Place	Scale and Size (Inches)
366	Blue Earth, 1879	. . .	Warner & Foote, Minneapolis & Phila.	1:38,990 6 parts, 4 are 25 x 19 ea. & 2 are 25 x 20-1/2 ea.
367	Brown, 1886	. . .	M. B. Haynes, Mankato, Minn.	1:39,600 2 parts, 43-1/2 x 30 ea.
368	Brown, 1900	. . .	L. G. Vogel, New Ulm, Minn.	1:42,240 40-1/2 x 54
369	Carver, 1880	. . .	Warner & Foote, Minneapolis & Phila.	1:31,680 6 parts, 4 are 16 x 25-1/2 ea. & 2 are 18 x 25-1/2 ea.
370	Cottonwood, 1898	Wm. A. Peterson	. . .	1:48,500 33 x 42
371	Dakota, 1874	Ed. A. H. Hoenck	Hoenck & Roosen, St. Paul	1:63,360 36-1/2 x 30-1/2

MINNESOTA (Cont.)

No.	County and Date	Author or Surveyor	Publisher and Place	Scale and Size (Inches)
372	Freeborn, 1878	. . .	Warner & Foote, Red Wing, Minn. & Phila.	1:36,205 3 parts, 16 x 51, 16-1/2 x 51 & 17-1/2 x 51
373	Houston, 1871	H. I. Bliss & J. M. Marti	H. I. Bliss & J. M. Marti, La Crosse, Wis.	1:47,520 46-1/2 x 46-1/2
374	Isanti and parts of Chisago, Anoka, Sherburne & Mille Lacs, 1898	. . .	C. M. Foote Publishing Co., E. J. Foote & Geo. F. Weston, Minneapolis	1:36,000 2 parts, 67 x 31-1/2 ea.
375	Lyon, 1884	Louis Larson	Marshall Messenger [Marshall, Minn.]	1:66,000 31 x 24-1/2
376	McLeod, 1880	. . .	Warner & Foote, Minneapolis & Phila.	1:31,680 3 parts, 1 is 18 x 54-1/2 & 2 are 16-1/2 x 54-1/2 ea.
377	Martin, 1887	. . .	M. B. Haynes, Mankato, Minn.	1:39,600 2 parts, 46-1/2 x 25-1/2 ea.
378	Murray, 1898	Chas. E. Ellis, J. C. Heffer, Geo. W. Atkinson & F. W. Leonard	E. Frank Peterson, Vermillion, S. Dak.	1:50,688 2 parts, 36 x 19-1/2 ea.
379	Nicollet, 1885	. . .	Haynes & Woodard, Mankato, Minn.	1:39,600 34-1/2 x 57
380	Ramsey, [c1885]	D. L. Curtice & H. S. Potts	D. L. Curtice & H. S. Potts	1:17,300 4 sheets, 1 is 31 x 34, 1 is 31 x 20 & 2 are 35 x 27 ea.
381	Ramsey & Washington & parts of Anoka, Dakota & Hennepin, Minn. & St. Croix & Pierce, Wis., 1887	. . .	C.M. Foote & Co., Minneapolis	1:36,205 4 parts, 37 x 31 ea.
382	Redwood, [c1898]	A. H. Anderson	The Pioneer Press Co., St. Paul, Minn.	1:43,000 8 parts, 28-1/2 x 15-1/2 ea.
383	Steele, 1879	. . .	Warner & Foote, Minneapolis	1:33,792 4 parts, 24 x 22 ea.
384	Todd, 1890	. . .	Henry H. Budgett, Long Prairie, Minn.	1:50,688 3 parts, 1 is 20 x 32 & 2 are 19 x 32 ea.
385	Watonwan, 1898	Chas. E. Ellis, J. A. Steinson, J. C. Heffer, F. W. Leonard & Geo. W. Atkinson	E. Frank Peterson, Vermillion, S. Dak.	1:42,240 34 x 38-1/2

MISSISSIPPI

No.	County and Date	Author or Surveyor	Publisher and Place	Scale and Size (Inches)
386	Coahoma, 1872	Hewson & FitzGerald	. . .	1:50,000 51-1/2 x 45
388	Issaquena, 1873	Jas. M. Searles & David Stratton	Hugh Lewis, New Orleans	1:65,000 34-1/2 x 39
389	Washington, 1871	Richard A. O'Hea	. . .	1:63,360 40-1/2 x 51-1/2

MISSISSIPPI (Cont.)

No.	County and Date	Author or Surveyor	Publisher and Place	Scale and Size (Inches)
390	Yazoo, 1874	Mercer & Fontaine & J. W. Mercer	. . .	1:50,688 57 x 58

MISSOURI

No.	County and Date	Author or Surveyor	Publisher and Place	Scale and Size (Inches)
391	Atchison, 1894	B. F. Rummerfield	. . .	1:140,000 Photocopy (pos.), 15 x 17
392	Buchanan, 1895	Tracy & Rutt	Tracy & Rutt, St. Joseph, Mo.	1:63,360 31 x 40
393	Cedar, 1879	Babbs & Stoddard	Reily & Co.	1:31,680 4 parts, 23 x 26-1/2 ea.
394	Cedar, 1897	Virgil L. Walker	E. P. Noll & Co., Phila.	1:31,680 2 parts, 23-1/2 x 52-1/2 ea.
395	Clay, 1887	. . .	G. M. Hopkins, Phila.	1:31,680 4 parts, 25-1/2 x 22 ea.
396	Gasconade, 1875	Geo. H. King	Geo. H. King	1:48,000 4 parts, 27 x 23 ea.
397	Grundy, [c1877]	B. F. Thomas	. . .	1:31,500 6 parts, 4 are 16 x 22-1/2 ea. & 2 are 17 x 22-1/2 ea.
398	Hickory, 1880	R. Thornton Higgins	J. S. & R. T. Higgins	1:63,360 19 x 27
399	Jackson, 1869	E. A. Hickman	. . .	1:64,200 Photocopy (pos.) in 12 sheets, 8 x 6-1/2 ea.
400	Jackson, 1887	John P. Edwards	John P. Edwards, Quincy, Ill.	1:31,680 6 parts, 4 are 18-1/2 x 28 ea. & 2 are 20-1/2 x 28 ea.
401	McDonald, 1884	H. v. Erdmannsdorff	Smith & Stroup, Phila.	1:42,900 40-1/2 x 53
402	Madison, [188-?]	. . .	B. B. Cahoon, Fredericktown, Mo.	1:110,000 24 x 18-1/2
403	Morgan, 1880	R. Thornton Higgins	J. S. & R. T. Higgins	1:84,480 2 parts, 26-1/2 x 18-1/2 ea.
404	Nodaway, [1876]	Morehouse, Sisson & Co.	Morehouse, Sisson & Co., Maryville, Mo.	1:63,360 2 sheets, 23-1/2 x 34 & 13 x 34
405	Pettis, 1876	. . .	Warner & Foote, Sedalia, Mo. & Phila.	1:31,680 6 parts, 2 are 21-1/2 x 26-1/2 ea. & 4 are 19-1/2 x 26-1/2 ea.
406	St. Louis, 1857	Gustavus Waagner	Schaerff & Bro., St. Louis	1:67,500 39-1/2 x 32
407	St. Louis, [1856-1865?]	. . .	. . .	1:32,000 8 parts, 18 x 34 ea.
408	Saline, 1871	M. J. Alexander	. . .	1:65,000 42 x 35-1/2

MISSOURI (Cont.)

No.	County and Date	Author or Surveyor	Publisher and Place	Scale and Size (Inches)
409	Vernon, 1886	. . .	Hall & Babbs, Stockton, Mo.	1:36,205 6 parts, 4 are 25-1/2 x 20 ea. & 2 are 25-1/2 x 21 ea.
410	Wayne, 1882	. . .	B. B. Cahoon	1:115,000 18-1/2 x 24
411	Webster, 1877	Tom. C. Strickland	. . .	1:130,000 16 x 11
412	Webster, 1878	T. C. Strickland	. . .	1:130,000 16 x 11

MONTANA

No.	County and Date	Author or Surveyor	Publisher and Place	Scale and Size (Inches)
413	Cascade, 1890	O. C. Mortson	. . .	1:190,000 28 x 42-1/2
414	Lewis & Clarke, 1890	Paul S. A. Bickel & William D. Rumsey	. . .	1:126,720 44-1/2 x 35-1/2
415	Silver Bow, 1890	G. A. Kornberg & John Hagel	. . .	1:126,720 20-1/2 x 39

NEBRASKA

No.	County and Date	Author or Surveyor	Publisher and Place	Scale and Size (Inches)
416	Cass, 1894	E. E. Hilton	T. H. Pollock, Plattsmouth, Nebr.	1:42,240 34-1/2 x 52
417	Cuming, [1900?]	W. W. Hixson & Co.	The West Point [Nebraska] Republican-Advertiser	1:43,000 2 parts, 24-1/2 x 41-1/2 ea.
418	Douglas, 1892	. . .	Rob't H. Willis, Omaha	1:32,000 31 x 67
419	Douglas, 1900	Geo. McBride & Jacob Hauck	. . .	1:32,000 29 x 65
420	Jefferson, 1889	J. R. Dunham	J. R. Dunham, Fairbury, Nebr.	1:42,240 47 x 40
421	Lincoln, 1894	I. A. Fort	. . .	1:126,720 27-1/2 x 33

NEVADA

No.	County and Date	Author or Surveyor	Publisher and Place	Scale and Size (Inches)
422	Elko, 1894	E. C. McClellan	. . .	1:600,000 15-1/2 x 17-1/2

NEW HAMPSHIRE

No.	County and Date	Author or Surveyor	Publisher and Place	Scale and Size (Inches)
423	Belknap, 1859	E. M. Woodford	Smith & Peavey, Phila.	1:39,600 6 parts, 4 are 17 x 26 ea. & 2 are 19 x 26 ea.
424	Belknap, 1860	E. M. Woodford	Smith & Peavey, Phila.	1:39,600 2 parts, 26-1/2 x 52 ea.

NEW HAMPSHIRE (Cont.)

No.	County and Date	Author or Surveyor	Publisher and Place	Scale and Size (Inches)
425	Carroll, 1861	H. F. Walling	Smith & Peavey, New York	1:63,360 6 parts, 27 x 18-1/2 ea.
426	Cheshire, 1858	L. Fagan	Smith & Morley, Phila.	1:42,240 2 parts, 28-1/2 x 56-1/2 ea.
427	Cheshire, 1858	L. Fagan	Smith & Morley, Phila.	1:42,240 2 parts, 28-1/2 x 56-1/2 ea.
428	Coos, 1861	H. F. Walling	Smith, Mason & Co., New York	1:84,480 2 parts, 31-1/2 x 42 ea.
429	Grafton, 1860	H. F. Walling	Smith, Mason & Co., New York	1:70,000 2 parts, 30-1/2 x 59-1/2 & 29-1/2 x 59-1/2
430	Hillsborough, 1858	J. Chace, Jr.	Smith, Mason & Co., Boston & Phila.	1:52,000 2 parts, 30-1/2 x 60 & 28 x 60
431	Merrimack, 1858	H. F. Walling	Smith & Peavey, Boston & New York	1:47,520 6 parts, 30 x 21 ea.
432	Rockingham, 1857	J. Chace, Jr.	Smith & Coffin, Phila.	1:50,688 2 parts, 28 x 57 & 29 x 57
433	Rockingham, 1860	J. Chace, Jr. [Coast Survey Coll.]	Smith & Coffin, Phila.	1:50,688 20 parts, 13 x 17 ea.
434	Rockingham (portion), 1876	J. Chace & J. W. A.	. . .	1:50,688 24 x 27
435	Strafford, 1856	J. Chace, Jr.	Smith & Bartlett, Phila. & Boston	1:42,500 2 parts, 28 x 50 & 30 x 50
436	Sullivan, 1860	H. F. Walling	Smith & Morley, New York	1:40,000 6 parts, 27-1/2 x 19 ea.

NEW JERSEY

No.	County and Date	Author or Surveyor	Publisher and Place	Scale and Size (Inches)
437	Atlantic, 1872	F. W. Beers	Beers, Comstock & Cline, New York	1:39,600 2 parts, 68 x 32-1/2 ea.
438	Bergen & Passaic, 1861	G.M. Hopkins	G. H. Corey, Phila.	1:42,240 2 parts, 58 x 23-1/2 ea.
439	Burlington (portion), [18-?]	. . .	. . .	1:40,550 Ms., 49 x 28-1/2
440	Burlington, 1849	J. W. Otley & R. Whiteford	Smith & Wistar, Phila.	1:53,000 34 x 66
441	Burlington, 1858	Wm. Parry, Geo. Sykes & F. W. Earl	R. K. Kuhn & J. D. Janney	1:50,688 4 parts, 30 x 25 ea.
442	Burlington, 1859	Wm. Parry, Geo. Sykes & F. W. Earl	R. K. Kuhn & J. D. Janney	1:50,688 6 parts, 20 x 24-1/2 ea.
443	Camden, 1857	. . .	R. L. Barnes, Phila. & Lloyd Vanderveer, Camden	1:42,240 2 parts, 23-1/2 x 37 ea.
444	Cape May, 1872	F. W. Beers	Beers, Comstock & Cline, New York	1:39,600 2 parts, 25-1/2 x 48-1/2 ea.

NEW JERSEY (Cont.)

No.	County and Date	Author or Surveyor	Publisher and Place	Scale and Size (Inches)
445	Cumberland, 1862	S.N. & F. W. Beers, L. B. Lake & C. S. Warner	A. Pomeroy, Phila.	1:38,990 2 parts, 29-1/2 x 54-1/2 ea.
446	Essex, 1850	J. C. Sidney	Hiram A. Belding, Newark	1:32,000 50-1/2 x 36-1/2
447	Essex, 1859	H. F. Walling	Baker & Tilden, New York	1:20,000 2 parts, 29-1/2 x 60 ea.
448	Essex, 1874	Matthew Hughes	Matthew Hughes, Orange, N. J.	1:14,400 6 sheets, 4 are 20-1/2 x 29-1/2 ea. & 2 are 21-1/2 x 29-1/2
449	Essex, 1877	W. A. Mirick	J. S. Schaeffer	1:36,500 22 x 25-1/2
450	Hudson (portion), 1841	L. F. Douglass	L. F. Douglass, Jersey City, N. J.	1:10,600 36-1/2 x 58-1/2
451	Hudson (portion), 1841	L. F. Douglass & George A. Buckingham	Benj. S. Demarest, New York (1876)	1:11,500 3 parts, 1 is 32 x 18-1/2 & 2 are 32 x 17-1/2 ea.
452	Hudson (portion), 1855	Wm. H. Wood	R. B. Kashow, Jersey City, N. J.	1:15,150 18-1/2 x 22-1/2
453	Hunterdon, 1851	Samuel C. Cornell	Lloyd Van Derveer & S. C. Cornell	1:42,240 51 x 37-1/2
454	Mercer, 1849	J. W. Otley & J. Keily	Lloyd Van der Veer, Camden	1:42,240 31-1/2 x 41
455	Middlesex, 1766	I. Hills & Az. Dunham	. . .	1:39,600 Photocopy (pos.), 31 x 61-1/2
456	Middlesex, 1850	J. W. Otley & J. Keily	Lloyd Van Derveer, Camden	1:43,000 40 x 38
457	Middlesex, 1861	H. F. Walling	Smith, Gallup & Co., New York	1:30,000 2 parts, 30 x 59-1/2 ea.
458	Monmouth, 1851	Jesse Lightfoot	J. B. Shields, Middletown-point, N. J.	1:42,240 2 sheets, 39 x 28 ea.
459	Monmouth, 1861	S. N. & F. W. Beers, & H. F. Walling	Smith, Gallup & Holt, New York	1:39,600 4 parts, 20 x 29-1/2 ea.
460	Morris, 1853	J. Lightfoot & Saml. Geil	J. B. Shields, Morristown, N. J.	1:42,240 37-1/2 x 51
461	Ocean, 1872	F. W. Beers	Beers, Comstock & Cline, New York	1:39,600 2 parts, 71-1/2 x 26 ea.
462	Salem & Gloucester, 1849	Alexr. C. Stansbie, James Keily & Samuel M. Rea	Smith & Wistar, Phila.	1:52,000 2 sheets, 38 x 26 & 38 x 28-1/2
463	Somerset, [1766]	I. Hills & Benjamin Morgan	. . .	1:39,600 Photocopy (pos.), 59-1/2 x 45-1/2
464	Somerset, 1850	J. W. Otley & J. Keily	Lloyd Van Derveer, Camden	1:42,240 45 x 37-1/2
465	Somerset, 1850	Otley, Van Derveer & Keily	Lloyd Van Derveer, Camden	1:42,240 2 parts, 22-1/2 x 37-1/2 ea.
466	Sussex, 1860	G. M. Hopkins, Jr.	Carlos Allen, Phila.	1:42,240 2 parts, 27 x 49-1/2 ea.

NEW JERSEY (Cont.)

No.	County and Date	Author or Surveyor	Publisher and Place	Scale and Size (Inches)
467	Union, 1862	Ernest L. Meyer & P. Witzel	. . .	1:21,120 41 x 57
468	Warren, 1852	D. McCarty	. . .	1:47,520 50 x 37-1/2
469	Warren, 1860	H. F. Walling & G. M. Hopkins, Jr.	Smith, Gallup & Co., New York	1:42,240 2 parts, 27 x 54-1/2 ea.

NEW MEXICO

470	Colfax & Mora, 1889	Edward Rollandet	. . .	1:253,440 27 x 37-1/2
471	Otero (portion), 1884-85	Surveyor General's Office, Santa Fe, N. M.	. . .	1:31,680 11 ms. maps, 16 x 22 ea.
472	Santa Fe, 1883	E. Kingman, Jr.	. . .	1:155,000 33-1/2 x 28

NEW YORK

473	Albany, [1854]	Jay Gould & I. B. Moore	. . .	. . . 38 x 55-1/2
474	Allegany, 1856	G. Bechler	Gillette, Matthews & Co., Phila.	1:50,688 56 x 53-1/2
475	Allegany (portion), 1879	Richd. H. Lee & Hiram J. Torrey	. . .	1:42,240 26 x 32-1/2
476	Broome, 1855	Franklin Gifford & Emile Wenig	A. O. Gallup & Co., Phila.	1:51,500 39 x 59-1/2
477	Cattaraugus, 1856	Samuel Geil & S. K. Godshalk	J. M. Tiffany, Fredonia, N. Y.	1:51,000 56 x 59
478	Cayuga, 1853	Samuel Geil, F. Gifford & S. K. Godshalk	Samuel Geil, Phila.	1:51,500 57 x 37
479	Cayuga & Seneca, 1859	O. W. Gray & G. D. Lothrop	A. R. Z. Dawson, I. D. Peck, S. Willard Treat, A. Y Peck, C. O. Titus, J. H. C. Dawson & L. G. Dawson, Phila.	1:63,360 2 parts, 30 x 58-1/2 ea.
480	Chautauqua, 1854	S. M. Rea & A. V. Trimble	Collins G. Keeney, Phila.	1:53,000 51-1/2 x 53
481	Chemung, 1853	Samuel M. Rea & A. V. Tremble	Wm. E. Baker, Phila.	1:42,000 4 parts, 21 x 29 ea.
482	Chenango, 1855	L. Fagan	LaFayette Leal	1:46,080 55-1/2 x 52
483	Chenango & Cortland, 1863	A. & C. S. Warner, S. N. & F. W. Beers, & B. Nichols	A. Pomeroy & S. W. Treat, Phila.	1:50,688 2 parts, 32 x 63 ea.
484	Clinton, 1856	A. Ligowsky	O. J. Lamb, Phila.	. . . 54-1/2 x 46
485	Clinton, 1885	H. K. Averill, Jr.	. . .	1:256,000 10-1/2 x 9

NEW YORK (Cont.)

No.	County and Date	Author or Surveyor	Publisher and Place	Scale and Size (Inches)
486	Columbia (portion), 1798	John Wigram. Copied by David Vaughan, 1850	. . .	1:63,360 16 x 23-1/2
487	Columbia, 1851	J. W. Otley & F. W. Keenan	John E. Gillett[e], Phila.	1:42,240 2 sheets, 27-1/2 x 38 ea.
488	Columbia, 1858	S. N. Beers, D. J. Lake & F. W. Beers	E. A. Balch, Phila.	1:39,500 2 parts, 56 x 28 ea.
489	Cortland, 1855	P. J. Browne	Eneas Smith, Cortland, N. Y. & J. B. Shields, Phila.	1:36,000 57 x 47-1/2
490	Delaware, 1856	Jay Gould	Collins G. Keeney, Phila.	1:63,360 2 parts, 28 x 57 ea.
491	Dutchess, 1850	J. C. Sidney	John E. Gillet[te]	1:42,240 2 sheets, 30 x 40 & 27-1/2 x 40
492	Dutchess, 1858	. . .	John E. Gillette, Phila.	1:46,080 2 parts, 60 x 28-1/2 ea.
493	Erie, 1854	Samuel Geil	Robert Pearsall Smith, Phila. & John Angell, Buffalo, N. Y.	1:62,000 55-1/2 x 40
494	Erie, 1855	Samuel Geil	Gillette, Matthews & Co., Phila.	1:59,000 6 parts, 3 are 27 x 19 ea. & 3 are 28-1/2 x 19 ea.
495	Essex, 1858	J. H. French	E. A. Balch, Phila.	1:65,000 2 parts, 28-1/2 x 50 ea.
496	Franklin, 1858	. . .	Taintor, Dawson & Co., Phila.	1:63,360 6 parts, 21 x 22 ea.
497	Fulton, 1856	J. Chace, Jr., J. O. Page & U. B. McChesny	Jno. T. Hill, Phila.	. . . 37-1/2 x 55-1/2
498	Genesee, 1854	J. W. Otley & S. M. Rea	John E. Gillett[e], Phila.	1:41,500 36-1/2 x 51
499	Greene, 1805 & 1809	Jas. Cockburn & Jacob Trumpbour, Jr. Copied Dec. 1910 by F. A. Gaylord	. . .	. . . Blue print, 33 x 65-1/2
500	Greene, 1856	Samuel Geil	E. A. Balch, Phila.	1:60,000 4 parts, 18-1/2 x 26-1/2 ea.
501	Herkimer, 1859	R. F. O'Connor & T. Golden	R. F. O'Connor, Little Falls, N. Y.	1:50,000 3 parts, 17-1/2 x 56, 18-1/2 x 56 & 19-1/2 x 56
502	Jefferson, 1855	Morris Levey	J. B. Shields, Phila.	1:50,688 2 parts, 26-1/2 x 50 ea.
503	Kings (portion), 1855	. . .	J. H. Colton & Co., New York	1:9,600 2 sheets, 37 x 25-1/2 & 37 x 26-1/2
504	Kings (portion), 1855	William Perris	Wm. Perris & J. H. Higginson, New York	1:3,960 4 sheets, 2 are 32 x 40-1/2 ea. & 2 are 29-1/2 x 40-1/2 ea.
505	Kings & Queens, 1859	H. F. Walling	W. E. & A. A. Baker, New York	1:40,000 2 parts, 29-1/2 x 60-1/2 ea.
506	Kings & part of Queens, 1860	. . .	J. H. Higginson, New York	1:63,360 29-1/2 x 32

NEW YORK (Cont.)

No.	County and Date	Author or Surveyor	Publisher and Place	Scale and Size (Inches)
507	Kings (portion), 1868	. . .	M. Dripps, New York	1:22,400 26 x 20
508	Kings, 1868	. . .	M. Dripps, New York	1:22,500 33-1/2 x 26-1/2
509	Kings (portion), 1869	. . .	M. Dripps, New York	1:22,600 23-1/2 x 19
510	Kings & part of Queens, [1872?]	. . .	M. Dripps, New York	1:22,400 64-1/2 x 35-1/2
511	Kings (portion), 1874	Henry Fulton	J. B. Beers & Co., New York	1:6,000 8 parts, 4 are 27 x 20-1/2 ea. & 4 are 27 x 21-1/2 ea.
512	Kings & Queens, 1886	. . .	J. B. Beers & Co., New York	1:39,600 2 parts, 27-1/2 x 50 ea.
513	Lewis, 1857	A. Ligowsky	S. & R. S. Taintor, Jr. & Co., Phila.	1:63,360 2 parts, 27 x 48-1/2 & 28 x 48-1/2
514	Livingston, 1852	Rea & Otley	Smith & Gillett[e], Phila.	1:45,000 52-1/2 x 38
515	Livingston, 1858	J. H. French	Jno. E. Gillette, Phila.	1:42,240 2 parts, 30 x 59 ea.
516	Madison, 1853	Gurdon Evans	Anthony D. Byles, Phila.	1:56,320 39-1/2 x 52
517	Madison, 1859	J. H. French	Jno. E. Gillette, Phila.	1:42,240 2 parts, 37-1/2 x 57-1/2 ea.
518	Monroe, 1852	P. J. Browne	A. G. Gillett[e], Addison, N. Y.	1:50,000 39 x 50
519	Monroe, 1858	P. J. Browne	John E. Gillette, C. K. Stone, A. J. Cowles, A. Pomeroy, I. D. Peck, C. O. Titus & A. Y. Peck, Phila.	1:42,240 2 parts, 29-1/2 x 58 ea.
520	Monroe, 1887	. . .	J. B. Beers & Co., New York	1:31,680 3 parts, 59-1/2 x 21-1/2 ea.
521	Montgomery, 1853	Samuel Geil & B. J. Hunter	Peter A. Griner & Robert P. Smith, Phila.	1:40,000 34 x 63-1/2
522	Niagara, 1852	F. Gifford & S. Geil	Franklin Gifford, Wilson, N. Y.	1:42,240 2 parts, 38 x 27 ea.
523	Niagara & Orleans, 1860	O. W. Gray & G. D. Lathrop	A. R. Z. Dawson, I. D. Peck, W. H. Green, A. Y. Peck, W. J. Tator, S. W. Treat, N. R. Wilbur, C. O. Titus & L. G. Dawson, Phila.	1:63,360 2 sheets, 60-1/2 x 28-1/2 ea.
524	Oneida, 1852	A. E. Rogerson & E. J. Murphy	Newell S. Brown, Phila.	1:63,360 51 x 40
525	Oneida, 1858	J. H. French, S. N. Beers, D. J. Lake & F. W. Beers	John E. Gillette, A. J. Cowles, A. Pomeroy, C. O. Titus & C. Bachman, Phila.	1:50,688 2 parts, 33-1/2 x 63-1/2 ea.
526	Onondaga, 1852	L. Fagan,& Sidney & Neff	E. H. Babcock & Co., Syracuse, N. Y. & Geo. C. Brown, Providence, R. I.	1:52,500 53-1/2 x 38
527	Onondaga, 1855	L. Fagan,& Sidney & Neff [Coast Survey Coll.]	E. H. Babcock & Co., Syracuse, N. Y. & J. W. Stackhouse, Phila.	1:42,500 15 parts, 17 x 13 ea.

NEW YORK (Cont.)

No.	County and Date	Author or Surveyor	Publisher and Place	Scale and Size (Inches)
528	Onondaga, 1859	J. H. French	. . .	1:42,240 2 parts, 32 x 61 ea.
529	Onondaga, 1860	Homer D. L. Sweet	A. R. Z. Dawson, I. D. Peck, W. H. Green, A. Y. Peck, W. J. Tator, S. W. Treat, N. R. Wilbur, C. O. Titus & L. G. Dawson, Phila.	1:42,240 2 parts, 32 x 61 ea.
530	Onondaga, 1889	Homer D. L. Sweet & H. Wadsworth Clarke	C. W. Bardeen	1:42,240 2 parts, 27 x 46 ea.
531	Ontario, [18-?]	. . .	. . .	1:330,000 Photocopy (pos.), 19 x 13-1/2
532	Ontario, [1815?]	. . .	. . .	1:432,000 Photocopy (pos.), 13-1/2 x 8-1/2
533	Ontario, 1852	H. F. Walling	John E. Gillett[e], Phila.	1:53,000 38 x 47-1/2
534	Ontario, 1859	S. N. & D. G. Beers	A. R. Z. Dawson, I. D. Peck, S. Willard Treat, A. Y. Peck, C. O. Titus, J. H. C. Dawson & L. G. Dawson, Phila.	1:42,240 2 parts, 29-1/2 x 61-1/2 ea.
535	Orange, [180-]	Simeon De Witt	. . .	. . . 9 x 11-1/2
536	Orange, before 1810	Anne Olmstead Peet (1936)	Roscoe W. Smith, Monroe, N. Y.	1:63,360 19 x 23
537	Orange, 1851	J. C. Sidney	Newell S. Brown, Newburgh, N. Y. & Phila.	1:52,000 2 parts, 22 x 57 ea.
538	Orange & Rockland, 1859	F. F. French, W. E. Wood & S. N. Beers	Corey & Bachman, Phila.	1:50,688 2 parts, 31-1/2 x 60 & 32-1/2 x 60
539	Orleans, 1852	Lightfoot & Geil	Lloyd Van Derveer, Phila.	1:44,000 37 x 43-1/2
540	Oswego, 1854	B. J. Hunter & Samuel Geil	Gillett[e], Matthews & Co., Phila.	. . . 2 parts, 25 x 55-1/2 ea.
541	Otsego, before 1850	Annie Olmstead Peet (c1963)	. . .	. . . 21 x 25-1/2
542	Otsego, 1856	C. & B. C. Gates	A. O. Gallup & Co., Phila.	1:50,500 2 parts, 51 x 30 ea.
543	Putnam, 1854	R. F. O'Connor	R. F. O'Connor, New York	1:31,680 2 sheets, 28 x 36 ea.
544	Queens, 1899	. . .	Hyde & Co., Brooklyn	1:25,000 38 x 28-1/2
545	Rensselaer, 1854	A. E. Rogerson	E. A. Balch, Troy, N. Y.	1:42,240 58-1/2 x 40
546	Rensselaer, 1861	D. J. Lake & S. N. Beers	Smith, Gallup & Co., Phila.	1:42,240 6 parts, 29 x 19-1/2 ea.
547	Richmond, 1668-1712	Frederick Skene & C. D. Burrus (1907). Copied by Everard A. McAroy (1914).	. . .	1:18,000 Blue print, 2 parts, 40-1/2 x 25-1/2 ea.
548	Richmond, 1780-1783	. . .	. . .	1:39,000 Photocopy (pos.), 22 x 16-1/2

NEW YORK (Cont.)

No.	County and Date	Author or Surveyor	Publisher and Place	Scale and Size (Inches)
549	Richmond, 1850	J. C. Sidney	M. Dripps, New York	1:26,000 27-1/2 x 39
550	Richmond, 1859	H. F. Walling	D. A. Fox, New York	1:15,840 55 x 55
551	Richmond, 1860	. . .	J. H. Higginson, New York	1:63,360 17 x 18
552	Richmond, 1884	. . .	G. W. & C. B. Colton & Co., New York	1:32,000 26 x 32-1/2
553	Richmond, 1887	. . .	J. B. Beers & Co.	1:18,000 2 sheets, 23-1/2 x 28-1/2 & 22-1/2 x 28-1/2
554	Richmond, 1887	. . .	J. B. Beers & Co., New York	1:18,000 4 parts, 2 are 38-1/2 x 29 ea. & 2 are 38-1/2 x 27-1/2
555	Rockland, 1854	R. F. O'Connor	R. F. O'Connor, New York	. . . 2 sheets, 27 x 39 ea.
556	St. Lawrence, 1858	A. E. Rogerson	J. B. Shields, Phila.	1:79,200 2 parts, 29-1/2 x 58 ea.
557	Saratoga, 1856	Samuel Geil	E. A. Balch, Phila.	1:50,688 2 parts, 30 x 38 & 27-1/2 x 38-1/2
558	Schenectady, 1856	L. Fagan	L. Fagan	1:31,680 6 parts, 4 are 22 x 19-1/2 ea. & 2 are 22 x 18-1/2 ea.
559	Schoharie, 1856	E. Wenig & W. Lorey	. . .	1:52,500 54-1/2 x 36
560	Schuyler, 1857	S. N. Beers	J. H. French, Syracuse, N. Y.	1:39,600 2 parts, 49-1/2 x 31-1/2 ea.
561	Seneca, 1850	Wm. T. Gibson	J. Delafield	1:145,000 16 x 10
562	Seneca, [185-]	P. J. Browne	A. G. Gillett[e], Addison, N. Y.	1:44,000 2 parts, 26 x 35 & 27 x 35
563	Seneca, 1852	Wm. T. Gibson	J. Delafield	1:44,000 52-1/2 x 34-1/2
564	Steuben, 1857	M. Levy	J. E. Gillette, Phila.	1:66,000 55-1/2 x 59
565	Suffolk, 1858	J. Chace, Jr.	John Douglass, Phila.	1:62,500 2 parts, 24-1/2 x 57-1/2 ea.
566	Sullivan, 1856	C. Gates & Son	Gillett[e] & Huntington, Phila.	1:50,000 6 parts, 2 are 17 x 26-1/2 ea., 2 are 18-1/2 x 26-1/2 ea. & 2 are 20-1/2 x 26-1/2 ea.
567	Tioga, 1855	Samuel Geil	E. D. Marsh, Phila.	1:40,500 58-1/2 x 40-1/2
568	Tompkins, 1853	L. Fagan	Horace & Charles T. Smith, & Robert Pearsall Smith, Phila.	1:44,000 2 parts, 41 x 29-1/2 ea.

NEW YORK (Cont.)

No.	County and Date	Author or Surveyor	Publisher and Place	Scale and Size (Inches)
569	Ulster, [1853]	Oliver J. Tillson & P. Henry Brink	P. H. Brink, Saugerti[e]s, N. Y. & O. J. Tillson, Rosendale, N. Y.	1:65,000 2 parts, 41-1/2 x 27-1/2 ea.
570	Ulster (portion), 1854	Oliver J. Tillson & P. Henry Brink	P. H. Brink, Saugerti[e]s, N. Y. & O. J. Tillson, Rosendale, N. Y.	1:65,000 4 parts, 20 x 23, 21 x 23, 21 x 28-1/2 & 22 x 32
571	Ulster, 1858	J. H. French	Taintor, Dawson & Co., Phila.	1:50,688 2 parts, 29-1/2 x 58-1/2 ea.
572	Warren, 1858	J. Chace, Jr.	E. A. Balch & W. O. Shearer, Phila.	1:67,000 37-1/2 x 53-1/2
573	Washington, 1853	Morris Levey	James D. Scott & Robert Pearsall Smith, Phila.	1:52,000 2 parts, 28 x 40 & 29 x 40
574	Wayne, [185-]	H. F. Walling & J. Delafield [Coast Survey Coll.]	. . .	1:40,000 16 parts, 17 x 13 ea.
575	Wayne, 1853	H. F. Walling	. . .	1:40,000 37 x 56
576	Wayne, 1858	J. H. French	John E. Gillette, C. K. Stone, A. J. Cowles, A. Pomeroy, I. D. Peck, C. O. Titus & A. Y. Peck, Phila.	1:42,240 2 parts, 30 x 59-1/2 ea.
577	Westchester, 1851	Sidney & Neff	Newell S. Brown, White Plains, N. Y. & Phila.	1:52,500 2 sheets, 24-1/2 x 37-1/2 ea.
578	Westchester, 1858	F. C. Merry	M. Dripps, New York	1:42,240 4 parts, 2 are 27-1/2 x 21 ea. & 2 are 30 x 21 ea.
579	Wyoming, 1853	P. J. Brown	Newel[l] S. Brown, Phila.	1:43,000 2 parts, 40 x 28-1/2 & 40-1/2 x 29-1/2
580	Yates, 1855	. . .	Burns & Miller, & L. & S. Denton, Penn Yan, N. Y.	1:42,240 4 parts, 19 x 21-1/2 ea.
581	Yates, 1865	S. N. & D. G. Beers, A. B. Prindle & H. A. Hawley	Stone & Stewart, Phila.	1:42,240 4 parts, 22-1/2 x 25 ea.

NORTH CAROLINA

No.	County and Date	Author or Surveyor	Publisher and Place	Scale and Size (Inches)
582	Alamance, 1893	Wm. L. Spoon	. . .	1:31,680 2 parts, 29 x 37 ea.
583	Bladen, 1885	John McDuffie & J. F. Gillespie	Board of County Commissioners	1:127,000 16-1/2 x 24
584	Brunswick (portion), [186-?]	B. L. Blackford	[Topographic Engineers, C. S. A.]	1:40,000 Photocopy (neg.) in 4 parts, 20 x 16-1/2 ea.
585	Catawba, 1886	R. A. Yoder	R. A. Yoder, Newton, N. C.	1:42,240 32 x 56
586	Cleveland, 1886	Paul B. Kyzer	. . .	1:84,480 24-1/2 x 22
587	Davidson, 1890	L. Johnson	. . .	1:63,360 39-1/2 x 26

NORTH CAROLINA (Cont.)

No.	County and Date	Author or Surveyor	Publisher and Place	Scale and Size (Inches)
588	Durham, 1887	L. Johnson	. . .	1:63,360 2 parts, 16 x 28-1/2 ea.
589	Hertford & parts of Northampton & Bertie, 1863	A.H. Campbell & Chas. E. Cassell	[Confederate States of America] Topog'l Dep't N.D. Va.	1:80,000 Photocopies (neg.) of 2 sheets, both in 2 overlapping parts, 18 x 17 ea.
590	Orange, 1891	George W. Tate	George W. Tate, Bingham School, N. C.	1:42,240 46-1/2 x 34
591	Wake, [1870]	Fendol Bevers	Nichols & Gorman	1:126,720 Photocopy (pos.), 18 x 21-1/2

NORTH DAKOTA

No.	County and Date	Author or Surveyor	Publisher and Place	Scale and Size (Inches)
592	Sargent, 1899	John R. Herring	E. P. Noll & Co., Phila.	1:63,360 37 x 41
593	Stark & Billings, 1897	J. G. Saunders	. . .	1:316,800 Blue print, 36 x 20
594	Traill, 1900	W. A. Kelly	W. A. Kelly	1:48,500 2 parts, 25-1/2 x 42 ea.

OHIO

No.	County and Date	Author or Surveyor	Publisher and Place	Scale and Size (Inches)
595	Allen, 1871	Haller & Willard [Coast Survey Coll.]	Haller & Willard	1:42,240 16 parts, 17 x 13 ea.
596	Ashland, 1861	John McDonnell	John McDonnell	1:42,240 54-1/2 x 50
597	Ashland, 1861	Philip Nunan & H. S. Plumb	. . .	1:42,240 2 parts, 28-1/2 x 41-1/2 ea.
598	Ashland, 1897	F. L. Niederheiser	Wertman & Niederheiser, Ashland, Ohio	1:31,680 4 parts, 2 are 36 x 28 ea. & 2 are 36 x 26-1/2 ea.
599	Ashtabula (portion), 1856	. . .	[Robert Pearsall Smith]	. . . 2 parts, 35-1/2 x 26 ea.
600	Auglaize, [186-?]	C. A. O. McClellan & C. S. Warner	C. A. O. McClellan, Waterloo, Ind. & C. S. Warner, Newton, Conn.	1:38,500 6 parts, 23-1/2 x 20 ea.
601	Belmont, 1868	D. J. Lake, J. S. & R. T. Higgins [Coast Survey Coll.]	C. O. Titus, Phila.	1:42,240 20 parts, 17 x 13 ea.
602	Butler, 1855	John Crane	. . .	1:32,000 47-1/2 x 60-1/2
603	Butler, 1868	D. J. Lake, J. S. & R. T. Higgins [Coast Survey Coll.]	C. O. Titus, Phila.	1:36,205 21 parts, 21 x 13 ea.
604	Champaign, 1858	F. Hess	S. H. Matthews	1:44,000 2 sheets, 42 x 23 & 42 x 27-1/2
605	Champaign, 1894	James Swisher	. . .	1:32,000 37 x 55

OHIO (Cont.)

No.	County and Date	Author or Surveyor	Publisher and Place	Scale and Size (Inches)
606	Clark, 1859	T. Kizer	J. Douglass Moler	1:36,000 33-1/2 x 52
607	Clermont, 1857	John Hill	Williams & Dorr	. . . 3 parts, 19-1/2 x 45 ea.
608	Clinton, 1859	H. F. Walling	Walling, Rice & Moon, New York	1:31,680 2 parts, 54 x 27 ea.
609	Columbiana, 1841	J. G. Williard	Lewis Vail	1:63,360 29-1/2 x 31-1/2
610	Columbiana, 1860	Carhart, Mead & Co.	Carhart, Mead & Co., Phila.	1:43,000 3 parts, 1 is 15 x 49-1/2, 1 is 17 x 49-1/2 & 1 is 18 x 49-1/2
611	Coshocton, [185-]	M. J. Becker	M. J. Becker, Mt. Vernon, Ohio	1:42,240 34-1/2 x 48-1/2
612	Crawford, [185-]	M. H. & J. V. B. Watson	M. H. & J. V. B. Watson, Dayton, Ohio	1:63,360 3 parts, 2 are 19-1/2 x 41-1/2 ea. & 1 is 20-1/2 x 41-1/2
613	Cuyahoga, 1852	Harris H. Blackmore [Coast Survey Coll.]	Stoddart & Everett, Cleveland	1:42,500 13 parts, 17 x 13 ea.
614	Cuyahoga, 1858	G. M. Hopkins, Jr.	S. H. Matthews, Phila.	1:42,240 2 sheets, 55 x 27 ea.
615	Darke, 1857	J. Chace, Jr.	S. H. Matthews, Phila.	1:42,240 2 parts, 28 x 44-1/2 ea.
616	Defiance, 1866	Jacob Willard [Coast Survey Coll.]	William McClellan, Waterloo, Ind.	1:42,240 13 parts, 17 x 13 ea.
617	Delaware & parts of Marion & Morrow, 1849	Geo. C. Eaton	James & Geo. C. Eaton, Delaware, Ohio	1:63,360 28-1/2 x 32-1/2
618	Erie & part of Ottawa, 1865	Philip Nunan	. . .	1:42,240 3 parts, 51 x 20-1/2 ea.
619	Fairfield, 1848	James W. Towson	Robert H. Caffee, Lancaster, Ohio	1:63,360 32 x 25
620	Fairfield, 1889	John N. Wolfe	Shaw & Cunningham, Lancaster, Ohio	1:42,240 42-1/2 x 40
621	Fayette, 1867	Henry F. Walling, Henry F. Walling, Jr., Andrew S. Mowry, John E. Earley & E. H. Burlingame [Coast Survey Coll.]	Henry F. Walling, Benj. H. Burnett, Charles H. Foote & Henry F. Walling, Jr.	1:31,680 15 parts, 17 x 13 ea.
622	Franklin, 1856	John Graham	R. C. Foote, Jr., Phila.	1:42,240 40 x 60
623	Franklin, 1883	R. R. Marble	G. J. Brand & Co., Columbus, Ohio	1:53,356 28-1/2 x 34-1/2
624	Franklin, 1895	Walter Braun, Herbert K. Knopf, Robert S. Blackford & Arthur A. Beck	. . .	1:40,550 38 x 52
625	Fulton, [185-?]	Skinner & Kenyon	Skinner & Kenyon, West Unity, Ohio	1:42,240 2 parts, 16-1/2 x 42-1/2 ea.
626	Fulton, 1867	Jacob Willard [Coast Survey Coll.]	William McClellan, Waterloo City, Ind.	1:42,240 13 parts, 17 x 13 ea.

OHIO (Cont.)

No.	County and Date	Author or Surveyor	Publisher and Place	Scale and Size (Inches)
627	Gallia & Meigs (portion), 1885	L. Morton	. . .	1:32,000 Blue print, 36 x 27
628	Geauga & Lake, 1857	. . .	S. H. Matthews, Phila.	1:43,000 60 x 43-1/2
629	Greene, 1855	A. E. Rogerson & E. J. Murphy	Anthony D. Byles, Phila.	1:42,240 2 parts, 37 x 26 ea.
630	Guernsey, 1855	. . .	Williams Dorr & Co.	1:50,688 2 sheets, 36 x 22-1/2 & 36 x 21
631	Hamilton, 1835	Samuel Morrison & Jesse Williams	. . .	1:135,000 13 x 17-1/2
632	Hamilton, 1847	Wm. D. Emerson	C. S. Williams & son	1:63,360 24 x 37
633	Hamilton, 1856	A. W. Gilbert	A. W. Gilbert, Cincinnati	1:42,240 4 parts, 19 x 23 ea.
634	Hamilton, [186-]	[Coast Survey Coll.]	. . .	1:31,680 14 parts, 17 x 13 ea.
635	Hamilton, 1884	. . .	Geo. Moessinger & Fred. Bertsch, Cincinnati	1:26,600 6 parts, 25-1/2 x 25-1/2 ea.
636	Hancock, 1863	D. J. Lake & A. & C. S. Warner	Cowles & Titus, Phila.	1:42,240 2 parts, 26-1/2 x 54 ea.
637	Hancock, 1890	U. K. Stringfellow	. . .	1:31,680 2 parts, 25 x 49 ea.
638	Hardin & Marion, 1869	D. J. Lake, J. S. & R. T. Higgins [Coast Survey Coll.]	C. O. Titus, Phila.	1:50,688 20 parts, 17 x 13 ea.
639	Harrison, 1862	Jacob Jarvis	Jacob Jarvis, Cadiz, Ohio	1:31,500 2 parts, 42-1/2 x 29-1/2 ea.
640	Henry, 1869	Jacob Willard [Coast Survey Coll.]	William McClellan	1:42,240 12 parts, 17 x 13 ea.
641	Holmes, 1861	E. H. Burlingame	H. F. Walling, New York	1:40,000 2 parts, 39 x 26-1/2 ea.
642	Huron, 1859	Philip Nunan	. . .	1:42,240 50 x 51-1/2
643	Jefferson, 1856	Jas. Keyly & Jos. M. Rickey	Lee & Marsh, Phila.	1:43,000 56 x 37
644	Licking, 1854	P. O'Beirne & Wm. Boell	O'Beirne & Boell, Jersey City, N. J.	1:47,520 36-1/2 x 44
645	Logan, 1864	D. J. Lake, A. & C. S. Warner, A. Y. Peck, Wm. H. Fraser, H. H. Simmons & H. H. Hardisty [Coast Survey Coll.]	Stone & Titus, Phila.	1:38,000 17 parts, 17 x 13 ea.
646	Lorain, 1857	John F. Geil	Matthews & Taintor, Phila.	1:39,000 57 x 47-1/2
647	Lucas, 1861	J. D. & E. Janney	J. D. & E. Janney	1:31,680 2 parts, 26 x 52-1/2 ea.
648	Lucas & parts of Wood, Ottawa & Sandusky, 1888	C. H. Judson	. . .	1:42,000 4 parts, 18 x 29 ea.

OHIO (Cont.)

No.	County and Date	Author or Surveyor	Publisher and Place	Scale and Size (Inches)
649	Lucas, 1896	Blue Oil Map Co.	. . .	1:31,680 4 parts, 24 x 36 ea.
650	Madison, 1862	H. F. Walling & Andrew S. Mowry	. . .	. . . 2 parts, 60 x 28-1/2 ea.
651	Mahoning, 1860	. . .	J. W. Canfield, Canfield, Ohio	1:31,680 4 parts, 21 x 31 ea.
652	Marion, 1852	Wm. Brown & W. M. Roberts	. . .	1:63,360 21 x 34
653	Medina, 1857	John F. Geil	Matthews & Taintor, Phila.	1:31,500 2 parts, 21 x 60-1/2 ea.
654	Miami, [1858?]	W. Arrott	S. H. Matthews	1:32,500 2 parts, 25-1/2 x 54 & 24 x 54
655	Monroe, 1869	Jno. B. Noll	. . .	1:31,680 6 parts, 24 x 20 ea.
656	Montgomery, 1851	. . .	Gustavus Heins	1:42,240 2 parts, 22-1/2 x 35 & 22 x 32
657	Montgomery, 1857	R. J. Skinner	R. J. Skinner	1:32,500 6 parts, 4 are 24 x 21 ea. & 2 are 24 x 22 ea.
658	Montgomery, 1869	D.J. Lake, J. S. & R. T. Higgins	C. O. Titus, Phila.	1:42,240 6 parts, 4 are 32 x 18 ea. & 2 are 32 x 19 ea.
659	Morgan, 1854	Wm. P. Johnson	. . .	1:63,360 26-1/2 x 35-1/2
660	Morrow, 1857	Harwood & Watson	Woodford & Bartlett, Phila.	1:42,500 6 parts, 4 are 24-1/2 x 17 ea. & 2 are 24-1/2 x 18 ea.
661	Muskingum, 1852	Geo. C. Eaton	U. P. Bennett, Zanesville, Ohio	1:63,360 31-1/2 x 37-1/2
662	Perry, 1859	H. F. Walling	Walling & Rice, New York	1:31,680 52-1/2 x 52-1/2
663	Pickaway, 1858	. . .	Kellogg & Randall, Phila.	1:43,200 39-1/2 x 55
664	Portage, 1857	P. J. Brown	Matthews & Taintor, Phila.	1:42,240 2 parts, 27 x 51-1/2 ea.
665	Preble, 1887	B. N. Griffing	Griffing, Gordon & Co., Phila.	1:31,680 8 parts, 4 are 14 x 25 ea., 2 are 15 x 25 ea. & 2 are 16 x 25 ea.
666	Preble, 1897	F. B. Robinson	F. B. Robinson	1:23,760 69 x 49
667	Putnam, [18-?]	[Coast Survey Coll.]	. . .	1:43,500 10 parts, 17 x 13 ea.
668	Richland, 1856	P. O'Byrne [i.e., O'Beirne]	Matthews & Taintor, Phila.	1:50,000 2 parts, 28-1/2 x 38 ea.
669	Ross, 1860	H. F. Walling	. . .	1:39,600 2 parts, 30-1/2 x 59-1/2 ea.
670	Sandusky, 1860	John McDonnell	John McDonnell	1:42,240 2 parts, 23 x 48-1/2 ea.

OHIO (Cont.)

No.	County and Date	Author or Surveyor	Publisher and Place	Scale and Size (Inches)
671	Sandusky, 1891	. . .	Henry Hughes, Fremont, Ohio	1:31,680 2 parts, 38 x 31 ea.
672	Scioto, 1875	Barton & Gibbs	. . .	1:39,600 4 sheets, 25-1/2 x 28 ea.
673	Seneca, 1864	D.J. Lake, A. & C. S. Warner, A. Y. Peck, Wm. H. Fraser, H. H. Simmons & H. H. Hardisty	Cyrus Stone & Clarence Titus, Phila.	1:42,240 6 parts, 28 x 18-1/2 ea.
674	Seneca, 1890-91	James Woods	. . .	1:50,000 27 x 40
675	Seneca, 1896	James Woods	James Woods, Tiffin, Ohio	1:50,000 30 x 44-1/2
676	Shelby, 1865	C. S. & L. C. Warner	C. A. O. McClellan & C. S. Warner	1:42,240 6 parts, 4 are 21 x 16 ea. & 2 are 21 x 17 ea.
677	Stark, [185-?]	. . .	Williams, Dorr & Co.	1:42,000 2 parts, 42 x 24 & 42 x 27
678	Stark, 1855	. . .	Williams, Dorr & Co.	1:42,000 4 sheets, 20-1/2 x 24, 20-1/2 x 27, 22-1/2 x 24 & 22-1/2 x 27
679	Summit, 1856	Hosea Paul	Matthews & Taintor, Phila.	1:42,240 59-1/2 x 40
680	Trumbull, 1856	P. J. Browne	Gillette, Matthews & Co., Phila.	1:43,000 39-1/2 x 59
681	Tuscarawas & parts of Carroll, Coshocton & Holmes, 1851	George W. Canfield [Coast Survey Coll.]	. . .	1:63,360 32-1/2 x 29-1/2
682	Tuscarawas, 1870	D. J. Lake, S. Hoover, G. P. Sanford & B. N. Griffin[g] [Coast Survey Coll.]	D. J. Lake, Phila.	1:45,000 24 parts, 17 x 13 ea.
683	Union, 1870	Andrew S. Mowry [Coast Survey Coll.]	F. W. Beers & Co., New York	1:31,680 21 parts, 17 x 13 ea.
684	Warren, 1856	P. O'Beirne	Anthony D. Byles, Phila.	1:31,680 50 x 51-1/2
685	Warren, 1867	G. P. Sanford, J. Silliman Higgins & R. H. Harrison [Coast Survey Coll.]	A. Warner, Phila.	1:37,000 21 parts, 17 x 13 ea.
686	Washington, 1858	Wm. Lorey	Edwin P. Gardner, Phila.	1:50,688 42-1/2 x 57
687	Wayne, 1856	W. Lorey & J. Hein	Baker & Gager, Phila.	1:51,500 36-1/2 x 56
688	Williams, 1864	D. J. Lake, A. & C. S. Warner, A. Y. Peck, Wm. H. Fraser, H. H. Simmons & H. H. Hardisty	Stone & Titus, Phila.	1:50,688 4 parts, 2 are 24-1/2 x 21 ea. & 2 are 25 x 21 ea.
689	Wood, 1871	[Coast Survey Coll.]	Earl W. Merry	. . . 19 parts, 17-1/2 x 13-1/2 ea.
690	Wyandot, 1870	D. J. Lake [Coast Survey Coll.]	R. H. Harrison, Cincinnati	1:42,240 13 parts, 17 x 13 ea.

OKLAHOMA

No.	County and Date	Author or Surveyor	Publisher	Scale and Size (Inches)
691	Cleveland, 1900	. . .	Democrat-Topic	1:63,360 32 x 31-1/2

OREGON

692	Clatsop, 1895	R. C. F. Astbury	. . .	1:48,000 Blue print, 4 parts, 24-1/2 x 22 ea.
693	Lincoln, 1895	Jno. F. Johnson	. . .	1:126,720 Blue print, 31 x 15-1/2
694	Multnomah, 1889	R. A. Habersham	. . .	1:48,000 2 sheets, 32-1/2 x 33-1/2 ea.
695	Yamhill, 1879	. . .	Lawrence & Ogilbe, Portland, Oreg.	1:84,480 22 x 27

PENNSYLVANIA

696	Adams, [185-?]	. . .	. . .	1:50,688 30-1/2 x 36
697	Adams, 1858	G. M. Hopkins	M.S. & E. Converse, Phila.	1:50,688 37-1/2 x 53
698	Allegheny, 1817	David Dougal & Jno. E. Whiteside	. . .	1:158,400 Photocopy (pos.), 20 x 17-1/2
699	Allegheny, 1851	Sidney & Neff	. . .	1:51,000 4 parts, 22 x 23 ea.
700	Allegheny, 1855	Sidney, Neff, S. M. Rea & L. H. Norfolk [Coast Survey Coll.]	R. L. Barnes, Phila.	1:51,000 14 parts, 17 x 13 ea.
701	Allegheny, 1862	S. N. Beers, F. W. Beers, A. B. Prindle, C. S. Warner & J. M. Beers	Smith, Gallup & Hewitt, Phila.	1:42,240 2 parts, 31 x 59-1/2 ea.
702	Allegheny, 1883	Alex. Y. Lee	Otto Krebs, Pittsburgh	1:37,714 59 x 57-1/2
703	Allegheny & parts of Westmoreland, Washington & Beaver, 1890	. . .	Otto Krebs, Pittsburgh	. . . 6 sheets, 23-1/2 x 35 ea.
704	Allegheny, 1898	Chas. T. Rainey	. . .	1:65,000 33 x 35
705	Armstrong, 1861	G. M. & H. W. Hopkins	A. Pomeroy & S. W. Treat, Phila.	1:50,688 2 parts, 56 x 24 ea.
706	Bedford, 1818	Jno. Morrison, Walter B. Hudson & [Jno. E. Whiteside]	. . .	1:200,000 Photocopy (pos.), 20-1/2 x 17-1/2
707	Bedford, 1861	E. L. Walker	. . .	1:63,360 4 parts, 22-1/2 x 28-1/2 ea.
708	Berks, [181-?]	Henry M. Richards	. . .	1:158,400 Photocopy (pos.), 18 x 23-1/2

PENNSYLVANIA (Cont.)

No.	County and Date	Author or Surveyor	Publisher and Place	Scale and Size (Inches)
709	Berks, [1820]	Henry M. Richards	. . .	1:25,344 16-1/2 x 21
710	Berks, 1854	M. S. Henry & M. K. Boyer	. . .	1:63,360 2 parts, 22-1/2 x 55-1/2 ea.
711	Berks, 1860	L. Fagan	H. F. Bridgens, Phila.	1:51,500 6 parts, 3 are 27 x 22 ea. & 3 are 29 x 22 ea.
712	Blair, 1859	Geil & Freed	Geil & Freed, Phila.	1:42,240 2 parts, 27 x 46-1/2 & 30 x 46-1/2
713	Bradford, 1858	Lake, Ames & Davison	Wm. J. Barker, Phila.	1:65,000 38 x 59-1/2
714	Bucks, 1817	Thos. G. Kennedy & Jno. E. Whiteside	. . .	1:158,400 Photocopy (pos.), 21 x 14
715	Bucks, 1850	W. E. Morris	Robert P. Smith, Phila.	1:52,000 55-1/2 x 36-1/2
716	Butler, 1817	David Dougal & Jno. E. Whiteside	. . .	1:158,400 Photocopy (pos.), 18-1/2 x 13
717	Butler, 1858	Jas. Dunlap, Hugh McKee, David Scott, E. Maurhoff & J. W. Kirker	. . .	. . . 6 parts, 19 x 26 ea.
718	Cambria, 1817	Walter B. Hudson, Jno. Morrison & Jno. E. Whiteside	. . .	1:158,400 Photocopy (pos.), 17 x 17
719	Cambria, 1867	D.G. Beers, J. H. Goodhue & F. B. Roe	A. Pomeroy, Phila.	1:50,688 6 parts, 4 are 17 x 24 ea. & 2 are 18-1/2 x 24 ea.
720	Centre, [181-?]	Walter B. Hudson & Jno. Morrison	. . .	1:175,000 Photocopy (pos.), 17 x 23-1/2
721	Centre, 1861	H. F. Walling	S. D. Tilden	1:63,360 2 parts, 25 x 62-1/2 ea.
722	Chester, 1820	James Hindman & Danl. Small	. . .	1:170,000 Photocopy (pos.), 17 x 22
723	Chester, 1847	S. M. Painter & J. S. Bowen	. . .	1:64,000 41 x 48
724	Chester, 1856	T. J. Kennedy, S. M. Painter & J. S. Bowen	T. J. Kennedy, Westchester, Pa. & R. L. Barnes, Phila.	1:64,000 4 parts, 20-1/2 x 24 ea.
725	Chester, 1860	T. J. Kennedy	. . .	. . . 2 parts, 28 x 55 ea.
726	Clarion, 1865	. . .	A. Pomeroy, Phila.	1:50,688 4 parts, 26 x 18 ea.
727	Clearfield, 1818	Charles Trcziyulny & [Jno. E. Whiteside]	. . .	1:158,400 Photocopy (pos.), 23 x 16
728	Clearfield, 1866	D. G. Beers, J. H. Goodhue & F. B. Roe	A. Pomeroy, Phila.	1:56,320 6 parts, 19 x 26-1/2 ea.
729	Clinton, 1862	H. F. Walling	Way, Palmer & Co., New York	1:63,360 2 parts, 28 x 56 & 26 x 56

PENNSYLVANIA (Cont.)

No.	County and Date	Author or Surveyor	Publisher and Place	Scale and Size (Inches)
730	Columbia & Montour, 1860	G. M. Hopkins, Jr.	J. A. J. Cummings, Chillisquaque, Pa.	1:42,240 6 parts, 29 x 21 ea.
731	Crawford, 1839	. . .	O. Spafford, Erie, Pa.	1:79,200 21-1/2 x 37
732	Crawford, 1865	F. W. Beers	A. Pomeroy & S. W. Treat, Phila.	1:56,320 6 parts, 18 x 27-1/2 ea.
733	Cumberland, 1858	H. F. Bridgens	. . .	1:42,500 45 x 61-1/2
734	Dauphin & Lebanon, [1819?]	Thomas Smith	. . .	1:158,400 Photocopy (neg.), 15 x 21-1/2
735	Dauphin, 1858	J. Southwick	Wm. J. Barker	1:64,000 2 parts, 39-1/2 x 29-1/2 ea.
736	Dauphin, 1862	S. N. & F. W. Beers	A. Pomeroy, Phila.	1:38,990 4 sheets, 2 are 42-1/2 x 30 ea. & 2 are 19 x 30 ea.
737	Delaware, 1818	John Melish, John Hills & Jno. E. White[side]	. . .	1:87,000 Photocopy (pos.), 16-1/2 x 22-1/2
738	Delaware, 1848	Joshua W. Ash	Robert P. Smith	1:25,250 2 parts, 42 x 28-1/2 ea.
739	Delaware, [1862]	George Smith	Henry P. Ashmead	1:86,000 14-1/2 x 18-1/2
740	Delaware, 1876	. . .	G. M. Hopkins & Co., Phila.	1:31,680 50 x 57
741	Elk, 1855	[H. A. Pattison]	. . .	. . . 2 parts, 24-1/2 x 19 ea.
742	Elk, 1856	H. A. Pattison	. . .	. . . 2 parts, 25-1/2 x 19 ea.
743	Erie & Crawford, 1818	David Dougal & Jno. E. Whiteside	. . .	1:158,400 Photocopy (pos.), 22 x 17-1/2
744	Erie, 1855	J. Chace, Jr.	O. McLeran & Isaac W. Moore, Phila.	1:63,360 39 x 53-1/2
745	Fayette, 1817	[Freeman Lewis] & Jno. E. Whiteside	. . .	1:158,400 Photocopy (pos.), 18-1/2 x 14-1/2
746	Fayette, [1858?]	. . .	. . .	1:65,000 33 x 39-1/2
747	Fayette, 1858	McLaughlin & Kinter	Wm. J. Barker, Phila.	1:65,000 2 parts, 29 x 37-1/2 ea.
747a	Fayette, 1865	G. M. Hopkins	R. L. Barnes, Phila.	1:84,480 24 x 29
748	Forest, [1864]	. . .	D. C. Gillespie, Brookville, Pa.	. . . 35 x 27
749	Forest, 1876	Irwin	J. L. Smith, Phila.	1:63,360 19-1/2 x 31-1/2
750	Forest, 1895	F. F. Whittekin	. . .	1:56,500 25 x 35
751	Franklin, 1858	D. H. Davison	Riley & Hoffman, Greencastle, Pa.	1:47,520 2 parts, 26-1/2 x 58 & 28 x 58

PENNSYLVANIA (Cont.)

No.	County and Date	Author or Surveyor	Publisher and Place	Scale and Size (Inches)
752	Fulton, 1873	. . .	A. Pomeroy & Co., Phila.	1:39,600 2 parts, 49-1/2 x 22-1/2 ea.
753	Greene, 1865	J. L. McConnell & G. F. Wolfe	Tuttle & Co., Phila.	1:72,411 24 x 29-1/2
754	Greene, 1897	C. T. Rainey	. . .	1:47,000 28-1/2 x 45
755	Huntingdon, 1856	William Christy	. . .	1:54,000 4 parts, 33 x 24-1/2
756	Indiana, 1856	David Peelor, J. B. McLaughlin & J. A. Kinter	William J. Barker, North Hector, N. Y.	. . . 2 parts, 42 x 26 ea.
757	Jefferson, 1857	. . .	D. C. Gillespie, Brookville, Pa.	. . . 51-1/2 x 36
758	Lancaster, 1819	J. Scott & Dan Small	. . .	1:158,400 Photocopy (pos.), 18 x 24
759	Lancaster, 1821	. . .	William Wagner, York, Pa.	1:158,400 16-1/2 x 22
760	Lancaster, 1824	. . .	Joshua Scott, Lancaster, Pa.	1:63,360 36 x 47-1/2
761	Lancaster, 1842	Josa. Scott	. . .	1:67,000 4 sheets, 19-1/2 x 25-1/2 ea.
762	Lancaster, 1851	. . .	. . .	1:65,000 2 parts, 41 x 23 ea.
763	Lancaster, 1858	Joshua Scott	James D. Scott, Phila.	. . . 6 parts, 24 x 18-1/2 ea.
764	Lawrence & Beaver, 1860	N. S. Ames	Wm. J. Barker, Phila.	. . . 2 parts, 51-1/2 x 26 & 51-1/2 x 29
765	Lebanon, 1860	Hy. F. Bridgens	Hy. F. Bridgens, Phila.	1:42,000 4 parts, 2 are 21-1/2 x 26 ea. & 2 are 21-1/2 x 27-1/2 ea.
765a	Lehigh, 1816 (copied 1960?)	Isaac A. Chapman & D. G. Williams	. . .	. . . Photocopy (pos.) in 4 parts, 43 x 26-1/2 ea.
766	Lehigh, 1862	G. A. Aschbach	G. A. Aschbach, Allentown	1:39,600 58 x 68-1/2
767	Lehigh, 1865	G. A. Aschbach	G. A. Aschbach, Allentown	1:39,600 58-1/2 x 69-1/2
768	Luzerne, 1864	Capt. David Schooley, McNair & Sturdevant	Lacoe & Schooley, & H. F. Walling, New York	1:59,400 6 parts, 31 x 21 ea.
769	Lycoming, 1861	H. F. Walling	S. D. Tilden, New York	1:63,360 6 parts, 25 x 20-1/2 ea.
770	McKean & part of Cameron, 1856	W. K. King	. . .	1:125,000 27 x 24-1/2
771	McKean & part of Cameron, 1857	W. K. King	. . .	1:125,000 27 x 24-1/2
772	McKean & Elk (portions), 1878	J. L. Brown	. . .	1:46,000 60 x 27

PENNSYLVANIA (Cont.)

No.	County and Date	Author or Surveyor	Publisher and Place	Scale and Size (Inches)
773	McKean, 1879	. . .	J. Opperman	1:39,600 30 x 39
774	Mercer, 1860	G. M. Hopkins, Jr. & Henry W. Hopkins	A. Pomeroy & S. W. Treat, Phila.	1:42,240 2 parts, 29-1/2 x 58-1/2 ea.
775	Mifflin, 1820	Michael M. Monahon & Dan Small	. . .	1:158,400 Photocopy (pos.), 17-1/2 x 21-1/2
776	Monroe & Carbon, 1860	H. F. Walling	Loomis, Way & Palmer	1:63,360 2 parts, 27-1/2 x 54-1/2 ea.
777	Montgomery, 1849	Wm. E. Morris	Smith & Wistar, Phila.	1:42,240 2 sheets, 37-1/2 x 26-1/2 & 37-1/2 x 28-1/2
778	Northampton, [181-?]	[Isaac A. Chapman]	. . .	1:200,000 Photocopy (pos.), 18 x 22-1/2
779	Northampton, 1860	G. M. Hopkins, Jr.	Smith, Gallup & Co., Phila.	1:38,990 6 parts, 20 x 28 ea.
780	Northumberland, 1858	G. M. Hopkins, Jr. & Kimber Cleaver	J. A. J. Cummings, Chillisquaque, Pa.	1:43,500 2 parts, 33-1/2 x 58-1/2 ea.
781	Northumberland, 1874	G. M. Hopkins, Abm. Shipman, A. J. Guffy, S. G. Frey, J. R. Hilbush, Kimber Cleaver & R. A. Ammerman	J. A. J. Cummings, Montandon, Pa.	1:43,500 6 parts, 33-1/2 x 22-1/2 ea.
782	Perry, Juniata & Mifflin, 1863	G. M. Hopkins	Smith, Gallup & Hewitt, Phila.	1:63,360 2 parts, 60 x 30 ea.
783	Philadelphia, 1819	John Melish	John Melish, Phila.	1:79,200 17-1/2 x 19-1/2
784	Philadelphia, 1843	Charles Ellet, Jr. & D. H. Kennedy	Charles Ellet, Jr., Phila.	1:25,344 34-1/2 x 59-1/2
785	Pike, 1856	John T. Cross	Charles Vinten, New York	1:91,000 25 x 20-1/2
786	Pike, 1872	F. W. Beers	F. W. Beers & Co., New York	1:49,500 4 parts, 29-1/2 x 23 ea.
787	Potter, 1856	S. Ross	. . .	1:114,000 27-1/2 x 21
788	Potter, 1893	F. W. Beers & W. A. Crosby	J. W. Vose & Co., New York	1:39,600 6 parts, 21 x 25-1/2 ea.
789	Schuylkill, 1817	Fk. Lauderbrun & Jno. E. Whiteside	. . .	1:158,400 Photocopy (pos.), 17-1/2 x 22-1/2
790	Schuylkill, 1830	. . .	H. S. Tanner, Phila.	1:126,720 15-1/2 x 21-1/2
791	Schuylkill, 1855	P. W. Sheafer	R. L. Barnes, Phila.	1:103,000 19-1/2 x 33
792	Schuylkill, 1863	Walter Scott, W. J. Cox, S. Lewis & J. S. Hawley	James D. Scott, Phila.	1:59,400 53-1/2 x 62
793	Schuylkill, 1864	Walter Scott, W. J. Cox, S. Lewis & J. S. Hawley	James D. Scott, Phila.	1:59,400 2 parts, 26-1/2 x 61-1/2 ea.

PENNSYLVANIA (Cont.)

No.	County and Date	Author or Surveyor	Publisher and Place	Scale and Size (Inches)
794	Somerset, 1818	John Wells & Jno. E. Whiteside	. . .	1:158,400 Photocopy (pos.), 21 x 18
795	Somerset, 1830	John Wells	H. S. Tanner, Phila.	1:158,400 17 x 20-1/2
796	Somerset, [185-?]	. . .	. . .	1:63,360 41-1/2 x 41
797	Somerset, 1860	Edward L. Walker	Edward L. Walker	1:63,360 4 parts, 22 x 25-1/2 ea.
798	Sullivan, 1872	F. W. Beers	A. Pomeroy & Co., New York	. . . 4 parts, 20-1/2 x 21 ea.
799	Susquehanna, 1858	G. M. Hopkins	Lee & Marsh, Phila.	1:46,080 6 parts, 28 x 19-1/2 ea.
800	Tioga, 1862	H. F. Walling	Way, Palmer & Co., New York	1:50,688 2 parts, 28 x 62-1/2 ea.
801	Union, [181-?]	Thomas Smith	. . .	. . . Photocopy (pos.), 21 x 18
802	Union, 1856	Thomas H. Paschall & James Keily	Th. Leonhardt & J. H. Camp, Phila.	1:52,500 29 x 40
803	Venango, [181-?]	Saml. Dale	. . .	. . . Photocopy (pos.), 15-1/2 x 18
804	Venango, 1857	R. Irwin, C. H. Heydrick & C. Heydrick	. . .	1:79,200 26 x 35
805	Venango, 1865	. . .	Beers, Ellis & Soule	1:63,360 31 x 42
806	Warren, [181-?]	Saml. Dale	. . .	. . . Photocopy (pos.), 12-1/2 x 20
807	Warren, 1838	Andrew H. Ludlow	. . .	1:63,360 26 x 36-1/2
808	Warren, 1865	. . .	R. L. Barnes, Phila. & R. R. Russell, Warren, Pa.	. . . 23-1/2 x 28
809	Warren, 1865	. . .	Beers, Ellis & Soule, New York	1:50,688 33 x 46
810	Warren, 1865	. . .	J. P. Hunt, Pittsburgh	1:65,000 23 x 29
811	Warren & Forest, 1881	John Gardiner	. . .	. . . 2 sheets, 21-1/2 x 31 ea.
812	Warren & Forest, 1882	. . .	J. L. Smith, Phila.	1:79,200 38 x 31-1/2
813	Warren, 1889	D. F. A. Wheelock	J. L. Smith, Phila.	1:39,600 2 sheets, 50-1/2 x 30-1/2 & 50-1/2 x 32
814	Warren, 1900	N. B. Brakenridge	N. B. Brakenridge, Warren, Pa.	1:39,600 4 parts, 22 x 30 ea.
815	Washington, 1817	Jonathan Knight & Jno. E. Whiteside	. . .	1:158,400 Photocopy (pos.), 16 x 19-1/2
816	Washington, 1856	James M. Sherman & A. R. Day	William J. Barker, North Hector, N. Y.	1:63,360 4 parts, 20-1/2 x 26 ea.

PENNSYLVANIA (Cont.)

No.	County and Date	Author or Surveyor	Publisher and Place	Scale and Size (Inches)
817	Washington, 1361	S. N. & F. W. Beers	A. Pomeroy & S. W. Treat, Phila.	1:42,240 2 parts, 29-1/2 x 61 ea.
818	Wayne & Pike, 1814	Jason Torrey	Joseph Rakestraw, Phila.	1:160,000 26-1/2 x 19
819	Wayne, 1860	G. M. Hopkins, Jr.	M. S. & E. Converse, Phila.	1:50,688 66-1/2 x 39-1/2
820	Westmoreland, 1818	[Cadwallader Evans] & Jno. E. Whiteside	. . .	1:158,400 Photocopy (pos.), 22 x 18
821	Westmoreland, 1857	D. J. Lake & N. S. Ames	Wm. J. Barker, North Hector, N. Y.	1:63,360 44-1/2 x 58
822	Wyoming, 1869	F. W. Beers	F. W. Beers, A. D. Ellis & G. G. Soule	1:42,240 39 x 62-1/2
823	York, [181-?]	Thomas Smith	. . .	. . . Photocopy (pos.), 17 x 23-1/2
824	York & Adams, 1821	. . .	D. Small & W. Wagner	1:190,080 16 x 23-1/2
825	York, 1860	D. J. Lake	W. O. Shearer & D. J. Lake, Phila.	1:51,500 60-1/2 x 59

RHODE ISLAND

No.	County and Date	Author or Surveyor	Publisher and Place	Scale and Size (Inches)
826	Bristol, 1851	Henry F. Walling	G. C. Brown, Providence	1:25,000 6 parts, 1 is 24-1/2 x 10, 1 is 25 x 14-1/2 & 4 are 17 x 13 ea.
827	Newport, 1850	H. F. Walling, O. Harkness & J. Hanson	. . .	1:42,500 28-1/2 x 38
828	Newport (portion), 1870	Wm. Dame & A. J. Ward	M. Dripps, New York, & Wm. Dame & A. J. Ward, Newport, R. I.	1:20,800 32 x 24
829	Newport (portion), [187-?]	. . .	A. J. Ward, Newport, R. I.	1:20,600 32-1/2 x 23
830	Providence, 1851	H. F. Walling	G. C. Brown	. . . 2 sheets, 38-1/2 x 25-1/2 & 38-1/2 x 26-1/2

SOUTH CAROLINA

No.	County and Date	Author or Surveyor	Publisher and Place	Scale and Size (Inches)
831	Abbeville, 1895	W. P. Bullock & P. L. Grier	. . .	1:63,360 44 x 44
832	Anderson, 1877	S. M. Pegg, J. H. von Hasseln, Geo. E. Brown, Rev. H. F. Chreitzberg & Jas. M. Cathcart	. . .	1:72,000 27 x 35-1/2
833	Anderson, 1897	J. H. von Hasseln	. . .	1:74,000 38 x 36
834	Beaufort, 1873	Vignoles & Ravenel, & Law & Kirk	. . .	1:126,720 32 x 25
835	Dorchester, 1900	J. Hamilton Knight	. . .	1:126,720 21-1/2 x 14

SOUTH CAROLINA (Cont.)

No.	County and Date	Author or Surveyor	Publisher and Place	Scale and Size (Inches)
836	Fairfield, 1876	Wm. B. & B. E. Elkin	J. L. Smith, Phila.	1:126,720 17-1/2 x 24
837	Greenville, 1882	Paul B. Kyzer	. . .	1:63,360 51-1/2 x 34
838	Laurens, 1883	Kyzer & Hellams	. . .	1:63,360 41 x 37
839	Marion, 1882	P. Y. Bethea	. . .	. . . 21 x 14
840	Marion, 1882	P.Y. Bethea	. . .	1:140,000 33 x 22
841	Newberry, [1887?]	Thomas M. Lake	. . .	1:63,360 31 x 37-1/2
842	Richland, 1897	M. L. Brasswell	. . .	1:63,360 33 x 35

SOUTH DAKOTA

No.	County and Date	Author or Surveyor	Publisher and Place	Scale and Size (Inches)
843	Aurora, 1900	Geo. W. Atkinson	E. Frank Peterson, Vermillion, S. Dak.	1:50,688 2 parts, 21-1/2 x 31-1/2 ea.
844	Bon Homme, 1893	E. Frank Peterson, E. S. Hodgin, E. A. Ufford, A. M. Ostness, H. M. Keene & F. C. Falkenstine	Rowley & Peterson, Vermillion, S. Dak.	1:39,000 6 parts, 4 are 15-1/2 x 21-1/2 ea. & 2 are 18 x 21-1/2 ea.
845	Brookings, 1897	E. Frank Peterson, Homer W. Stevens, Frank B. Stevens, C. B. Ainsworth, Geo. W. Atkinson & J. A. Steinson	E. Frank Peterson, Vermillion, S. Dak.	1:50,688 36 x 44
846	Clark, 1900	Geo. W. Atkinson, C. F. Sundy & J. R. Moses	E. Frank Peterson, Vermillion, S. Dak.	1:57,000 52 x 28-1/2
847	Codington, 1898	E. Frank Peterson, C. B. Ainsworth & Geo. W. Atkinson	E. Frank Peterson, Vermillion, S. Dak.	1:46,500 2 parts, 23 x 38 ea.
848	Deuel, 1898	E. Frank Peterson, Byron S. Payne, Jr., C. F. Sundy & C. E. Ellis	E. Frank Peterson, Vermillion, S. Dak.	1:50,688 42-1/2 x 28
849	Douglas, 1900	E. Frank Peterson, J. A. Johnson & Homer W. Stevens	. . .	1:46,000 33 x 43
850	Grant, 1899	E. Frank Peterson, Chas. E. Ellis, O. S. Cowley, J. C. Heffer & F. W. Leonard	E. Frank Peterson, Vermillion, S. Dak.	1:51,000 4 parts, 16 x 24-1/2 ea.
851	Hamlin, 1897	. . .	C. L. Abbott, Estelline, S. Dak.	1:69,000 19 x 28-1/2
852	Hamlin, 1897	K. E. Hilthon, F. B. Stevens, C. F. Sundy & E. Frank Peterson	E. Frank Peterson, Vermillion, S. Dak.	1:42,240 4 parts, 18 x 23-1/2 ea.
853	Hamlin, 1897	K. E. Hilthon, F. B. Stevens, C. F. Sundy & E. Frank Peterson	E. Frank Peterson, Vermillion, S. Dak.	1:84,480 18 x 24

SOUTH DAKOTA (Cont.)

No.	County and Date	Author or Surveyor	Publisher and Place	Scale and Size (Inches)
854	Hanson, 1893	H. W. Stevens, E. M. Stevens, F. B. Stevens & E. S. Hodgin	Rowley & Peterson, Vermillion, S. Dak.	1:42,000 2 parts, 20-1/2 x 29 & 21 x 29
855	Kingsbury, 1899	E. Frank Peterson, Geo. W. Atkinson, Wm. Williamson, Henry J. Ramsey, T. J. Lewis & H. A. Whiting	E. Frank Peterson, Vermillion, S. Dak., for Geo. W. Atkinson	1:52,000 4 parts, 2 are 18 x 23 ea. & 2 are 18 x 24 ea.
856	Lake, 1899	E. Frank Peterson, Geo. W. Atkinson & Wm. Williamson	E. Frank Peterson, Vermillion, S. Dak., for Geo. W. Atkinson	1:47,000 4 parts, 2 are 19 x 17 ea. & 2 are 19-1/2 x 17 ea.
857	Lawrence, 1894	G. R. Kimball & Alvin Clark	. . .	1:31,680 Blue print, 2 parts, 33 x 57-1/2 & 33 x 60-1/2
858	Lincoln, 1893	E. Frank Peterson, E. M. Stevens & J. K. Stickney	Rowley & Peterson, Vermillion, S. Dak.	1:36,205 4 parts, 2 are 26-1/2 x 22-1/2 ea. & 2 are 25-1/2 x 22-1/2 ea.
859	Lincoln, [c1900]	. . .	[Mark D. Scott, Sioux Falls, S. Dak.]	1:90,000 23 x 18-1/2
860	McCook, 1900	E. Frank Peterson, Geo. W. Atkinson, Byron S. Payne & J. F. Larson	E. Frank Peterson, Vermillion, S. Dak., for Geo. W. Atkinson	1:47,000 4 parts, 19-1/2 x 17-1/2 ea.
861	Miner, 1898	E. Frank Peterson, Geo. W. Atkinson & John C. Heffer	E. Frank Peterson, Vermillion, S. Dak.	1:46,000 38-1/2 x 34-1/2
862	Minnehaha, 1893	. . .	H. M. Avery, Sioux Falls, S. Dak.	1:42,240 2 sheets, 41-1/2 x 28-1/2 & 41-1/2 x 25-1/2
863	Moody, 1896	. . .	E. Frank Peterson, Vermillion, S. Dak.	1:42,240 43 x 35
864	Sanborn, 1900	E. Frank Peterson	E. Frank Peterson, Vermillion, S. Dak.	1:126,720 13-1/2 x 13
865	Spink, 1899	E. Frank Peterson, A. B. Gunderson & T. O. Erickson	E. Frank Peterson, Vermillion, S. Dak.	1:63,360 2 parts, 23-1/2 x 37 ea.
866	Turner, 1893	. . .	Rowley & Peterson, Vermillion, S. Dak.	1:36,205 6 parts, 2 are 19 x 21-1/2 ea. & 4 are 16-1/2 x 21-1/2 ea.
867	Union, 1892	E. Frank Peterson	Tackabury, Rowley & Co.	1:32,000 6 parts, 2 are 26 x 20 ea., 2 are 27 x 20 ea. & 2 are 28 x 20 ea.

TENNESSEE

No.	County and Date	Author or Surveyor	Publisher and Place	Scale and Size (Inches)
868	Bedford & Coffee (portion), 1863	N. Michler, John E. Weyss & C. S. Mergell	. . .	1:105,000 Photocopy (pos.), 11-1/2 x 18-1/2
869	Bedford, 1878	D. G. Beers & Co.	D. G. Beers & Co., Phila.	1:50,688 4 parts, 24-1/2 x 17 ea.

TENNESSEE (Cont.)

No.	County and Date	Author or Surveyor	Publisher and Place	Scale and Size (Inches)
870	Davidson, 1871	Wilbur F. Foster	. . .	1:37,000 2 parts, 27-1/2 x 48-1/2 ea.
871	Davidson, [1900?]	W. B. Southgate	W. W. Southgate & Son, Nashville	1:63,360 Blue print, 31-1/2 x 33
872	Gibson, 1877	D. G. Beers & Co.	D. G. Beers & Co., Phila.	1:50,688 6 parts, 2 are 31-1/2 x 15 ea. & 4 are 31-1/2 x 13-1/2 ea.
873	Knox, 1895	. . .	Vance, Coffee & Pill	1:42,000 6 parts, 4 are 19 x 23 ea. & 2 are 20 x 23 ea.
874	Madison, 1877	D. G. Beers & Co.	D. G. Beers & Co., Phila.	1:50,688 2 parts, 28 x 37 ea.
875	Marshall, 1899	W. M. Carter	. . .	1:42,240 48-1/2 x 32
876	Maury, 1878	D. G. Beers & Co.	D. G. Beers & Co., Phila.	1:50,688 57 x 38-1/2
877	Montgomery, 1877	D. G. Beers & Co.	D. G. Beers & Co., Phila.	1:42,240 4 parts, 28 x 19-1/2 ea.
878	Rutherford, 1878	D. G. Beers & Co.	D. G. Beers & Co., Phila.	1:50,688 4 parts, 27 x 19 ea.
879	Shelby, 1888	. . .	M. T. Williamson, Memphis	1:31,680 6 parts, 3 are 28-1/2 x 22 ea. & 3 are 29-1/2 x 22 ea.
880	Sumner, 1878	D. G. Beers & Co.	D. G. Beers & Co., Phila.	1:50,688 4 parts, 26 x 18 ea.

TEXAS

No.	County and Date	Author or Surveyor	Publisher and Place	Scale and Size (Inches)
881	Anderson, 1879	. . .	General Land Office	1:133,320 17-1/2 x 20-1/2
882	Anderson, 1895 (traced 1903)	E. Schütze & Addison Walker	General Land Office	. . . Blue print, 43 x 37
883	Angelina, 1879	. . .	General Land Office	1:133,320 18-1/2 x 26-1/2
884	Angelina, 1899 (traced 1935)	J. L. Woodland	General Land Office	1:66,660 Blue print, 38 x 50-1/2
885	Aransas, 1880	. . .	General Land Office	1:133,320 16-1/2 x 17-1/2
886	Aransas, 1896	E. Schütze	General Land Office	. . . 36 x 33
887	Archer, 1879	. . .	General Land Office	1:133,320 19 x 17
888	Atascosa, 1879	. . .	General Land Office	1:133,320 22 x 23
889	Atascosa, 1894 (traced 1919)	E. von Rosenberg & Grady W. Davis	General Land Office	1:66,660 Blue print, 2 parts, 23-1/2 x 42 ea.
890	Austin, 1880	. . .	General Land Office	1:133,320 20-1/2 x 22-1/2

TEXAS (Cont.)

No.	County and Date	Author or Surveyor	Publisher and Place	Scale and Size (Inches)
891	Bandera, 1879	. . .	General Land Office	1:133,320 16 x 29-1/2
892	Bastrop, 1879	. . .	General Land Office	1:133,320 24 x 23-1/2
893	Bee, 1879	. . .	General Land Office	1:133,320 25 x 22
894	Bell, 1879	. . .	General Land Office	1:133,320 23 x 28
895	Bell, 1896 (traced 1919)	E. von Rosenberg & Lee Hawkins	General Land Office	1:66,660 Blue print, 2 parts, 46 x 26-1/2 ea.
896	Bexar, 1879	. . .	General Land Office	1:133,320 22-1/2 x 26
897	Bexar, 1887	John D. Rullmann	. . .	1:66,660 2 parts, 45 x 23-1/2 ea.
898	Bexar, 1887	John D. Rullmann	. . .	. . . 11 x 11-1/2
899	Bexar, 1897	John D. Rullmann	. . .	1:66,660 2 parts, 22-1/2 x 40-1/2 ea.
900	Blanco, 1880	. . .	General Land Office	1:133,320 25-1/2 x 17
901	Borden, 1892	. . .	General Land Office	1:66,660 20 x 18
902	Bosque, 1879	. . .	General Land Office	1:133,320 22-1/2 x 27
903	Bosque, 1890 (traced 1919)	J. W. Maxcy & Lee Hawkins	General Land Office	1:66,660 Blue print, 47-1/2 x 37
904	Bowie, 1879	. . .	General Land Office	1:133,320 16 x 21
905	Bowie, 1894	M. Stakemann	. . .	1:133,320 16-1/2 x 21
906	Brazoria, 1877	F. W. Stevens	Shapard, Stevens & Co., Brazoria, Tex.	1:193,314 20-1/2 x 19-1/2
907	Brazoria, 1879	. . .	General Land Office	1:133,320 26 x 24-1/2
908	Brazos, 1879	. . .	General Land Office	1:133,320 21-1/2 x 15
909	Briscoe, 1879	. . .	General Land Office	1:133,320 21 x 16-1/2
910	Brown, 1876	A. R. Roessler	Texas Land & Immigration Co. of New York, New York	1:133,320 25-1/2 x 21
911	Burleson, 1879	. . .	General Land Office	1:133,320 16 x 21
912	Caldwell, 1879	. . .	General Land Office	1:133,320 16-1/2 x 19-1/2
913	Caldwell, 1880	. . .	General Land Office	1:133,320 16-1/2 x 19-1/2
914	Calhoun, [18-?]	. . .	. . .	1:150,000 Ms., 23-1/2 x 17-1/2

TEXAS (Cont.)

No.	County and Date	Author or Surveyor	Publisher and Place	Scale and Size (Inches)
915	Calhoun, 1879	. . .	General Land Office	1:133,320 22-1/2 x 18-1/2
916	Callahan, [187-?]	. . .	Land Dept., Texas & Pacific Railway Co., Marshall, Tex.	1:133,320 18-1/2 x 15-1/2
917	Callahan, 1879	. . .	General Land Office	1:133,320 20-1/2 x 16-1/2
918	Cameron, 1895	. . .	General Land Office	1:133,333 Blue print, 48 x 25
919	Camp, 1879	. . .	General Land Office	1:133,320 7-1/2 x 14-1/2
920	Camp, 1897	C. W. Pressler	[General Land Office]	. . . Blue print, 17-1/2 x 26
921	Castro, 1891	. . .	General Land Office	1:133,320 20-1/2 x 17-1/2
922	Chambers, 1879	. . .	General Land Office	1:133,320 19-1/2 x 24-1/2
923	Cherokee, 1879	. . .	General Land Office	1:133,320 26 x 18-1/2
924	Childress, 1892	. . .	General Land Office	. . . 24 x 18-1/2
925	Clay, 1880	. . .	General Land Office	1:133,320 29-1/2 x 17-1/2
926	Coleman, 1879	. . .	General Land Office	1:133,320 25 x 16-1/2
927	Coleman, 1897 (traced 1936)	E. Schutze & J. L. Woodland	General Land Office	. . . Blue print, 47 x 33-1/2
928	Collin, 1881	Sam. R. Hamilton & T. B. Wilson	. . .	1:133,320 21-1/2 x 19
929	Collingsworth, 1892	. . .	General Land Office, Austin	1:133,320 22-1/2 x 18
930	Colorado, 1880	. . .	General Land Office	1:133,320 22-1/2 x 21-1/2
931	Comal, 1879	. . .	General Land Office	1:133,320 17 x 22
932	Comal, 1897 (traced 1914)	Herman Pressler & O. O. Terrell	General Land Office	1:66,660 Blue print, 37 x 42-1/2
933	Comanche, 1876	A.R. Roessler	Texas Land & Immigration Co. of New York, New York	1:133,320 27 x 23-1/2
934	Comanche, 1879	. . .	General Land Office	1:133,320 23 x 24
935	Concho, 1879	. . .	General Land Office	1:133,320 21 x 16
936	Concho, 1897	E. von Rosenberg & Grady W. Davis	General Land Office, Austin	1:66,660 44 x 36-1/2
937	Cooke, 1888	D. L. R. Butt	. . .	1:39,996 Blue line print, 17 x 13-1/2
938	Coryell, 1879	. . .	General Land Office	1:133,320 23 x 23-1/2
939	Cottle, 1891	. . .	General Land Office	1:133,320 22 x 16

TEXAS (Cont.)

No.	County and Date	Author or Surveyor	Publisher and Place	Scale and Size (Inches)
940	Crane, 1889	. . .	General Land Office	1:133,320 22 x 16-1/2
941	Crockett, 1894	. . .	General Land Office	1:133,320 Blue print, 32 x 43-1/2
942	Crosby, 1892	. . .	General Land Office	1:133,320 20 x 17-1/2
943	Dallam, 1888	. . .	General Land Office	1:133,320 23 x 26
944	Dallas, 1884 (traced 1931)	. . .	General Land Office, Austin	1:66,660 Blue print, 36-1/2 x 33-1/2
945	Dallas, 1886	J. M. Strong	Murphy & Bolanz, Dallas	1:133,320 21-1/2 x 16-1/2
946	Dallas, 1900	. . .	Sam Street, Dallas	1:75,000 29-1/2 x 27
947	Dawson, 1892	. . .	General Land Office	. . . 22 x 18-1/2
948	De Witt, 1881	. . .	General Land Office	1:133,320 27-1/2 x 26
949	Deaf Smith, 1898 (traced 1906)	Herman Pressler	General Land Office	1:66,660 Blue print, 36-1/2 x 48
950	Delta, 1889 (traced 1932)	W. M. Beck	General Land Office	1:66,660 Blue print, 28 x 37-1/2
951	Denton, [187-?]	. . .	Land Dept., Texas & Pacific Railway Co., Marshall, Tex.	1:133,320 16-1/2 x 17-1/2
952	Denton, 1879	. . .	General Land Office	1:133,320 20 x 17
953	Denton, 1897 (traced 1932)	W. B. Smith	General Land Office	1:66,660 Blue print, 2 parts, 20-1/2 x 38 ea.
954	Dickens, 1891	. . .	General Land Office	1:133,320 21 x 18
955	Dimmit, 1879	. . .	General Land Office	1:133,320 20 x 23-1/2
956	Dimmit, 1894 (traced 1901)	G. N. Beaumont & J. W. Morris	General Land Office, Austin	1:66,660 Blue print, 39-1/2 x 46-1/2
957	Dimmit, 1897	. . .	Land & Tax Dept., Texas & Pacific R'y Co.	. . . 16 x 21
958	Duval, 1880	. . .	General Land Office	1:133,320 29-1/2 x 20-1/2
959	Eastland, 1879	. . .	General Land Office	1:133,320 16-1/2 x 21
960	Eastland, Brown & Comanche (portions), [189-?]	M. Stakemann	Texas & Pacific R'y. Co., Marshall, Tex.	1:133,320 19-1/2 x 14-1/2
961	Eastland, 1889-96	. . .	General Land Office	1:66,660 Blue print, 21 x 42 ea.
962	Edwards, 1893	. . .	General Land Office, Austin	. . . 26 x 29-1/2
963	El Paso, 1893-94	M. Stakemann	. . .	. . . 9 sheets, 21 x 16 ea.

TEXAS (Cont.)

No.	County and Date	Author or Surveyor	Publisher and Place	Scale and Size (Inches)
964	Ellis, 1879	. . .	General Land Office	1:133,320 18-1/2 x 22-1/2
965	Ellis, 1889	E. A. Hausmann	General Land Office	1:66,660 Blue print, 38-1/2 x 46
966	Erath, 1879	. . .	General Land Office	1:133,320 25-1/2 x 22
967	Erath, 1896	E. von Rosenberg, P. J. Anthony & O. O. Terrell	General Land Office, Austin	1:66,660 Blue print, 2 parts, 23-1/2 x 41-1/2 ea.
968	Falls, 1879	. . .	General Land Office	1:133,320 17-1/2 x 20
969	Fannin, [187-?]	. . .	Land Dept., Texas & Pacific Railway Co., Marshall, Tex.	1:133,320 21 x 16
970	Fannin, 1892 (traced 1901)	C. W. Pressler & Legg	[General Land Office]	. . . Blue print, 39-1/2 x 35
971	Fayette, 1879	. . .	General Land Office	1:133,320 18-1/2 x 21-1/2
972	Fisher, [187-?]	. . .	Land Dept., Texas & Pacific Railway Co., Marshall, Tex.	1:133,320 19 x 16
973	Fisher, 1880	. . .	General Land Office	1:133,320 20 x 17-1/2
974	Floyd, 1892	. . .	General Land Office	1:133,320 20-1/2 x 17-1/2
975	Foard, 1891	. . .	General Land Office	. . . 17-1/2 x 19-1/2
976	Franklin, 1879	. . .	General Land Office	1:133,320 19-1/2 x 9-1/2
977	Franklin, 1897 (traced 1899)	C. W. Pressler & Amos Wynne	[General Land Office]	1:66,660 Blue print, 35-1/2 x 14
978	Frio, 1879	. . .	General Land Office	1:133,320 20-1/2 x 20
979	Frio, 1893 (traced 1935)	G. N. Beaumont & Jas. Woodland	General Land Office	1:66,660 Blue print, 2 parts, 22 x 41-1/2 ea.
980	Galveston, 1879	. . .	General Land Office	1:133,320 17-1/2 x 26
981	Galveston, 1891	Island City Abstract & Loan Co.	. . .	1:120,000 23 x 31
982	Galveston, 1891 (traced 1935)	Chas. W. Pressler & Jas. Woodland	[General Land Office]	. . . Blue print, 36 x 51-1/2
983	Galveston, 1892	. . .	General Land Office, Austin	1:133,320 15-1/2 x 23-1/2
984	Gillespie, 1879	. . .	General Land Office	1:133,320 19-1/2 x 24
985	Gillespie, 1887 (traced 1918)	O. O. Terrell	General Land Office, Austin	. . . Blue print, 34 x 46
986	Glasscock, 1889	. . .	General Land Office	1:133,320 21 x 16-1/2
987	Glasscock, [189-?]	M. Stakemann	. . .	1:133,320 20-1/2 x 16

TEXAS (Cont.)

No.	County and Date	Author or Surveyor	Publisher and Place	Scale and Size (Inches)
988	Goliad, 1896 (traced 1900)	. . .	General Land Office, Austin	1:66,660 Blue print, 2 parts, 21 x 44 ea.
989	Gonzales, 1880	. . .	General Land Office	1:133,320 24 x 21-1/2
990	Gray, 1889	. . .	General Land Office	1:133,320 22 x 16-1/2
991	Grimes, 1880	. . .	General Land Office	1:133,320 29 x 15
992	Guadalupe, 1880	. . .	General Land Office	1:133,320 22 x 21
993	Hale, 1892	. . .	General Land Office	1:133,320 21 x 18
994	Hamilton, 1876	A. R. Roessler	Texas Land & Immigration Co. of New York, New York	1:133,320 19 x 22
995	Hardeman, 1880	. . .	General Land Office, Austin	1:133,320 25-1/2 x 23-1/2
996	Hardeman, 1891	. . .	General Land Office, Austin	. . . 18 x 17
997	Hardin, 1898	. . .	General Land Office	1:66,660 Photocopy (pos.) in 2 parts, 38-1/2 x 21 ea.
998	Harris, 1879	. . .	General Land Office	1:133,320 23 x 33-1/2
999	Harrison, 1879	. . .	General Land Office	1:133,320 19-1/2 x 21
1000	Hartley, 1892	. . .	General Land Office, Austin	1:133,320 18-1/2 x 21
1001	Haskell, 1876	A. R. Roessler	Texas Land & Immigration Co. of New York, New York	1:120,000 Photocopy (pos.), 18 x 22-1/2
1002	Haskell, 1879	. . .	General Land Office	1:133,320 20-1/2 x 17-1/2
1003	Hays, 1880	. . .	General Land Office, Austin	1:133,320 22 x 19
1004	Hemphill, 1888	. . .	General Land Office, Austin	1:133,320 21 x 17
1005	Henderson, [187-?]	J. S. Daugherty	. . .	. . . Blue print, 15 x 28
1006	Hidalgo, 1896	. . .	General Land Office, Austin	1:133,320 Blue print, 43 x 25
1007	Hill, 1886	A. M. Craig	General Land Office, Austin	1:133,320 19 x 24
1008	Hood, 1879	. . .	General Land Office	1:66,660 26-1/2 x 29
1009	Hood, 1893 (traced 1918)	G. N. Beaumont & Jno. C. Newton	General Land Office	1:66,660 Blue print, 34 x 31-1/2
1010	Hood, 1894	. . .	General Land Office	. . . Photocopy (pos.), 17 x 16-1/2
1011	Hopkins, 1885 (traced 1936)	Geo. J. Thielepape & A. C. Clark	General Land Office, Austin	1:66,660 Blue print, 34 x 35-1/2

TEXAS (Cont.)

No.	County and Date	Author or Surveyor	Publisher and Place	Scale and Size (Inches)
1012	Houston, 1896 (traced 1915)	H. M. Bramlette	General Land Office	1:66,660 Blue print, 2 parts, 23 x 46 ea.
1013	Howard, [189-?]	M. Stakemann	. . .	. . . 19 x 16
1014	Hunt, 1873	A. L. Lucas & Chas. W. Pressler	General Land Office, Austin	1:133,320 Photocopy (pos.), 21 x 14-1/2
1015	Hunt, 1879	. . .	General Land Office	1:133,320 21 x 14
1016	Hunt, 1894 (traced 1914)	C. W. Pressler & O. O. Terrell	General Land Office	1:66,660 Blue print, 46-1/2 x 28-1/2
1017	Hutchinson, 1891	. . .	General Land Office	1:133,320 21 x 17-1/2
1018	Irion, 1893	E. Shütze [i.e., Schütze]	General Land Office	1:66,660 Blue print, 40-1/2 x 36
1019	Jack, 1876	A. R. Roessler	Texas Land & Immigration Co., New York	1:133,320 20 x 16
1020	Jack, 1879	. . .	General Land Office	1:133,320 21 x 16-1/2
1021	Jack, 1896	. . .	General Land Office	1:133,320 21 x 18
1022	Jackson, 1880	. . .	General Land Office	1:133,320 22 x 19
1023	Jackson, 1896	. . .	General Land Office, Austin	1:133,320 Blue print, 23-1/2 x 19-1/2
1024	Jasper, 1879	. . .	General Land Office	1:133,320 32 x 17-1/2
1025	Jasper, 1898	. . .	General Land Office	. . . Photocopy (pos.), 63-1/2 x 35-1/2
1026	Jeff Davis & Presidio (portions), 1894	M. Stakemann	. . .	1:133,320 20 x 16-1/2
1027	Jefferson, 1879	. . .	General Land Office	1:133,320 21-1/2 x 18-1/2
1028	Jefferson, 1898	Pattillo Higgins	. . .	1:133,320 26 x 23
1029	Johnson, 1887	F. G. Blaux	General Land Office	1:66,660 Blue print, 33 x 35
1030	Jones, 1879	. . .	General Land Office	1:133,320 21 x 16-1/2
1031	Jones, [188-?]	. . .	Panhandle Abstract Co., Anson, Tex.	1:150,000 16-1/2 x 15
1032	Karnes, 1880	. . .	General Land Office	1:133,320 23 x 22-1/2
1033	Kaufman & Rockwall, 1878	Jones & Murphy	. . .	1:133,320 22 x 15-1/2
1034	Kaufman, 1896 (traced 1931)	W. M. Beck	General Land Office	. . . Blue print, 42 x 28

TEXAS (Cont.)

No.	County and Date	Author or Surveyor	Publisher and Place	Scale and Size (Inches)
1035	Kendall, 1879	. . .	General Land Office	1:133,320 19 x 19
1036	Kendall, 1899 (traced 1919)	Hunnicutt & J. Bascom Giles	General Land Office	1:66,660 Blue print, 34-1/2 x 32-1/2
1037	Kent, 1888	. . .	General Land Office	1:133,320 22 x 17-1/2
1038	Kerr, 1879	. . .	General Land Office	1:133,320 19-1/2 x 27-1/2
1039	Kimble, 1879	. . .	General Land Office	1:133,320 16 x 28
1040	Kimble, 1892	. . .	General Land Office, Austin	. . . 14-1/2 x 23
1041	Kinney, 1879	. . .	General Land Office	1:133,320 20 x 30-1/2
1042	Kinney, 1884	. . .	New York & Texas Land Co., Palestine, Tex.	1:140,000 24 x 33
1043	Knox, 1880	. . .	General Land Office	1:133,320 22 x 18-1/2
1044	La Salle, 1895	G. N. Beaumont	General Land Office	1:66,660 Blue print, 46 x 40-1/2
1045	Lamar, [187-?]	. . .	Land Dept., Texas & Pacific Railway Co., Marshall, Tex.	1:133,320 21 x 16-1/2
1046	Lampasas, 1879	. . .	General Land Office	1:133,320 18 x 24
1047	Lavaca, 1879	. . .	General Land Office	1:133,320 20-1/2 x 21-1/2
1048	Lavaca, 1896 (traced 1914)	C. W. Pressler & H. M. Bramlette	[General Land Office]	. . . Blue print, 2 parts, 21-1/2 x 41 ea.
1049	Lee, 1879	. . .	General Land Office	1:133,320 21-1/2 x 16-1/2
1050	Lee, 1888 (traced 1890)	J. W. Maxcy & Amos Wynne	General Land Office	1:66,660 Blue print, 40 x 38-1/2
1051	Leon, 1879	. . .	General Land Office	1:133,320 22-1/2 x 19
1052	Liberty, 1879	. . .	General Land Office	1:133,320 24 x 24
1053	Liberty, 1895	. . .	General Land Office	1:133,320 24 x 25-1/2
1054	Live Oak, 1879	. . .	General Land Office	1:133,320 25-1/2 x 18-1/2
1055	Live Oak, 1899 (traced 1910)	Wise, Hedick & F. D. Russell	General Land Office, Austin	. . . Blue print, 50 x 36-1/2
1056	Llano, 1875	A. R. Roessler & M. v. Mittendorfer	. . .	1:133,320 Photocopy (pos.), 15-1/2 x 20
1057	Llano, 1879	. . .	General Land Office	1:133,320 20 x 20-1/2
1058	Llano, 1890	G. N. Beaumont & G. W. Davis	General Land Office, Austin	1:66,660 Blue print, 2 parts, 20-1/2 x 40-1/2 ea.

TEXAS (Cont.)

No.	County and Date	Author or Surveyor	Publisher and Place	Scale and Size (Inches)
1059	Llano, 1890	. . .	General Land Office	1:66,600 31 x 42
1060	Lubbock, 1892	. . .	General Land Office	1:133,320 20 x 17-1/2
1061	Lynn, 1891	. . .	General Land Office	1:133,320 22 x 17-1/2
1062	McCulloch, 1879	. . .	General Land Office	1:133,320 21 x 16
1063	McLennan, 1880	. . .	General Land Office	1:133,320 21 x 23-1/2
1064	McLennan, 1896	Herman Pressler	General Land Office	1:66,660 Blue print, 2 parts, 47 x 26 ea.
1065	McMullen, 1879	. . .	General Land Office	1:133,320 24-1/2 x 15-1/2
1066	Madison, 1879	. . .	General Land Office	1:133,320 16 x 20-1/2
1067	Marion, 1879	. . .	General Land Office	1:133,320 13 x 19
1068	Martin, 1894	M. Stakemann	. . .	1:133,320 20 x 16-1/2
1069	Mason, 1879	. . .	General Land Office	1:133,320 22 x 17
1070	Matagorda, 1879	. . .	General Land Office	1:133,320 29 x 26
1071	Maverick, 1879	. . .	General Land Office	1:133,320 31 x 20
1072	Maverick, 1893	. . .	General Land Office	1:133,320 32-1/2 x 19-1/2
1073	Medina, 1879	. . .	General Land Office	1:133,320 25-1/2 x 21
1074	Menard, 1879	. . .	General Land Office	1:133,320 17 x 29
1075	Menard, 1894 (traced 1936)	W. H. Warren & A. C. Clark	General Land Office	1:66,660 Blue print, 30 x 40-1/2
1076	Milam, 1879	. . .	General Land Office	1:133,320 26 x 22-1/2
1077	Mills, 1888	. . .	General Land Office	1:66,660 31-1/2 x 40
1078	Mitchell, 1889	. . .	General Land Office	. . . Photocopy (pos.), 20 x 17
1079	Mitchell, [189-?]	M. Stakemann	. . .	1:133,320 21 x 17
1080	Montgomery, 1880	. . .	General Land Office	1:133,320 21 x 24
1081	Morris, 1880	. . .	General Land Office	1:133,320 23 x 10-1/2
1082	Motley, 1893	Blau	General Land Office, Austin	1:66,660 36-1/2 x 30-1/2

TEXAS (Cont.)

No.	County and Date	Author or Surveyor	Publisher and Place	Scale and Size (Inches)
1083	Nacogdoches, 1881	G. N. Beaumont	General Land Office	1:133,320 23-1/2 x 20-1/2
1084	Navarro, 1880	G. N. Beaumont	General Land Office	1:133,320 19 x 25
1085	Nolan, 1880	. . .	General Land Office	1:133,320 24 x 18-1/2
1086	Nolan, [189-?]	M. Stakemann	. . .	1:133,320 20 x 16
1087	Nueces, 1879	. . .	General Land Office	1:133,320 28-1/2 x 37-1/2
1088	Oldham, 1888	. . .	General Land Office	1:133,320 23 x 26
1089	Orange, 1880	. . .	General Land Office	1:133,320 13-1/2 x 17-1/2
1090	Orange, 1895	. . .	General Land Office	. . . Photocopy (pos.), 34 x 36
1091	Palo Pinto, 1879	. . .	General Land Office	1:133,320 21 x 16-1/2
1092	Palo Pinto, [188-?]	. . .	Land Dept., Texas & Pacific Railway Co., Marshall, Tex.	1:133,320 21 x 17-1/2
1093	Palo Pinto, 1898	Herman Pressler & Grady W. Davis	General Land Office, Austin	1:66,660 Blue print, 43 x 36
1094	Panola, 1897 (traced 1932)	W. B. Smith	General Land Office	1:66,660 Blue print, 38 x 37-1/2
1095	Parker, 1889 Sept. (traced 1919)	Herman Pressler & Jno. C. Newton	General Land Office, Austin	1:66,660 Blue print, 39-1/2 x 34-1/2
1096	Parker, 1889 Nov.	. . .	General Land Office	1:66,660 34-1/2 x 31
1097	Pecos (portion), 1891	F. G. Blau	. . .	1:66,660 Photocopy (neg.) in 6 parts, 3 are 22 x 17 ea. & 3 are 24 x 17 ea.
1098	Polk, [18-?]	. . .	[General Land Office]	1:66,660 Photocopy (pos.), 49 x 39
1099	Polk, 1879	. . .	General Land Office	1:133,320 25 x 19-1/2
1100	Presidio & Brewster (portions), 1891	M. Stakemann	Texas & Pacific Land Office, Dallas	. . . 21 x 16
1101	Rains & Van Zandt (portion), [187-?]	. . .	Land Dept., Texas & Pacific Railway Co., Marshall, Tex.	1:133,320 19 x 15-1/2
1102	Rains, 1880	. . .	General Land Office	1:133,320 11 x 11
1103	Rains, 1888	John W. Maxey [i.e., Maxcy]	General Land Office	1:66,660 Blue print, 25-1/2 x 27
1104	Red River, [187-?]	. . .	Land Dept., Texas & Pacific Railway Co., Marshall, Tex.	1:133,320 21-1/2 x 16-1/2
1105	Red River, 1879	. . .	General Land Office	1:133,320 23-1/2 x 19-1/2

TEXAS (Cont.)

No.	County and Date	Author or Surveyor	Publisher and Place	Scale and Size (Inches)
1106	Refugio, 1879	. . .	General Land Office	1:133,320 19 x 27-1/2
1107	Roberts, 1888	. . .	General Land Office	1:133,320 21 x 16-1/2
1108	Robertson, 1889 (traced 1919)	Jno. W. Maxey [i.e., Maxcy] & Jno. C. Newton	General Land Office	. . . Blue print, 42-1/2 x 39
1109	Rockwall, 1874 (traced 1930)	. . .	General Land Office	1:66,660 Blue print, 22-1/2 x 18-1/2
1110	Rockwall, 1880	. . .	General Land Office	1:66,660 20 x 16-1/2
1111	Runnels, 1879	. . .	General Land Office	1:133,320 20-1/2 x 16-1/2
1112	Runnels, [189-?]	. . .	J. N. Winters & Co., Ballinger, Tex.	1:133,320 21-1/2 x 17
1113	Runnels, 1898	Herman Pressler & Grady W. Davis	General Land Office, Austin	1:66,660 Blue print, 41-1/2 x 35-1/2
1114	Rusk, 1895	C. W. Pressler	General Land Office, Austin	1:66,660 Blue print, 44-1/2 x 32-1/2
1115	Sabine, 1879	. . .	General Land Office	1:133,320 20 x 15
1116	Sabine, 1896 (traced 1899)	S. T. Beer & Co.	General Land Office, Austin	1:66,660 Photocopy (pos.), 44-1/2 x 30
1117	San Jacinto, [18-?]	. . .	. . .	1:66,660 Blue print, 42-1/2 x 34
1118	San Jacinto, 1879	. . .	General Land Office	1:133,320 21-1/2 x 17-1/2
1119	San Jacinto, 1889 (traced 1914)	F. G. Blau & O. O. Terrell	General Land Office	1:66,660 Blue print, 43-1/2 x 34
1120	San Patricio, 1879	. . .	General Land Office	1:133,320 16 x 26
1121	San Patricio, 1896	. . .	General Land Office	1:66,660 Blue print, 30 x 49
1122	San Saba, 1876	A. R. Roessler	Texas Land & Immigration Co. of New York, New York	1:133,320 23 x 20
1123	San Saba, 1879	. . .	General Land Office	1:133,320 19-1/2 x 22
1124	Schleicher, 1898	S. J. Rowe & J. Bascom Giles	General Land Office	1:66,660 Blue print, 33-1/2 x 51
1125	Shackelford, 1879	. . .	General Land Office	1:133,320 21 x 17
1126	Shelby, 1880	. . .	General Land Office	1:133,320 19 x 24-1/2
1127	Shelby, 1897 (traced 1899)	P. F. Appell	General Land Office	1:66,660 Blue print, 2 parts, 40 x 23-1/2 ea.
1128	Smith, 1880	. . .	General Land Office	1:133,320 19 x 20

TEXAS (Cont.)

No.	County and Date	Author or Surveyor	Publisher and Place	Scale and Size (Inches)
1129	Somervell, 1884 (traced 1934)	Geo. J. Thielepape & Jas. Woodland	General Land Office	1:66,660 Blue print, 25 x 24
1130	Starr, 1900	. . .	General Land Office	1:133,320 Blue print, 46-1/2 x 23
1131	Stephens, [187-?]	. . .	Land Dept., Texas & Pacific Railway Co., Marshall, Tex.	1:133,320 19 x 16
1132	Stephens, 1879	. . .	General Land Office	1:133,320 20-1/2 x 17
1133	Sterling, 1892	. . .	General Land Office	. . . 23 x 14-1/2
1134	Stonewall, 1880	. . .	General Land Office	1:133,320 18-1/2 x 17-1/2
1135	Sutton, 1898	P. F. Appell	General Land Office	1:66,660 Blue print, 2 parts, 38 x 22-1/2 & 38 x 32
1136	Sutton, 1898	P. F. Appell & G. W. Davis	General Land Office	1:66,660 Blue print, 38 x 54-1/2
1137	Tarrant, [187-?]	. . .	Land Dept., Texas & Pacific Railway Co., Marshall, Tex.	1:133,320 19 x 16-1/2
1138	Tarrant, 1885	. . .	General Land Office	1:66,660 Blue print, 35 x 32-1/2
1139	Tarrant, 1892	J. J. Goodfellow	Goodfellow & Williams, Fort Worth	1:33,330 62 x 61
1140	Taylor, 1879	. . .	General Land Office	1:133,320 19-1/2 x 16-1/2
1141	Taylor, [189-?]	M. Stakemann	. . .	1:133,320 19-1/2 x 15-1/2
1142	Throckmorton, 1880	. . .	General Land Office	1:133,320 24 x 18-1/2
1143	Throckmorton, 1898 (traced 1914)	C. W. Pressler & O. O. Terrell	Gen. Land Office	. . . Blue print, 39-1/2 x 34
1144	Titus, 1880	. . .	General Land Office	1:133,320 22-1/2 x 14-1/2
1145	Tom Green, 1892 (traced 1910 & 1931)	E. Schütze & W. M. Beck	General Land Office	. . . Blue print, 2 parts, 23 x 42-1/2 ea.
1146	Tom Green (eastern portion), 1894	. . .	General Land Office	1:133,320 21-1/2 x 23
1147	Tom Green (western portion), 1894	. . .	General Land Office	1:133,320 21 x 16
1148	Travis, 1880	Reuben W. Ford	. . .	1:53,298 2 parts, 27-1/2 x 65-1/2 ea.
1149	Travis, 1894 (traced 1914)	Herman Pressler & H. M. Bramlette	General Land Office	1:66,660 Blue print, 2 parts, 23 x 40 ea.
1150	Trinity, 1879	. . .	General Land Office	1:133,320 13-1/2 x 23
1151	Tyler, 1879	. . .	General Land Office	1:133,320 21 x 17-1/2

TEXAS (Cont.)

No.	County and Date	Author or Surveyor	Publisher and Place	Scale and Size (Inches)
1152	Tyler, 1897	S. J. Rowe	General Land Office, Austin	1:66,660 Blue print, 39-1/2 x 36-1/2
1153	Tyler, 1898	[S. J.] Rowe	General Land Office, Austin	1:66,660 Photocopy (pos.), 39 x 35
1154	Upshur, 1897 (traced 1914)	C. W. Pressler & O. O. Terrell	General Land Office, Austin	1:66,660 Blue print, 35 x 29
1155	Van Zandt, [c1884]	. . .	General Land Office	1:133,320 18-1/2 x 19
1156	Walker, 1879	. . .	General Land Office	1:133,320 18-1/2 x 15-1/2
1157	Walker, 1889 (traced 1903)	Frank R. Sweeney	General Land Office	1:66,660 Blue print, 40-1/2 x 33-1/2
1158	Waller, 1879	. . .	General Land Office	1:133,320 20-1/2 x 14
1159	Waller, 1897 (traced 1900)	Herman Pressler & J. W. Morris	General Land Office, Austin	1:66,660 Blue print, 45 x 27
1160	Washington, 1879	. . .	General Land Office	1:133,320 13 x 21
1161	Webb (eastern portion, formerly Encinal Co.), 1879	. . .	General Land Office	1:133,320 32-1/2 x 22
1162	Wharton, 1880	. . .	General Land Office	1:133,320 23 x 27-1/2
1163	Wharton, 1895	. . .	General Land Office	1:133,320 23-1/2 x 25-1/2
1164	Wilbarger, 1887	J. A. Nabers	. . .	. . . 12 x 9
1165	Wilbarger, [189-?]	[J. A. Nabers]	J. E. Lutz, Vernon, Tex.	. . . 12 x 8-1/2
1166	Williamson, 1880	. . .	General Land Office	1:133,320 20-1/2 x 28-1/2
1167	Williamson, 1888 (traced 1917)	Herman Pressler & P. J. Anthony	General Land Office	1:66,660 Blue print, 38-1/2 x 55
1168	Wilson, 1879	. . .	General Land Office	1:133,320 21 x 22
1169	Winkler, 1889	. . .	General Land Office	1:133,320 23 x 18
1170	Wise, [187-?]	. . .	Land Dept., Texas & Pacific Railway Co., Marshall, Tex.	1:133,320 19 x 16-1/2
1171	Wise, 1879	. . .	General Land Office	1:133,320 20-1/2 x 17
1172	Wise, 1895	Herman Pressler & O. O. Terrell	General Land Office	1:66,660 Blue print, 40-1/2 x 36
1173	Wood, 1879	. . .	General Land Office	1:133,320 16 x 16-1/2
1174	Wood, 1895 (traced 1914)	C. W. Pressler & H. M. Bramlette	[General Land Office]	1:66,660 Blue print, 32 x 33

TEXAS (Cont.)

No.	County and Date	Author or Surveyor	Publisher and Place	Scale and Size (Inches)
1175	Young, 1880	. . .	General Land Office	1:133,320 22 x 20-1/2
1176	Young, 1896	J. F. Clark & Grady W. Davis	General Land Office, Austin	1:66,660 Blue print, 41-1/2 x 35
1177	Young, 1898	. . .	General Land Office, Austin	. . . 34 x 29-1/2
1178	Zavala, 1879	. . .	General Land Office	1:133,320 20 x 24-1/2

UTAH

1179	Salt Lake [c1890]	. . .	. . .	1:42,000 2 sheets, 27 x 59 ea.
1180	Weber, 1888	Washington Jenkins	. . .	1:39,600 4 parts, 36-1/2 x 21 ea.

VERMONT

1181	Addison, 1857	H. F. Walling	Baker & Tilden, Boston & New York	1:50,000 2 sheets, 54-1/2 x 27 ea.
1182	Addison, 1857	H. F. Walling	Wm. E. Baker & Co., Boston & New York	1:50,000 4 parts, 27 x 27 ea.
1183	Bennington, 1856	E. Rice & C. E. Harwood	C. B. Peckham & H. F. Walling, New York	1:63,360 42-1/2 x 55-1/2
1184	Caledonia, 1858	H. F. Walling	Baker & Tilden, New York	1:50,000 54-1/2 x 55
1185	Chittenden, 1857	H. F. Walling	Baker, Tilden & Co., Boston & New York	1:50,000 2 sheets, 27 x 54-1/2 ea.
1186	Essex, 1878	. . .	F. W. Beers & Co., New York	1:50,688 2 parts, 27-1/2 x 48-1/2 ea.
1187	Franklin & Grand Isle, 1857	H. F. Walling	Baker, Tilden & Co., Boston & New York	1:50,000 2 sheets, 55-1/2 x 28-1/2 ea.
1188	Orange, 1858	H. F. Walling	Baker & Tilden, New York	1:50,000 55-1/2 x 54-1/2
1189	Orleans, Lamoille & Essex, 1859	H. F. Walling	Loommis & Way, New York	1:84,480 2 parts, 28-1/2 x 54 ea.
1190	Rutland, 1854	J. Chace, Jr.	Isaac W. Moore, Owen McLeran & James D. Scott, Phila.	1:63,360 6 parts, 19-1/2 x 23-1/2 ea.
1191	Washington, 1858	H. F. Walling	Baker & Tilden, New York	1:50,000 54-1/2 x 54-1/2
1192	Windham, 1856	J. Chace, Jr.	C. McClellan & Co., Phila.	1:67,000 53-1/2 x 44
1193	Windsor, 1855	Hosea Doton	. . .	1:65,000 6 parts, 18-1/2 x 22-1/2 ea.
1194	Windsor, [1856]	J. Chace, Jr.	. . .	1:65,000 55-1/2 x 45

VERMONT (Cont.)

No.	County and Date	Author or Surveyor	Publisher and Place	Scale and Size (Inches)
1195	Windsor, 1856	Hosea Doton	. . .	1:65,000 2 parts, 27-1/2 x 44-1/2 ea.

VIRGINIA

No.	County and Date	Author or Surveyor	Publisher and Place	Scale and Size (Inches)
1196	Accomack, 1820	John Wood	. . .	1:41,000 Photocopy (pos.) in 24 parts, 18 x 23 ea.
1197	Albemarle & Augusta (portions), [186-]	[Hotchkiss Coll. no. 20]	. . .	1:150,000 Ms., 18 x 22
1198	Albemarle, [1864]	C. S. Dwight & A. H. Campbell	Chief Engineer's Office, D.N.V.	1:80,000 Photocopy (neg.) in 4 parts, 22 x 18 ea.
1199	Albemarle, 1864	Albert H. Campbell & C. S. Dwight	Chief Engr's. Office [D.N.V.]	1:80,000 Ms., 30 x 24
1200	Albemarle, 1875	G. Peyton	. . .	1:50,688 4 parts, 26 x 24 ea.
1201	Amelia, [1820?]	. . .	. . .	1:40,000 Photocopy (pos.) in 8 parts, 17-1/2 x 16 ea.
1202	Amelia, [185-?]	William L. Booker	R. L. Barnes, Phila.	1:82,000 18 x 26-1/2
1203	Amelia, [186-]	D. E. Henderson	. . .	1:40,000 Photocopy (neg.) in 8 parts, 21 x 18 ea.
1204	Amelia, [1864]	A. H. Campbell & D. E. Henderson	Chief Engineers Office, D.N.V.	1:80,000 Photocopy (neg.) in 2 parts, 17-1/2 x 17 ea.
1205	Amelia, 1864	A. H. Campbell & D. E. Henderson	Chief Engineer's Office, D.N.V.	1:80,000 Blue print, 14-1/2 x 30-1/2
1206	Amherst & Nelson, [186-]	C. S. Dwight [Hotchkiss Coll. no. 49]	. . .	1:80,000 Ms., 31 x 37-1/2
1207	Amherst & Nelson, [1864]	. . .	Chief Engineer's Office, D.N.V.	1:80,000 Photocopy (neg.) in 4 parts, 18 x 22 ea.
1208	Amherst & Nelson, 1864	C. S. Dwight & A. H. Campbell	Chief Engineer's Office, D.N.V.	1:80,000 Blue print, 26 x 40-1/2
1209	Arlington, [17--] ([1960])	W. Bell & B. Sims	. . .	1:14,400 Blue line print, 34 x 21-1/2
1210	Arlington & Fairfax (portions), 1861	V. P. Corbett	. . .	. . . 11 x 15
1211	Arlington, 1900	Howell & Taylor, & G. P. Strum	. . .	1:11,000 4 parts, 30-1/2 x 20 ea.
1212	Augusta (portion), [1736-82]	Meredith Leitch (1947)	. . .	1:135,416 10-1/2 x 15-1/2
1213	Augusta, 1870	Jed Hotchkiss	Board of Survey of Washington College, Va.	1:63,360 2 parts, 23 x 45-1/2 & 24-1/2 x 45-1/2
1214	Augusta, 1865-75	P. S. Michie & Jed. Hotchkiss	Office of the Chief of Engineers, U.S. Army	1:84,480 33-1/2 x 34-1/2

VIRGINIA (Cont.)

No.	County and Date	Author or Surveyor	Publisher and Place	Scale and Size (Inches)
1215	Bedford, 1864	W. Izard & A. H. Campbell	Chief Engineer's Office, D.N.V.	1:80,000 Photocopy (neg.) in 4 parts, 22 x 17-1/2 ea.
1216	Bedford, 1864	W. Izard & A. H. Campbell	Top. Dept. [D.N.V.]	1:80,000 Photocopy (neg.) in 4 parts, 17-1/2 x 21-1/2 ea.
1217	Bland, 1866	John S. Peck	Leisenring, Phila.	. . . 13 x 19
1218	Botetourt (eastern portion), [186-]	Walter Izard, Jno. M. Coyle & W. Hutchinson	[Chief Engr's. Off., D.N.V.]	1:40,000 Photocopy (neg.) in 6 parts, 17-1/2 x 21 ea.
1219	Botetourt (northwestern portion), [186-]	. . .	[Chief Engr's. Off., D.N.V.]	1:40,000 Photocopy (neg.) in 4 parts, 21 x 17-1/2 ea.
1220	Botetourt (southwestern portion), [186-]	. . .	[Chief Engr's. Off., D.N.V.]	1:40,000 Photocopy (neg.) in 4 parts, 17-1/2 x 21-1/2 ea.
1221	Botetourt, 1864	Walter Izard, A. H. Campbell & J. Innes Randolph	Chief Engineer's Office, D.N.V.	1:80,000 Photocopy (neg.) in 4 parts, 16-1/2 x 21 ea.
1222	Botetourt, 1865	Walter Izard & A. H. Campbell	Chief Engineer's Office, D.N.V.	1:80,000 Blue print, 25-1/2 x 30
1223	Botetourt & Roanoke, 1865-85	Walter Travd [i.e., Izard], A.H. Campbell, Jed. Hotchkiss & Sev. P. Ker [Hotchkiss Coll. no. 284]	. . .	1:80,000 Ms., 43 x 22
1224	Brunswick, 1820	John Wood	. . .	1:39,600 Photocopy (pos.) in 12 parts, 19 x 15 ea.
1225	Brunswick, 1864	A. H. Campbell & H. M. Graves	Topl. Dept., D.N.Va.	1:80,000 Photocopy (neg.) in 4 parts, 21-1/2 x 17-1/2 ea.
1226	Brunswick, 1864	A. H. Campbell & H. M. Graves	Topl. Dept., D.N.Va.	1:80,000 Blue print, 30 x 26-1/2
1227	Buckingham & Appomattox, 1863	A. H. Campbell & Charles E. Cassell [Hotchkiss Coll. no. 21]	. . .	1:80,000 Ms., 27-1/2 x 35-1/2
1228	Campbell, [186-]	A.H. Campbell [Hotchkiss Coll. no. 22]	. . .	1:80,000 Ms., 25 x 27-1/2
1229	Campbell, 1864	C. S. Dwight & A. H. Campbell	Chief Engineer's Office, D.N.V.	1:80,000 Photocopy (neg.) in 4 parts, 17-1/2 x 20-1/2 ea.
1230	Campbell, 1864	C. S. Dwight & A. H. Campbell	Chief Engineer's Office, D.N.V.	1:80,000 Blue print, 25 x 27-1/2
1231	Caroline, [186-]	A. H. Campbell	Chief Engineer's Office, D.N.V.	1:80,000 Photocopy (neg.) in 4 parts, 20-1/2 x 17-1/2 ea.
1232	Caroline, [186-]	[Hotchkiss Coll. no. 24]	[Eng. Office, 2d Corps, A.N.Va.]	1:80,000 Ms., 24 x 21

VIRGINIA (Cont.)

No.	County and Date	Author or Surveyor	Publisher and Place	Scale and Size (Inches)
1233	Caroline, Hanover & Henrico (portions), [186-]	[Hotchkiss Coll. no. 25]	. . .	1:160,000 Ms., 10-1/2 x 12
1234	Caroline, 1862	A. H. Campbell [Hotchkiss Coll. no. 23]	Chief Engineer's Office, D.N.Va.	1:80,000 Ms., 23-1/2 x 26
1235	Charlotte, [186-]	Jed. Hotchkiss [Hotchkiss Coll. no. 289]	. . .	1:80,000 Ms., 31 x 20
1236	Charlotte, 1864	A. H. Campbell & C. E. Cassell	Topl. Departmt. [D.N.V.]	1:80,000 Photocopy (neg.) in 4 parts, 19-1/2 x 16 ea.
1237	Chesterfield (portion), [186-]	. . .	[Chief Engr's. Off., D.N.V.]	1:50,000 Photocopy (pos.), 24-1/2 x 33
1238	Chesterfield (portion), 1863-64	A. H. Campbell & D. E. Henderson	Chief Engineer's Office, D.N.V.	1:40,000 Blue print, 25 x 36
1239	Chesterfield, 1888	J. E. La Prade	Board of Supervisors	1:47,520 34-1/2 x 50-1/2
1240	Clarke & Warren (portions), 1834	George Love	. . .	1:39,600 Photocopy (neg.) in 4 parts, 17-1/2 x 22 ea.
1241	Culpeper & Madison (portion), 1863	A. H. Campbell & Lieut. Dwight [Hotchkiss Coll. no. 27]	Chief Engineers Office, D.N.V.	1:80,000 Ms., 33 x 32
1242	Culpeper, Madison & Rappahannock, 1864	C. S. Dwight & A. H. Campbell	Chief Engineer's Office, D.N.V.	1:80,000 Photocopy (neg.) in 6 parts, 4 are 17 x 21 ea. & 2 are 18 x 21 ea.
1243	Cumberland, 1864	A. H. Campbell & Charles E. Cassell	[Chief Engr's. Off., D.N.V.]	1:80,000 Photocopy (neg.) in 2 parts, 18-1/2 x 17 ea.
1244	Dinwiddie, [1820?]	. . .	. . .	1:39,600 Photocopy (pos.) in 8 parts, 24 x 18 ea.
1245	Dinwiddie, 1854	James Keily	James D. Scott, Phila.	. . . 38-1/2 x 49
1246	Dinwiddie, 1864	A. H. Campbell, S. L. Sommers & H. M. Graves	[Chief Engr's. Off., D.N.V.]	1:80,000 Photocopy (neg.) in 2 parts, 20 x 17 ea.
1247	Dinwiddie, 1864	A. H. Campbell, S. L. Sommers, H. M. Graves & J. Innes Randolph [Hotchkiss Coll. no. 28]	. . .	1:80,000 Ms., 22-1/2 x 23-1/2
1248	Elizabeth City, [c1892]	E. A. Semple, Wm. Ivy & C. Hubbard	E. W. Smith & Co., Phila.	1:15,840 4 parts, 20 x 27 ea.
1249	Essex, King & Queen, & King William (portions), 1863	A. H. Campbell & Jed. Hotchkiss [Hotchkiss Coll. no. 29]	Chief Engineers Office, D.N.Va.	1:80,000 Ms., 30 x 33
1250	Fairfax (portion), 1861	F. F. Mead	. . .	1:28,160 Ms., 38 x 36-1/2
1251	Fairfax & Arlington, & parts of Loudoun & Prince William, 1864	J. Paul Hoffmann & S. Howell Brown [Hotchkiss Coll. no. 30]	. . .	1:126,720 Ms., 24-1/2 x 14
1252	Fauquier (central portion), [186-?]	C. S. Dwight	[Chief Engr's. Off., D.N.V.]	1:40,000 Photocopy (neg.) in 2 parts, 19-1/2 x 17 ea.

VIRGINIA (Cont.)

No.	County and Date	Author or Surveyor	Publisher and Place	Scale and Size (Inches)
1253	Fauquier (northwestern portion), [186-?]	. . .	[Chief Engr's. Off., D.N.V.]	1:40,000 Photocopy (neg.) in 6 parts, 20-1/2 x 17-1/2 ea.
1254	Fauquier (portion), [186-]	[Hotchkiss Coll. no. 32]	. . .	1:80,000 Ms., 13 x 17
1255	Fauquier, Prince William & Rappahannock (portions), [186-]	[Hotchkiss Coll. no. 34]	. . .	1:126,720 Ms., 15 x 17-1/2
1256	Fauquier, 1863	J. K. Boswell & Jed. Hotchkiss [Hotchkiss Coll. no. 31]	. . .	1:126,720 Ms., 25-1/2 x 19
1257	Fluvanna, 1863	A. H. Campbell, Cha's. E. Cassell & H. M. G[raves]	[Chief Engr's. Off., D.N.V.]	1:80,000 Photocopy (neg.) in 2 parts, 20 x 17 ea.
1258	Frederick, Va. & Berkeley & Jefferson, W. Va., 1809	Chas. Varle	. . .	1:136,000 33-1/2 x 24-1/2
1259	Frederick, 1820	John Wood	. . .	1:63,360 Photocopy (neg.) in 12 parts, 18 x 22 ea.
1260	Frederick, 1820	John Wood	. . .	1:107,000 Photocopy (pos.), 26-1/2 x 39
1261	Frederick, [186-]	[John] Wood [Hotchkiss Coll. no. 35]	. . .	1:160,000 Ms., 16-1/2 x 18
1262	Goochland, [1820?]	. . .	. . .	1:39,600 Photocopy (pos.) in 6 parts, 17-1/2 x 20 ea.
1263	Goochland, 1863	A. H. Campbell, Chas. E. Cassell & H. M. Graves	[Chief Engr's. Off., D.N.V.]	1:80,000 Photocopy (neg.) in 2 parts, 16-1/2 x 17-1/2 ea.
1264	Goochland, [1881]	John W. George	. . .	1:115,000 17 x 22
1265	Grayson, 1897	S. M. Dickey & C. R. Boyd	Board of Supervisors of Grayson County	1:130,000 14 x 24-1/2
1266	Greene, [186-]	[Hotchkiss Coll. no. 36]	. . .	1:40,000 Ms., 34 x 34
1267	Greene, 1863	Engr. Office, 2nd. Corps	. . .	1:160,000 Ms., 12-1/2 x 8-1/2
1268	Greene, 1866-75	P. S. Michie & Jed. Hotchkiss	Office of the Chief of Engineers, U.S. Army	1:63,360 24-1/2 x 24
1269	Greensville & Northampton, N. C. (portion), 1864	A. H. Campbell	Chief Engineer's Office, D.N.V.	1:80,000 Photocopy (neg.) in 4 parts, 21 x 17 ea.
1270	Hanover, [1820?]	. . .	. . .	1:63,360 Photocopy (pos.) in 4 parts, 24 x 15 ea.
1271	Hanover (portion), [186-?]	A. H. Campbell & D. E. Henderson	[Chief Engr's. Off., D.N.V.]	1:40,000 Photocopy (neg.) in 4 parts, 21-1/2 x 17-1/2 ea.
1272	Hanover (portion), [186-]	[Hotchkiss Coll. no. 37]	. . .	1:80,000 Ms., 22 x 37-1/2

VIRGINIA (Cont.)

No.	County and Date	Author or Surveyor	Publisher and Place	Scale and Size (Inches)
1273	Hanover, [186-]	[Hotchkiss Coll. no. 38]	. . .	1:80,000 Ms., 14-1/2 x 10-1/2
1274	Hanover (portion), [186-]	[Hotchkiss Coll. no. 39]	. . .	1:160,000 Ms., 20 x 20-1/2
1275	Henrico, 1819	John Wood	. . .	1:39,600 Photocopy (pos.) in 6 parts, 18 x 24 ea.
1276	Henrico, [1820?]	[John Wood]	. . .	1:39,600 Photocopy (pos.) in 6 parts, 18 x 24 ea.
1277	Henrico, 1853	James Keily	Robert P. Smith & C. Carpenter, Richmond	1:41,500 Photocopy (pos.) in 8 parts, 4 are 17-1/2 x 23 ea. & 4 are 17-1/2 x 15 ea.
1278	Henrico, [1853] (photographed 1864)	[James Keily]	[Robert P. Smith & C. Carpenter]	1:60,000 Photocopy (pos.), 35 x 16-1/2
1279	Henrico (portion), 1862	. . .	. . .	1:100,000 Photocopy (pos.), 11 x 13
1280	Henrico & Chesterfield (portions), 1862	Albert H. Campbell [Hotchkiss Coll. no. 40]	Chief Engineer's Office, D.N.V.	1:40,000 Ms., 39-1/2 x 28
1281	Henrico, [1864]	[Hotchkiss Coll. no. 41]	. . .	1:40,000 Ms., 25-1/2 x 52
1282	Henrico, 1887	James T. Redd	. . .	1:95,040 28-1/2 x 14
1283	Isle of Wight & Nansemond (portion), 1864	A. H. Campbell	Chief Engineer's Office, D.N.V.	1:80,000 Photocopy (neg.) in ? parts, 17-1/2 x 20-1/2 ea.
1284	King William, 1863	John Grant, A. S. Barrows, A. H. Campbell & Jed. Hotchkiss [Hotchkiss Coll. no. 42]	Chief Engineer's Office, D.N.V.	1:80,000 Ms., 20 x 20-1/2
1285	King William, 1865	B. Lewis Blackford	[Chief Engr's. Off., D.N.V.]	1:80,000 Photocopy (neg.) in 2 parts, 20 x 17 ea.
1286	King William, 1865	A. H. Campbell & B. L. Blackford	[Chief Engrs Off., D.N.V.]	1:80,000 Blue print, 23 x 34
1287	Loudoun, 1853	Yardley Taylor	Thomas Reynolds & Robert Pearsall Smith, Phila.	1:47,000 39-1/2 x 49-1/2
1288	Loudoun & Fauquier (portion), [186-]	Wm. P. Smith & A. S. Barrows [Hotchkiss Coll. no. 33]	Topogl. Office, A.N.V.	1:126,720 Ms., 18-1/2 x 15-1/2
1289	Loudoun, Va. & Jefferson, W. Va. & parts of Berkeley, W. Va., & Frederick & Montgomery, Md., 1864	J. Paul Hoffmann & S. Howell Brown [Hotchkiss Coll. no. 43]	Chf. Topl. Dept., A.N.Va.	1:126,720 Ms., 17 x 19
1290	Louisa, [186-]	Jed. Hotchkiss [Hotchkiss Coll. no. 296]	. . .	1:80,000 Ms., 21-1/2 x 26-1/2
1291	Louisa & Hanover (portion), [186-]	[Hotchkiss Coll. no. 45]	. . .	1:160,000 Ms., 16 x 22

VIRGINIA (Cont.)

No.	County and Date	Author or Surveyor	Publisher and Place	Scale and Size (Inches)
1292	Louisa, 1863	B. L. Blackford, A. H. Campbell & James O'Conner	Chief Engineers Office, D.N.V.	1:80,000 Photocopy (neg.) in 4 parts, 21 x 17 ea.
1293	Louisa, 1863-64	B. L. Blackford & A. H. Campbell	Chief Engineers Office, D.N.V.	1:80,000 Blue print, 23-1/2 x 28-1/2
1294	Lunenburg, 1864	A. H. Campbell, H. M. Graves & J. I. Randolph	Chief Engineers Office, D.N.V.	1:80,000 Blue print, 21 x 25
1295	Lunenburg, 1871	Jed. Hotchkiss [Hotchkiss Coll. no. 298]	. . .	1:80,000 Ms., 23-1/2 x 25-1/2
1296	Lunenburg, 1871	Jed. Hotchkiss & Board of Survey of Washington and Lee University	. . .	1:98,000 19-1/2 x 22
1297	Madison, [186-]	[Hotchkiss Coll. no. 46]	. . .	1:160,000 Ms., 11 x 8-1/2
1298	Madison, 1866-1875	P. S. Michie & Jed. Hotchkiss	Office of the Chief of Engineers, U.S. Army	1:63,360 30-1/2 x 23-1/2
1299	Mecklenburg, [186-]	Jed. Hotchkiss [Hotchkiss Coll. no. 299]	. . .	1:80,000 Ms., 20 x 32-1/2
1300	Mecklenburg, Brunswick & Greensville, [186-]	. . .	[Chief Engr's. Off., D.N.V.]	1:180,000 Photocopy (neg.), 20-1/2 x 17-1/2
1301	Mecklenburg, 1864	A. H. Campbell & H. M. Graves	[Chief Engr's. Off., D.N.V.]	1:80,000 Photocopy (neg.) in 2 parts, 19-1/2 x 17-1/2 ea.
1302	Mecklenburg, 1864	A. H. Campbell & H. M. Graves	[Chief Engr's. Off., D.N.V.]	1:80,000 Blue print, 19-1/2 x 33-1/2
1303	Mecklenburg, 1870	Confederate States Engineer Corps	Geo. B. Finch, Boydton, Va.	1:80,000 22 x 34-1/2
1304	Montgomery, 1821	John Wood	. . .	1:90,000 Photocopy (pos.) in 4 parts, 17 x 24 ea.
1305	Montgomery, [186-]	[Hotchkiss Coll. no. 48]	. . .	1:80,000 Ms., 21 x 21
1306	Montgomery, 1864	C. S. Dwight, A. H. Campbell & J. Innis Randolph	Chief Engineer's Office, D.N.V.	1:80,000 Photocopy (neg.) in 2 parts, 17 x 20-1/2 ea.
1307	Montgomery, 1864	C. S. Dwight, A. M. Smith & S. W. Hill [Hotchkiss Coll. no. 47]	. . .	1:40,000 Ms., 34 x 44
1308	Nansemond (portion), [16-?] (c1946)	J. H. Granbery	. . .	1:96,000 Photocopy (pos.), 8 x 10
1309	Nansemond & Norfolk (portions), [16-?] (c1948)	J. H. Granbery	. . .	1:31,680 24 x 35-1/2
1310	Nansemond, 1820	John Wood	. . .	1:39,600 Photocopy (neg.) in 15 parts, 22 x 18 ea.
1311	Nelson, 1866	Hotchkiss & Robinson, & C. W. Oltmanns [Hotchkiss Coll. no. 301]	. . .	1:63,360 Ms., 36 x 34

VIRGINIA (Cont.)

No.	County and Date	Author or Surveyor	Publisher and Place	Scale and Size (Inches)
1312	New Kent, Charles City, James City & York (portion), [186-?]	. . .	Chief Engineer's Office, D.N.V.	1:80,000 Photocopy (neg.) in 4 parts, 17 x 20-1/2 ea.
1313	Norfolk, 1887	Sykes & Gwathmey	[Norfolk County] Board of Supervisors	1:40,000 2 parts, 30 x 45 ea.
1314	Nottoway, 1864	A. H. Campbell & H. M. Graves	[Chief Engr's. Off., D.N.V.]	1:80,000 Photocopy (neg.) in 2 parts, 16-1/2 x 16-1/2 ea.
1315	Nottoway, 1864	A. H. Campbell & H. M. Graves	Chief Engrs Off., D.N.Va.	1:80,000 Blue print, 17 x 22-1/2
1316	Orange, [186-]	[Hotchkiss Coll. no. 50]	. . .	1:80,000 Ms., 16 x 30
1317	Orange, [186-]	Walter Izard [Hotchkiss Coll. no. 51]	. . .	1:40,000 Ms., 30 x 59-1/2
1318	Orange & Spotsylvania, [186-?]	Jacob Paul Hoffmann	. . .	1:155,000 Photocopy (neg.), 14-1/2 x 23-1/2
1319	Orange, Spotsylvania & Caroline, [186-?]	. . .	[Chief Engr's. Off., D.N.V.]	1:80,000 Photocopy (neg.) in 12 parts, 17-1/2 x 21-1/2 ea.
1320	Orange, 1863	A. H. Campbell & Lieut. Isard [sic] [Hotchkiss Coll. no. 52]	Chief Engineer's Office, D.N.V.	1:80,000 Ms., 17 x 32
1321	Orange, 1864	Walter Izard & A. H. Campbell	Chief Engineer's Office, D.N.V.	1:80,000 Photocopy (neg.) in 2 parts, 18-1/2 x 17 ea.
1322	Patrick, 1821	John Wood	. . .	1:39,600 Photocopy (pos.) in 8 parts, 23 x 18 ea.
1323	Powhatan, 1864	A. H. Campbell & C. E. Cassell	Chief Engineers Office, D.N.V.	1:80,000 Blue print, 17 x 20-1/2
1324	Powhatan, 1864	A. H. Campbell & C. E. Cassell	[Chief Engr's. Off., D.N.V.]	1:80,000 Photocopy (neg.), 17 x 20
1325	Prince Edward, [1820?]	. . .	. . .	1:48,000 Photocopy (pos.) in 4 parts, 18 x 24 ea.
1326	Prince Edward, 1864	A. H. Campbell & C. E. Cassell	[Chief Engr's. Off., D.N.V.]	1:80,000 Photocopy (neg.) in 2 parts, 18 x 17 ea.
1327	Prince Edward, 1879	H. Jacob	[Prince Edward County] Board of Supervisors	1:63,360 2 parts, 24-1/2 x 15-1/2 ea.
1328	Prince George, 1863	A. H. Campbell & S. L. Sommers	Chief Engineer's Office, D.N.V.	1:80,000 Blue print, 19-1/2 x 24-1/2
1329	Prince George, 1863	A. H. Campbell, S. L. Sommers & J. Houston Patton	Chief Engineer's Office, D.N.V.	1:80,000 Photocopy (pos.), 19 x 24-1/2
1330	Prince George, Surry, Sussex & Southampton, 1863	A. H. Campbell	Chief Engineers Office, D.N.V.	1:240,000 Blue print, 17 x 21

VIRGINIA (Cont.)

No.	County and Date	Author or Surveyor	Publisher and Place	Scale and Size (Inches)
1331	Prince George, 1864	A. H. Campbell & S. L. Sommers [Hotchkiss Coll. no. 54]	. . .	1:80,000 Ms., 19 x 22
1332	Prince George, Surry, Sussex & Southampton, 1865	J. A. Wilson [Hotchkiss Coll. no. 175]	Top. Eng. Office, V.D.	1:240,000 Ms., 18-1/2 x 15.
1333	Princess Anne & Norfolk, [1781?]	. . .	. . .	1:190,080 Photocopy (pos.), 20 x 34-1/2
1334	Rappahannock, 1863	[Hotchkiss Coll. no. 55]	Engr. Office, 2nd Corps	1:160,000 Ms., 12-1/2 x 9-1/2
1335	Rappahannock, 1866-75	P. S. Michie & Jed. Hotchkiss	Office of the Chief of Engineers, U.S. Army	1:63,360 32-1/2 x 25
1336	Roanoke, [186-?]	Walter Izard, Jno. M. Coyle & W. Hutchinson	[Chief Engr's. Off., D.N.V.]	1:40,000 Photocopies (neg.) of 2 sheets, 1 in 3 parts & 1 in 4 parts, 17-1/2 x 21-1/2 ea.
1337	Roanoke, [186-]	[Hotchkiss Coll. no. 56]	. . .	1:160,000 Ms., 10 x 12
1338	Roanoke, 1864	A. H. Campbell & W. Izard	Chief Engineers Office, D.N.V.	1:80,000 Blue print, 21 x 22-1/2
1339	Rockbridge, [1860?]	William Gilham, Lumsden, Brockenbrough, Lynch, Poynor, Davidson, W. A. Smith, Heth & W. N. P. [i.e. William Newton Mercer] Otey	. . .	1:63,360 30 x 36 (includes ornate border)
1340	Rockbridge, [1860?]	William Gilham, Lumsden, Brockenbrough, Lynch, Poynor, Davidson, W. A. Smith, Heth & W. N. P. Otey	. . .	1:63,360 27-1/2 x 33 (lacks ornate border)
1341	Rockbridge, 1860	William Gilham, Lumsden, Brockenbrough, Lynch, Poynor, Davidson, W. A. Smith, Heth & W. N. P. Otey	. . .	1:63,360 2 parts, 30 x 18 ea.
1342	Rockbridge, [186-]	[Hotchkiss Coll. no. 57]	. . .	1:160,000 Ms., 17-1/2 x 14-1/2
1343	Rockbridge, [186-?]	Walter Izard, Jno. M. Coyle & W. Hutchinson	[Chief Engr's. Off., D.N.V.]	1:40,000 Photocopies (neg.) of 4 sheets ea. in 4 parts, 21 x 17-1/2 ea.
1344	Rockingham, 1866-75	P. S. Michie & Jed. Hotchkiss	Office of the Chief of Engineers, U.S. Army	1:84,480 33 x 33
1345	Shenandoah, Page & Warren (portion), 1866-75	P. S. Michie & Jed. Hotchkiss	Office of the Chief of Engineers, U.S. Army	1:84,480 35-1/2 x 32
1346	Smyth, 1899	Chas. R. Boyd & John D. Barns	. . .	1:63,360 29-1/2 x 29
1347	Spotsylvania, [1820?]	. . .	. . .	1:39,600 Photocopy (pos.) in 6 parts, 3 are 22 x 17 ea. & 3 are 16 x 18-1/2 ea.
1348	Spotsylvania, [186-]	[Hotchkiss Coll. no. 59]	. . .	1:80,000 Ms., 23 x 16

VIRGINIA (Cont.)

No.	County and Date	Author or Surveyor	Publisher and Place	Scale and Size (Inches)
1349	Spotsylvania, [186-]	[Hotchkiss Coll. no. 60]	. . .	1:80,000 Ms., 23 x 16
1350	Spotsylvania, [186-]	[Hotchkiss Coll. no. 61]	. . .	1:80,000 Ms., 23 x 16-1/2
1351	Spotsylvania & Caroline, [186-]	[Hotchkiss Coll. no. 62]	. . .	1:126,720 Ms., 16-1/2 x 27
1352	Spotsylvania (portion), [186-?]	Stanford's Geogl. Estabt.	Hugh Rees, London	1:90,000 Photocopy (pos.), 11-1/2 x 17-1/2
1353	Spotsylvania, 1862	John Grant & S. T. Pendleton [Hotchkiss Coll. no. 58]	. . .	1:40,000 Ms., 42 x 46
1354	Spotsylvania, 1863	A.H. Campbell	Chief Engineer's Office, D.N.V.	1:80,000 Photocopy (neg.) in 2 parts, 17 x 17-1/2 ea.
1355	Spotsylvania (portion), 1864	N. Michler	Army of the Potomac	1:63,360 Photocopy (neg.), 13 x 16-1/2
1356	Stafford, [1820?]	. . .	. . .	1:39,600 Photocopy (pos.) in 8 parts, 23-1/2 x 14 ea.
1357	Stafford (portion), [186-?]	. . .	. . .	1:20,200 Ms., 26 x 38
1358	Stafford (portion), [186-?]	. . .	. . .	1:20,200 Ms., 21-1/2 x 28
1359	Stafford, [186-]	[Hotchkiss Coll. no. 63]	. . .	1:126,720 Ms., 13-1/2 x 17-1/2
1360	Stafford, 1863	B. L. Blackford, Morton & A. H. Campbell	[Chief Engr's. Off.] Depart* of N. Va.	1:40,000 Photocopy (neg.) in 6 parts, 18 x 21-1/2 ea.
1361	Stafford, 1864	B. L. Blackford	[Chief Engr's. Off.] Dept. of N. Va.	1:80,000 Photocopy (neg.), 23 x 16
1362	Washington, 1821	John Wood	. . .	1:100,000 Photocopy (pos.) in 4 parts, 18 x 23 ea.
1363	Washington, 1890	C. R. Boyd	J. L. Smith, Phila.	1:63,360 2 sheets, 40-1/2 x 30-1/2 ea.
1364	Washington, [1891]	. . .	. . .	. . . 6 x 11
1365	Wythe, 1821	John Wood	. . .	1:100,000 Photocopy (pos.) in 6 parts, 22-1/2 x 17-1/2 ea.
1366	Wythe (portion), [186-]	[Hotchkiss Coll. no. 65]	. . .	1:80,000 Ms., 17-1/2 x 29
1367	Wythe (portion), [186-]	Mayhew, Magill Smith & Walter Izard [Hotchkiss Coll. no. 64]	. . .	1:40,000 Ms., 17-1/2 x 48
1368	Wythe & Pulaski (portion), 1890	C. R. Boyd	J. L. Smith, Phila.	1:63,360 23-1/2 x 40
1369	York & Warwick (portions), [1862]	. . .	. . .	. . . Blue line print, 11 x 16

WASHINGTON

No.	County and Date	Author or Surveyor	Publisher and Place	Scale and Size (Inches)
1370	Clark, 1888	R. A. Habersham	. . .	1:63,360 39-1/2 x 27-1/2
1371	Columbia, 1900	W. E. Cahill & H. L. Jeffress	. . .	1:47,520 2 parts, 31 x 43-1/2 ea.
1372	Cowlitz, 1895	F. M. Lane	. . .	1:79,200 Blue print, 31 x 39
1373	Cowlitz, 1897	O. P. Anderson Map & Blue Print Co. Inc.	O. P. Anderson Map & Blue Print Co. Inc., Seattle	1:130,000 Blue print, 20-1/2 x 25-1/2
1374	King, 1888	Anderson, Bertrand & Co.	Anderson, Bertrand & Co., Seattle	1:180,000 18 x 24-1/2
1375	King, 1894	O. P. Anderson & Co.	. . .	1:102,000 2 parts, 34-1/2 x 26-1/2 ea.
1376	Pierce, 1890	Fred. G. Plummer	. . .	1:210,000 16 x 22
1377	Stevens (portion), 1900	L. L. Tower	Colville Map Co., Colville, Wash.	1:96,000 2 parts, 33 x 23 ea.
1378	Wahkiakum, 1898	L. P. Ouellette	. . .	1:31,680 Blue print, 37-1/2 x 53-1/2

WEST VIRGINIA

No.	County and Date	Author or Surveyor	Publisher and Place	Scale and Size (Inches)
1379	Berkeley, 1820	John Wood	. . .	1:65,000 Photocopy (pos.) in 4 parts, 18 x 24 ea.
1380	Berkeley, 1847	Jno. P. Kearfott & D. H. Strother	James N. Riddle, Martinsburg, W. Va.	1:95,000 Photocopy (neg.), 21-1/2 x 17-1/2
1381	Berkeley, 1894	J. Baker Kearfott	E. P. Noll & Co., Phila.	1:42,000 38-1/2 x 34-1/2
1382	Boone, 1895	W. C. Chapman & J. C. Thomas	W. C. Chapman & J. C. Thomas, Madison, W. Va.	1:48,000 Ms., 45-1/2 x 34 in.
1383	Cabell, 1822	John Wood	. . .	1:72,500 Photocopy (pos.) in 12 parts, 18 x 24 ea.
1384	Greenbrier, 1821	John Wood	. . .	1:65,000 Photocopy (pos.) in 12 parts, 24 x 18 ea.
1385	Greenbrier, 1887	H. H. Harrison & J. O. Handley	. . .	1:100,000 29 x 36
1386	Hancock, Brooke, Ohio & Marshall, 1871	F. W. Beers & Jas. M. Lathrop	F. W. Beers & Co., & Geo. Nichols, I. D. Hall, D. L. Miller, W. R. Dumond, I. F. Manchester & C. J. Corbin	1:63,360 65-1/2 x 33 in.
1387	Hardy, 1822	John Wood	. . .	1:63,360 Photocopy (pos.) in 8 parts, 24 x 18 ea. Va. State Library copy.

WEST VIRGINIA (Cont.)

No.	County and Date	Author or Surveyor	Publisher and Place	Scale and Size (Inches)
1388	Hardy, 1822	John Wood	. . .	1:130,000 Photocopy (neg.) in 2 parts, 17-1/2 x 24 ea. National Archives copy.
1389	Harrison, 1821	John Wood	. . .	1:63,360 Photocopy (pos.) in 8 parts, 24 x 18 ea. Va. State Library copy.
1390	Harrison, 1821	John Wood	. . .	1:92,000 Photocopy (neg.) in 4 parts, 17-1/2 x 22-1/2 ea. National Archives copy.
1391	Jackson, [178-?]	. . .	. . .	. . . Photocopy (neg.) in 6 parts, 23 x 17 ea.
1392	Jefferson, 1820	John Wood	. . .	1:65,000 Photocopy (pos.) in 6 parts, 14 x 24 ea.
1393	Jefferson, 1852	S. Howell Brown	. . .	1:26,700 39 x 52-1/2
1394	Jefferson, 1862	Bureau of Topographical Engineers	. . .	1:26,500 Photocopy (pos.), 34 x 22-1/2
1395	Jefferson, 1883	S. Howell Brown	J. L. Smith, Phila.	1:26,700 2 parts, 31 x 45-1/2 & 29-1/2 x 45-1/2
1396	Kanawha, 1822	John Wood	. . .	1:69,000 Photocopy (pos.) in 12 parts, 18 x 24 ea.
1397	Lewis, [1820?]	. . .	. . .	. . . Photocopy (pos.) in 4 parts, 21 x 18 ea.
1398	Mason, 1822	John Wood	. . .	1:65,000 Photocopy (pos.) in 12 parts, 18 x 24 ea.
1399	Monongalia, 1821	John Wood	. . .	1:65,000 Photocopy (pos.) in 8 parts, 24 x 18 ea.
1400	Monroe, 1821	John Wood	. . .	1:65,000 Photocopy (pos.) in 8 parts, 24 x 18 ea.
1401	Morgan, 1820	John Wood	. . .	1:65,000 Photocopy (pos.) in 4 parts, 18 x 24 ea.
1402	Nicholas, 1822	John Wood	. . .	1:68,000 Photocopy (pos.) in 8 parts, 24 x 18 ea.
1403	Ohio, 1821	John Wood	. . .	1:69,000 Photocopy (pos.) in 3 parts, 17-1/2 x 24 ea.
1404	Pendleton, 1822	John Wood	. . .	1:63,360 Photocopy (pos.) in 8 parts, 24 x 18 ea.
1405	Pocahontas, 1825	H. Boye	. . .	1:92,000 Photocopy (neg.) in 4 parts, 24-1/2 x 16 ea.

WEST VIRGINIA (Cont.)

No.	County and Date	Author or Surveyor	Publisher and Place	Scale and Size (Inches)
1406	Preston, 1821	John Wood	. . .	1:65,000 Photocopy (pos.) in 6 parts, 24 x 18 ea.
1407	Randolph, 1822	John Wood	. . .	1:63,360 Photocopy (pos.) in 12 parts, 24 x 18 ea.
1408	Tyler, 1821	John Wood	. . .	1:65,000 Photocopy (pos.) in 8 parts, 18 x 24 ea.
1409	Wetzel, 1865	Thomas Tucker	John P. Hunt, Pittsburgh	. . . 25 x 31
1410	Wood, 1821	John Wood	. . .	1:63,360 Photocopy (pos.) in 8 parts, 18 x 24 ea.

WISCONSIN

No.	County and Date	Author or Surveyor	Publisher and Place	Scale and Size (Inches)
1411	Ashland, 1898	. . .	W. S. Nohl	1:52,500 4 sheets, 22-1/2 x 35 ea.
1412	Brown, 1870	Arthur Jacobi	County Board of Supervisors	1:47,000 40-1/2 x 32
1413	Brown, 1900	. . .	W. W. Hixson, Rockford, Ill.	1:42,240 46 x 36-1/2
1414	Dane (portion), 1861	A. Ligowsky	Menges & Ligowsky, Madison, Wis.	1:50,688 2 parts, 31 x 47 ea.
1415	Dodge, 1900	. . .	W. W. Hixson, Rockford, Ill.	1:45,500 2 parts, 22 x 43-1/2 ea.
1416	Eau Claire, 1878	Fisher & Brown	Fisher & Brown, Pardeeville, Wis.	1:50,688 2 parts, 33 x 23 ea.
1417	Fond du Lac, [1856?]	W. T. Coneys & M. L. Bogert	Bogert & Haight	1:50,688 2 parts, 24 x 58-1/2 ea.
1418	Grant, 1857	J. Wilson, Jr.	. . .	1:100,000 33-1/2 x 26-1/2
1419	Grant, 1868	Warren Gray & G. Delevan Pattengill	. . .	1:49,000 6 parts, 3 are 22 x 30 ea. & 3 are 22 x 29 ea.
1420	Green, 1861	[Coast Survey Coll.]	J. T. Dodge, Monroe, Wis.	1:50,000 13 parts, 17 x 13 ea.
1421	Iowa, 1870	E. T. & W. J. Wrigglesworth [Coast Survey Coll.]	. . .	1:42,240 13 parts, 17 x 13 ea.
1422	Jefferson, 1872	E. M. Harney [Coast Survey Coll.]	E. M. Harney	1:42,240 15 parts, 17 x 13 ea.
1423	Jefferson, 1900	. . .	Banner Printing Co., Jefferson, Wis.	1:42,240 2 parts, 19-1/2 x 37 ea.
1424	Juneau, 1876	G. V. Nash & F. B. Morgan	G. V. Nash & F. B. Morgan	1:42,240 4 parts, 32-1/2 x 20-1/2 ea.
1425	Kenosha, 1861	H. F. Walling [Coast Survey Coll.]	J. Lathrop, Jr., Kenosha, Wis.	1:31,680 11 parts, 1 is 15 x 25-1/2 & 10 are 17 x 13 ea.

WISCONSIN   (Cont.)

No.	County and Date	Author or Surveyor	Publisher and Place	Scale and Size (Inches)
1426	Kewaunee, 1895	. . .	W. T. Rooney & A. M. Schleis, Kewaunee, Wis.	1:31,680 4 parts, 28-1/2 x 21 ea.
1427	La Crosse, 1874	H. I. Bliss	H. I. Bliss, La Crosse, Wis.	1:43,000 4 parts, 20 x 20 ea.
1428	La Crosse, 1890	Brice & Smith	Brice & Smith, La Crosse, Wis.	1:31,680 53-1/2 x 53-1/2
1429	Manitowoc, 1872	E. M. Harney [Coast Survey Coll.]	. . .	1:42,240 18 parts, 17 x 13 ea.
1430	Milwaukee, 1858	H. F. Walling	M. H. Tyler, New York	1:31,680 2 parts, 50 x 30-1/2 & 50 x 32-1/2
1431	Milwaukee, 1879	Geo. F. Epeneter	. . .	1:32,000 2 parts, 27-1/2 x 40-1/2 ea.
1432	Milwaukee, 1893	Wm. R. Knell	Wm. R. Knell Publishing Co.	1:18,103 2 parts, 43 x 53 ea.
1433	Monroe, 1877	. . .	Warner & Foote, Red Wing, Minn.	1:42,240 6 parts, 4 are 24-1/2 x 18 ea. & 2 are 24-1/2 x 19 ea.
1434	Racine, 1858	T. B. Redding & J. J. Watson	T. B. Redding & J. J. Watson, Racine, Wis.	1:43,000 4 parts, 2 are 23-1/2 x 25-1/2 ea. & 2 are 23-1/2 x 28 ea.
1435	Racine & Kenosha, 1873	E. M. Harney, G. V. Nash, M. G. Tucker, F. A. Morgan, F. D. Harney, S. W. Briggs, Geo. H. Ingalls & W. F. Nash	E. M. Harney, Winneconne, Wis.	1:42,240 6 parts, 4 are 18 x 24-1/2 ea. & 2 are 19 x 24-1/2 ea.
1436	Rock, 1900	. . .	W. W. Hixson, Rockford, Ill.	1:42,000 4 parts, 20 x 23-1/2 ea.
1437	Sauk, 1859	Wm. H. Canfield	. . .	1:85,000 2 parts, 31 x 21 & 31 x 21-1/2
1438	Sheboygan, 1862	C. Palmer & E. M. Harney	G. A. Randall & C. Palmer	1:43,500 6 parts, 4 are 18 x 24 ea. & 2 are 17 x 24 ea.
1439	Trempealeau, 1877	M. G. Tucker	. . .	1:52,000 2 sheets, 25 x 41-1/2 & 31-1/2 x 41-1/2
1440	Walworth, 1857	T. B. Redding & J. J. Watson	T. B. Redding & J. J. Watson, Elkhorn, Wis.	1:42,240 6 parts, 23 x 21-1/2 ea.
1441	Walworth, 1900	. . .	W. W. Hixon [i.e., Hixson] & Co., Rockford, Ill.	1:42,240 39 x 37
1442	Waukesha, 1859	H. F. Walling, A. S. Mowry & W. O. Bartlett [Coast Survey Coll.]	M. H. Tyler, New York	1:31,680 18 parts, 17 x 13 ea.
1443	Waukesha, 1900	. . .	Waukesha Weekly Press	1:42,000 40 x 37
1444	Waupaca, 1874	E. M. Harney	E. M. Harney, Winneconne, Wis.	1:42,240 Photocopy (pos.) in 9 parts, 6 are 24 x 18 ea. & 3 are 11 x 18 ea.

WISCONSIN (Cont.)

No.	County and Date	Author or Surveyor	Publisher and Place	Scale and Size (Inches)
1445	Winnebago, 1862	G. A. Randall & C. Palmer	G. A. Randall & J. A. Bogert	1:43,000 6 parts, 4 are 16-1/2 x 24 ea. & 2 are 17-1/2 x 24 ea.
1446	Winnebago, 1873	E. M. Harney, S. W. Briggs, G. V. Nash, F. A. Morgan, F.D. Harney & M. G. Tucker	E.M. Harney, Winneconne, Wis.	1:42,240 2 sheets, 31-1/2 x 50 & 25-1/2 x 50
1447	Wood, [1878?]	J. A. Gaynor & C. T. Purdy	J. A. Gaynor & C. T. Purdy	1:54,309 2 parts, 23-1/2 x 38 ea.

INDEX

NUMBERS REFER TO ENTRIES

Abbeville Co., S. C., 831
Abbott, C.L., 851
Accomack Co., Va., 1196
Adams Co., Ill., 99
Adams Co., Pa., 696-697, 824
Addison Co., Vt., 1181-1182
Adkins, I. F., 93
Ainsworth, C. B., 845, 847
Alachua Co., Fla., 72
Alamance Co., N. C., 582
Alameda Co., Calif., 11
Albany Co., N. Y., 473
Albemarle Co., Va., 1197-1200
Alexander, Joseph M., 335
Alexander, M. J., 408
Alexandria Co., Va., See Arlington Co., Va.
Allamakee Co., Iowa, 177
Allegan Co., Mich., 321, 352
Allegany Co., N. Y., 474-475
Allegheny Co., Pa., 698-704
Allen, C. R., 207
Allen, Carlos, 466
Allen, D. B., 128
Allen Co., Ohio, 595
Amador Co., Calif., 12-13
Amelia Co., Va., 1201-1205
Ames, N. S., 764, 821
Amherst Co., Va., 1206-1208
Ammerman, R. A., 781
Anderson, A. H., 382
Anderson (O. P.) & Co., 1375
Anderson (O. P.) Map & Blue Print Co., 1373
Anderson Co., S. C., 832-833
Anderson Co., Tex., 881-882
Anderson, Bertrand & Co., 1374
Andrews, R. T., 36
Androscoggin Co., Maine, 265
Angelina Co., Tex., 883-884
Angell, John, 493
Anne Arundel Co., Md., 279-281
Anoka Co., Minn., 374, 381
Anthony, James, 8
Anthony, P. J., 967, 1167
Appell, P. F., 1127, 1135-1136
Appomattox Co., Va., 1227
Aransas Co., Tex., 885-886
Arapahoe Co., Colo., 53
Archer Co., Tex., 887
Arlington Co., Va., 1209-1211, 1251
Armstrong Co., Pa., 705
Arnold, Charles R., 114
Arrott, W., 654
Ascension Parish, La., 254
Aschbach, G. A., 766-767
Ash, Joshua W., 738
Ashland Co., Ohio, 596-598

Ashland Co., Wis., 1411
Ashley, P. N., 51
Ashmead, Henry P., 739
Ashtabula Co., Ohio, 599
Aspen, Colo., Times, 55
Astbury, R. C. F., 692
Atascosa Co., Tex., 888-889
Atchison Co., Mo., 391
Atkinson, George W., 378, 385, 843, 845-847, 855-856, 860-861
Atlantic Co., N. J., 437
Auglaize Co., Ohio, 600
Augusta Co., Va., 1197, 1212-1214
Aurora Co., S. Dak., 843
Austin Co., Tex., 890
Averill, H. K., Jr., 485
Avery, H. M., 862
Avoyelles Parish, La., 244-245

Babbs & Stoddard, 393
Babcock (E. H.) & Co., 526-527
Bachman, C., 525
Bacon, Delos H., 1
Baker, A. A., 505
Baker, C. H., 297
Baker, J. W., 92
Baker, Sidney, 266, 269, 274
Baker, Thomas W., 312-313, 316, 320
Baker, William E., 66, 481, 505
Baker (William E.) & Co., 267, 320, 1182
Baker & Co., 269
Baker & Gager, 687
Baker & Tilden, 447, 1181, 1184, 1188, 1191
Baker, Tilden & Co., 1185, 1187
Balch, E. A., 488, 495, 500, 545, 557, 572
Ball, LeRoy D., 77
Ballard Co., Ky., 223
Baltimore Co., Md., 282-285
Bandera Co., Tex., 891
Banner Printing Co., 1423
Bannister, Alfred, 49
Bardeen, C. W., 530
Barker, William J., 58-59, 713, 735, 747, 756, 764, 816, 821
Barnes, C. M., 235
Barnes, R. L., 193, 443, 700, 724, 747a, 791, 808, 1202
Barns, John D., 1346
Barnstable Co., Mass., 306
Barren Co., Ky., 224
Barrows, A. S., 1284, 1288
Barry Co., Mich., 327
Bartlett, W. O., 1442

Barton & Gibbs, 672
Bastrop Co., Tex., 892
Batchelor, J. J., 275
Batchelor, L. J., 274
Bauskett, W. T., 82
Beall, George W., 281, 301-302
Beasley, T. D., 35
Beaufort Co., S. C., 834
Beauman, Guy, 90, 113, 118, 131
Beaumont, G. N., 956, 979, 1009, 1044, 1058, 1083-1084
Beaver Co., Pa., 703, 764
Bechler, G., 474
Bechler, G. R., 342, 360-361
Bechler & Wenig, 323
Bechler, Wenig & Co., 342, 360
Beck, Arthur A., 624
Beck, W. M., 950, 1034, 1145
Becker, M. J., 611
Bedford Co., Pa., 706-707
Bedford Co., Tenn., 868-869
Bedford Co., Va., 1215-1216
Bee Co., Tex., 893
Beer (S. T.) & Co., 1116
Beers, D. G., 534, 581, 719, 728
Beers (D. G.) & Co., 226-227, 232, 237-238, 242-243, 869, 872, 874, 876-878, 880
Beers, F. W., 329, 332, 349, 351, 358-359, 437, 444-445, 459, 461, 483, 488, 525, 701, 732, 736, 786, 788, 798, 817, 822, 1386
Beers (F. W.) & Co., 329, 332, 349, 351, 358-359, 683, 1186, 1386
Beers (J. B.) & Co., 511-512, 520, 553-554
Beers, J. M., 701
Beers, Silas N., 445, 459, 483, 488, 525, 534, 538, 546, 560, 581, 701, 736, 817
Beers & Lanagan, 224, 239, 241
Beers, Comstock & Cline, 437, 444, 461
Beers, Ellis & Soule, 805, 809
Belding, Hiram A., 446
Belknap Co., N. H., 423-424
Bell, W., 1209
Bell Co., Tex., 894-895
Belmont Co., Ohio, 601
Benedict, C., 82
Bennett, U. P., 661
Bennington Co., Vt., 1183
Bergen Co., N. J., 438
Bergmann, G. T., 234
Berkeley Co., W. Va., 1258, 1289, 1379-1381
Berkley, H. J., 282
Berks Co., Pa., 708-711

Berkshire Co., Mass., 307
Berrien Co., Mich., 324
Bertie Co., N. C., 589
Bertsch, Frederic, 635
Bethea, P. Y., 839-840
Bevers, Fendol, 591
Bexar Co., Tex., 896-899
Bickel, Paul S. A., 414
Billings Co., N. Dak., 593
Black Hawk Co., Iowa, 178
Blackford, B. Lewis, 584, 1285-1286, 1292-1293, 1360-1361
Blackford, Robert S., 624
Blackmore, Harris H., 613
Bladen Co., N. C., 583
Bladen Co., N. C. Board of County Commissioners, 583
Blair Co., Pa., 712
Blanco Co., Tex., 900
Bland Co., Va., 1217
Blau, F. G., 1082, 1097, 1119
Blaux, F. G., 1029
Bliss, H. I., 373, 1427
Blue Earth Co., Minn., 366
Blue Oil Map Co., 649
Blunt, N. B., 25
Boell, William, 644
Böye, Herman, 1405
Bogert, J. A., 1445
Bogert, M. L., 1417
Bogert & Haight, 1417
Bon Homme Co., S. Dak., 844
Bond, Isaac, 292-293
Booker, William L., 1202
Boone Co., Ind., 137
Boone Co., W. Va., 1382
Borden Co., Tex., 901
Bosque Co., Tex., 902-903
Boswell, J. K., 1256
Botetourt Co., Va., 1218-1223
Boulder Co., Colo., 53
Bourbon Co., Ky., 225
Bourquin, Frederick, 76, 78-80
Bowen, J. S., 723-724
Bowie Co., Tex., 904-905
Boyd, Charles R., 1265, 1346, 1363, 1368
Boyer, M. K., 710
Boyle Co., Ky., 226
Bradford, John, 77
Bradford Co., Pa., 713
Brady, E. W., 204
Brakenridge, N. B., 814
Bramlette, H. M., 1012, 1048, 1149, 1174
Branch Co., Mich., 322
Brand (G. J.) & Co., 623
Brasswell, M. L., 842
Braun, Walter, 624
Brazoria Co., Tex., 906-907
Brazos Co., Tex., 908
Breckinridge Co., Ky., 231
Brevard Co., Fla., 73
Brewster Co., Tex., 1100
Brice & Smith, 1428
Bridgens, H. F., 711, 733, 765
Briggs, S. W., 1435, 1446
Brigham, H. G., 326
Brink, P. Henry, 569-570
Briscoe Co., Tex., 909
Bristol Co., Mass., 308-309
Bristol Co., R. I., 826
Britton & Rey, 19
Brockenbrough, William A., 1339-1341
Bromfield, Davenport, 37
Bromley (G. W.) & Co., 80
Brooke Co., W. Va., 1386

Brookings Co., S. Dak., 845
Broome Co., N. Y., 476
Brown, George C., 526, 826, 830
Brown, George E., 832
Brown, J. A., 13
Brown, J. L., 772
Brown, Mason L., 365
Brown, Newell S., 524, 537, 577, 579
Brown, P. J., 579, 664
Brown, S. Howell, 1251, 1289, 1393, 1395
Brown, William, 652
Brown Co., Minn., 367-368
Brown Co., Tex., 910, 960
Brown Co., Wis., 1412-1413
Brown Co., Wis. Board of Supervisors, 1412
Browne, P. J., 489, 518-519, 562, 680
Brunswick Co., N. C., 584
Brunswick Co., Va., 1224-1226, 1300
Buchanan Co., Iowa, 179
Buchanan Co., Mo., 392
Buckingham, George A., 451
Buckingham Co., Va., 1227
Buckman, O. H., 30
Bucks Co., Pa., 714-715
Budgett, Henry H., 384
Budington, A., 64
Buena Vista Co., Iowa, 180
Bullock, W. P., 87, 831
Burhans, S. H., 104-105, 135, 350
Burleson Co., Tex., 911
Burlingame, E. H., 621, 641
Burlington Co., N. J., 439-442
Burnett, Benjamin H., 621
Burns & Miller, 580
Burrus, C. D., 547
Bushnell, J. W., 78-79
Butler Co., Iowa, 181
Butler Co., Ohio, 602-603
Butler Co., Pa., 716-717
Butt, D. L. R., 937
Butte Co., Calif., 14-15
Byles, Anthony D., 69, 516, 629, 684

Cabell Co., W. Va., 1383
Caffee, Robert H., 619
Cahill, W. E., 1371
Cahoon, B. B., 402, 410
Caldwell Co., Tex., 912-913
Caldwell Parish, La., 246
Caledonia Co., Vt., 1184
Calhoun Co., Ark., 7
Calhoun Co., Mich., 323
Calhoun Co., Tex., 914-915
Callahan Co., Tex., 916-917
Callen, J. B., 214
Cambria Co., Pa., 718-719
Camden Co., N. J., 443
Cameron Co., Pa., 770-771
Cameron Co., Tex., 918
Camp, J. H., 802
Camp Co., Tex., 919-920
Campbell, Albert H., 589, 1198-1199, 1204-1205, 1208, 1215-1216, 1221-1223, 1225-1231, 1234, 1236, 1238, 1241-1243, 1246-1247, 1249, 1257, 1263, 1269, 1271, 1280, 1283-1284, 1286, 1292-1294, 1301-1302, 1306, 1314-1315, 1320-1321, 1323-1324, 1326, 1328-1331, 1338, 1354, 1360

Campbell Co., Va., 1228-1230
Canfield, George W., 681
Canfield, J. W., 651
Canfield, William H., 1437
Cape May Co., N. J., 444
Carbon Co., Pa., 776
Carhart, Mead & Co., 610
Carnahan, James, 233
Caroline Co., Md., 286
Caroline Co., Va., 1231-1234, 1319, 1351
Carpenter, C., 1277-1278
Carroll Co., Ill., 100
Carroll Co., Ind., 138-139
Carroll Co., Md., 287-288
Carroll Co., N. H., 425
Carroll Co., N. H., 425
Carroll Co., Ohio, 681
Carter, W. M., 875
Carver Co., Minn., 369
Cascade Co., Mont., 413
Cass Co., Mich., 324-325
Cass Co., Nebr., 416
Cassell, Charles E., 589, 1227, 1236, 1243, 1257, 1263, 1323-1324, 1326
Castro Co., Tex., 921
Catahoula Parish, La., 247
Catawba Co., N. C., 585
Cathcart, ---, 154
Cathcart, James M., 832
Cattaraugus Co., N. Y., 477
Cayuga Co., N. Y., 478-479
Cecil Co., Md., 289-290
Cedar Co., Iowa, 182
Cedar Co., Mo., 393-394
Centre Co., Pa., 720-721
Chace, J., Jr., 58-59, 265-266, 269, 274-276, 278, 430, 432-435, 497, 565, 572, 615, 744, 1190, 1192, 1194
Chambers Co., Tex., 922
Champaign Co., Ohio, 604-605
Chapman, Isaac A., 765a, 778
Chapman, W. C., 1382
Charles City Co., Va., 1312
Charlotte Co., Va., 1235-1236
Chastain, A. W., 228
Chatham Co., Ga., 84-86
Chautauqua Co., N. Y., 480
Chemung Co., N. Y., 481
Chenango Co., N. Y., 482-483
Cherokee Co., Ga., 87
Cherokee Co., Tex., 923
Cherokee Map Co., 87
Cheshire Co., N.H., 426-427
Chester Co., Pa., 722-725
Chesterfield Co., Va., 1237-1239, 1280
Chesterfield Co., Va. Board of Supervisors, 1239
Chief Engineer's Office, D.N.V., See Confederate States of America. Army.
Childress Co., Tex., 924
Chisago Co., Minn., 374
Chittenden Co., Vt., 1185
Christian Co., Ill., 101-102
Christian Co., Ky., 227
Christy, William, 755
Chreitzberg, H. F., 832
Church, A. F., 275
Clarion Co., Pa., 726
Clark, A. C., 1011, 1075
Clark, Alvin, 857
Clark, J. F., 1176
Clark, Richard, 58-59, 62
Clark Co., Ind., 140
Clark Co., Ky., 225

Clark Co., Ohio, 606
Clark Co., S. Dak., 846
Clark Co., Wash., 1370
Clarke, H. Wadsworth, 530
Clarke Co., Ga., 88
Clarke Co., Va., 1240
Clatsop Co., Oreg., 692
Clay Co., Iowa, 183
Clay Co., Ky., 228
Clay Co., Mo., 395
Clay Co., Tex., 925
Clearfield Co., Pa., 727-728
Cleaver, Kimber, 780-781
Clermont Co., Ohio, 607
Cleveland Co., N. C., 586
Cleveland Co., Okla., 691
Clinton Co., Ind., 137
Clinton Co., Iowa, 184
Clinton Co., Mich., 326
Clinton Co., N. Y., 484-485
Clinton Co., Ohio, 608
Clinton Co., Pa., 729
Coahoma Co., Miss., 386
Coast Survey Coll., 132, 155-156, 171, 193, 324, 330, 339, 350, 352, 354, 433, 527, 574, 595, 601, 603, 613, 616, 621, 626, 634, 638, 640, 645, 667, 681-683, 685, 689-690, 700, 1420-1422, 1425, 1429, 1442
Cockburn, James, 499
Codington Co., S. Dak., 847
Coffee Co., Ga., 89
Coffee Co., Tenn., 868
Colbert Co., Ala., 1
Colbert County Abstract Co., 1
Cole, M. S., 231
Coleman Co., Tex., 926-927
Colfax Co., N. Mex., 470
Collin Co., Tex., 928
Collingsworth Co., Tex., 929
Colorado Co., Tex., 930
Colton (G. W. & C. B.) & Co., 552
Colton (J. H.) & Co., 503
Columbia Co., N. Y., 486-488
Columbia Co., Pa., 730
Columbia Co., Wash., 1371
Columbiana Co., Ohio, 609-610
Colusa Co., Calif., 16
Colville Map Co., 1377
Comal Co., Tex., 931-932
Comanche Co., Tex., 933-934, 960
Compton, H. T., 36
Concho Co., Tex., 935-936
Concordia Parish, La., 248-249
Condit, Wright & Hayden, 157, 166
Coneys, W. T., 1417
Confederate States of America.
  Army, 584, 589, 1198-1199, 1204-1205, 1207-1208, 1215-1216, 1218-1222, 1225-1226, 1229-1232, 1234, 1236-1238, 1241-1243, 1246, 1249, 1252-1253, 1257, 1263, 1267, 1269, 1271, 1280, 1283-1286, 1288-1289, 1292-1294, 1300-1303, 1306, 1312, 1314-1315, 1319-1321, 1323-1324, 1326, 1328-1330, 1332, 1334, 1336, 1338, 1343, 1354, 1360-1361
Conn, A. C., 87
Consolidated Publishing Co., 340
Contra Costa Co., Calif., 11
Converse, E., 697, 819
Converse, M. S., 697, 819
Cook Co., Ill., 103-109
Cooke Co., Tex., 937
Coos Co., N. H., 428
Corbett, V. P., 1210

Corbin, C. J., 1386
Corey, G. H., 438
Corey & Bachman, 538
Cornell, Samuel C., 453
Cortland Co., N. Y., 483, 489
Coryell Co., Tex., 938
Cosby, C. Reynolds, 152
Coshocton Co., Ohio, 611, 681
Cottle Co., Tex., 939
Cottonwood Co., Minn., 370
Cowles, A. J., 519, 525, 576
Cowles & Titus, 137, 159, 164, 636
Cowley, O. S., 850
Cowlitz Co., Wash., 1372-1373
Cox, W. J., 792-793
Coyle, John M., 1218, 1336, 1343
Craig, A. M., 1007
Crane, John, 602
Crane Co., Tex., 940
Crawford Co., Iowa, 185-186
Crawford Co., Ohio, 612
Crawford Co., Pa., 731-732, 743
Crockett Co., Tex., 941
Crosby, W. A., 788
Crosby Co., Tex., 942
Cross, John T., 785
Culpeper Co., Va., 1241-1242
Cumberland Co., Ky., 229
Cumberland Co., Maine, 266
Cumberland Co., N. J., 445
Cumberland Co., Pa., 733
Cumberland Co., Va., 1243
Cuming Co., Nebr., 417
Cummings, J. A. J., 730, 780-781
Currie, G. H., 160
Curtice, D. L., 380
Cuyahoga Co., Ohio, 613-614

Dakota Co., Minn., 371, 381
Dale, Samuel, 803, 806
Dallam Co., Tex., 943
Dallas Co., Tex., 944-946
Dame, William, 828
Dane Co., Wis., 1414
Darke Co., Ohio, 615
Daugherty, J. S., 1005
Dauphin Co., Pa., 734-736
Davidson, Charles A., 1339-1341
Davidson, J. M., 42
Davidson Co., N. C., 587
Davidson Co., Tenn., 870-871
Davis, George W., 140
Davis, Grady W., 889, 936, 1058, 1093, 1113, 1136, 1176
Davison, D. H., 276, 751
Dawson, A. R. Z., 479, 523, 529, 534
Dawson, F. M., 257
Dawson, J. H. C., 479, 534
Dawson, L. G., 479, 523, 529, 534
Dawson Co., Tex., 947
Day, A. R., 816
Deaf Smith Co., Tex., 949
Dearborn Co., Ind., 142
Decatur Co., Ind., 167
Decatur, Ill., Herald Despatch, 102, 124
Defiance Co., Ohio, 616
De Jarnatt & Crane, 16
De Kalb Co., Ill., 110
De Kalb Co., Ind., 141
Delafield, J., 561, 563, 574
Delaware Co., Iowa, 187
Delaware Co., N. Y., 490
Delaware Co., Ohio, 617
Delaware Co., Pa., 737-740

Delphi, Ind., Journal, 139
Delta Co., Tex., 950
Demarest, Benjamin S., 451
Denison, Iowa, Bulletin, 186
Denton, L., 580
Denton, S., 580
Denton Co., Tex., 951-953
Deuel Co., S. Dak., 848
De Witt, Simeon, 535
De Witt Co., Tex., 948
Dickens Co., Tex., 954
Dickey, S. M., 1265
Dickinson, C. H., 254
Dickinson Co., Iowa, 188
Dickinson Co., Kans., 212
Dickson, George K., 127
Dickson (M. M.) & Co., 362
Dickson, Melzar M., 200
Dill, W. W., 156
Dilworth, William H., 303
Dimmit Co., Tex., 955-957
Dinwiddie Co., Va., 1244-1247
Dodge, George M., 26
Dodge, J. T., 1420
Dodge Co., Wis., 1415
Dorchester Co., S. C., 835
Dorr (Williams) & Co., 630
Dorsetts, C. H., 84
Dorsey, Caleb, 279
Doton, Hosea, 1193, 1195
Dougal, David, 698, 716, 743
Doughty, W. E., 341
Douglas Co., Kans., 213
Douglas Co., Nebr., 418-419
Douglas Co., S. Dak., 849
Douglass, John, 565
Douglass, L. F., 450-451
Downin, S. S., 304
Doyle, J. M., 52
Dripps, M., 507-510, 549, 578, 828
Dubuque Co., Iowa, 189
Dugdale, C. R., 196
Dukes Co., Mass., 306
Dumond, W. R., 1386
Dunham, Az., 455
Dunham, C. T., 132
Dunham, J. R., 420
Dunlap, James, 717
Du Page Co., Ill., 103, 108-109
Durham Co., N. C., 588
Dutchess Co., N. Y., 491-492
Duval Co., Fla., 74-75
Duval Co., Tex., 958
Dwelle, E. H., 210
Dwight, C. S., 1198-1199, 1206, 1208, 1229-1230, 1241-1242, 1252, 1306-1307

Eager, E. N., 43
Earl, F. W., 441-442
Earley, John E., 621
East Baton Rouge Parish, La., 250
East Carroll Parish, La., 251-252
Eastland Co., Tex., 959-961
Eaton, George C., 617, 661
Eaton, James, 617
Eaton, L. H., 272-273
Eaton, William C., 67-68
Eaton Co., Mich., 327
Eau Claire Co., Wis., 1416
Edgar Co., Ill., 111
Edwards, John P., 99, 170, 213, 217, 221, 400
Edwards Co., Ill., 112
Edwards Co., Tex., 962
El Dorado Co., Calif., 17

Elizabeth City Co., Va., 1248
Elk Co., Pa., 741-742, 772
Elkhart Co., Ind., 143
Elkin, B. E., 836
Elkin, William B., 836
Elko Co., Nev., 422
Ellet, Charles, Jr., 784
Elliott, Gordon L., 181
Ellis, A. D., 822
Ellis, Charles E., 378, 385, 848, 850
Ellis Co., Tex., 964-965
El Paso Co., Tex., 963
Emerson, William D., 632
Encinal Co., Tex., 1161
Ensign, D. W., 195
Epeneter, George F., 1431
Erath Co., Tex., 966-967
Erickson, T. O., 865
Erie Co., N. Y., 493-494
Erie Co., Ohio, 618
Erie Co., Pa., 743-744
Essex Co., Mass., 310
Essex Co., N. J., 446-449
Essex Co., N. Y., 495
Essex Co., Vt., 1186, 1189
Essex Co., Va., 1249
Evans, Cadwallader, 820
Evans, Gurdon, 516

Fagan, Lawrence, 426-427, 482, 526-527, 558, 568, 711
Fairfax Co., Va., 1210, 1250-1251
Fairfield Co., Conn., 58-59
Fairfield Co., Ohio, 619-620
Fairfield Co., S. C., 836
Falkenstine, F. C., 844
Falls Co., Tex., 968
Fannin Co., Tex., 969-970
Farmer, John, 363a
Farmer (Silas) & Co., 365
Fauquier Co., Va., 1252-1256, 1288
Fayette Co., Ky., 225, 230
Fayette Co., Ohio, 621
Fayette Co., Pa., 745-747a
Fayette Co., Tex., 971
Finch, George B., 1303
Finley, S. H., 32
Fisher & Brown, 1416
Fisher Co., Tex., 972-973
Florida Land & Improvement Co., 76
Flower, W. L., 104-105
Floyd Co., Ga., 90
Floyd Co., Ga. Commissioners of Roads and Revenues, 90
Floyd Co., Ind., 144-145
Floyd Co., Ky., 240
Floyd Co., Tex., 974
Fluvanna Co., Va., 1257
Foard Co., Tex., 975
Fond du Lac Co., Wis., 1417
Fondé, Henry, 5
Foote (C. M.) & Co., 381
Foote (C. M.) Publishing Co., 374
Foote, Charles H., 621
Foote, E. J., 374
Foote, R. C., Jr., 622
Ford, Reuben W., 1148
Forest Co., Pa., 748-750, 811-812
Forshey, Caleb G., 248
Forsyth, William, 223
Fort, I. A., 421
Foster, Wilbur F., 870
Fountain Co., Ind., 146
Fox, D. A., 550
Franke, E. V., 181

Franklin Co., Ill., 113
Franklin Co., Maine, 267
Franklin Co., Mass., 311
Franklin Co., N. Y., 496
Franklin Co., Ohio, 622-624
Franklin Co., Pa., 751
Franklin Co., Tex., 976-977
Franklin Co., Vt., 1187
Franklin Parish, La., 253
Fraser, William H., 645, 673, 688
Frederick Co., Md., 291-293, 1289
Frederick Co., Va., 1258-1261
Freeborn Co., Minn., 372
Freed, Isaac G., 333, 343, 364, 712
French, F. F., 538
French, J. H., 69, 495, 515, 517, 525, 528, 560, 571, 576
Frey, S. G., 781
Fries, J. O., 81
Frio Co., Tex., 978-979
Frost, H. J., 337, 346
Frost & McLennan, 123
Fuller, John F., 212
Fulton, Henry, 511
Fulton Co., Ga., 91
Fulton Co., N. Y., 497
Fulton Co., Ohio, 625-626
Fulton Co., Pa., 752

Gallia Co., Ohio, 627
Gallup (A. O.) & Co., 476, 542
Galveston Co., Tex., 980-983
Gardiner, John, 811
Gardner, Edwin P., 686
Gasconade Co., Mo., 396
Gast Bank Note & Litho. Co., 112, 257
Gates, B. C., 542
Gates, C., 542
Gates (C.) & Son, 566
Gaylord, F. A., 499
Gaynor, J. A., 1447
Geary Co., Kans., 214
Geauga Co., Ohio, 628
Geil, John F., 646, 653
Geil, Samuel, 143, 321, 326, 328, 330-331, 333, 335, 341, 343, 352, 361, 460, 477-478, 493-494, 500, 521-522, 539-540, 557, 567
Geil & Co., 333, 343
Geil & Freed, 712
Geil & Harley, 321, 336, 341, 352, 364
Geil & Jones, 322, 324, 327-328, 344, 348, 356, 364
Geil, Harley & Siverd, 323-324, 327, 333, 343-344, 348, 356, 364
Geil, Harley, Leamings, Cathcart & J. D. Nash, 154
Geil, Leamings & Cathcart, 154
Genesee Co., Mich., 328, 353-354
Genesee Co., N. Y., 498
George, A. L., 25
George, John W., 1264
Gerber, E. B., 141, 151, 153, 155, 161
Gerrish, E. P., 68
Gibbs, E. H., 199
Gibson, William T., 561, 563
Gibson Co., Tenn., 872
Gifford, Franklin, 476, 478, 522
Gilbert, A. W., 633
Giles, J. Bascom, 1036, 1124
Gilham, William, 1339-1341

Gillespie, D. C., 748, 757
Gillespie, J. F., 583
Gillespie Co., Tex., 984-985
Gillett, A. G., 518, 562
Gillette, John E., 487, 491-492, 498, 515, 517, 519, 525, 533, 564, 576
Gillette & Huntington, 271, 566
Gillette, Matthews & Co., 474, 494, 540, 680
Glasscock Co., Tex., 986-987
Gloucester Co., N. J., 462
Godshalk, S. K., 477-478
Golden, T., 501
Goliad Co., Tex., 988
Gonzales Co., Tex., 989
Goochland Co., Va., 1262-1264
Goodfellow, J. J., 1139
Goodfellow & Williams, 1139
Goodhue, J. H., 719, 728
Gould, Jay, 473, 490
Grafton Co., N. H., 429
Graham, John, 622
Granbery, J. H., 1308-1309
Grand Isle Co., Vt., 1187
Grant, John, 1284, 1353
Grant Co., Ind., 147
Grant Co., S. Dak., 850
Grant Co., Wis., 1418-1419
Gratiot Co., Mich., 326, 329
Graves, H. M., 1225-1226, 1246-1247, 1257, 1263, 1294, 1301-1302, 1314-1315
Gray, O. W., 479, 523
Gray, Warren, 1419
Gray Co., Tex., 990
Grayson Co., Ky., 231
Grayson Co., Va., 1265
Grayson Co., Va. Board of Supervisors, 1265
Green, W. H., 523, 529
Green Co., Wis., 1420
Greenbrier Co., W. Va., 1384-1385
Greene Co., Ala., 2
Greene Co., Ill., 114
Greene Co., N. Y., 499-500
Greene Co., Ohio, 629
Greene Co., Pa., 753-754
Greene Co., Va., 1266-1268
Greensville Co., Va., 1269, 1300
Greenup Co., Ky., 236
Greenville Co., S. C., 837
Greenwood Co., Kans., 215
Grier, Paul L., 831
Griffing, B. N., 665, 682
Griffing, Gordon & Co., 665
Griffith, J. M., 12
Grimes Co., Tex., 991
Griner, Peter A., 521
Gross, I. M., 321, 336, 341, 352
Gross, W. W., 84
Grundy Co., Mo., 397
Guadalupe Co., Tex., 992
Guernsey Co., Ohio, 630
Guffy, A. J., 781
Gunderson, A. B., 865

Haas, David L., 29
Habersham, R. A., 694, 1370
Hagel, John, 415
Hagnauer, Robert, 127
Hale, George, 122
Hale, John, 204
Hale Co., Ala., 3
Hale Co., Tex., 993
Haley, H. A., 312-313

Hall, I. D., 1386
Hall & Babbs, 409
Haller & Willard, 595
Hamilton, Samuel R., 928
Hamilton Co., Ind., 148
Hamilton Co., Ohio, 631-635
Hamilton Co., Tex., 994
Hamlin Co., S. Dak., 851-853
Hampden Co., Mass., 312-313
Hampshire Co., Mass., 314-315
Hancock Co., Ill., 115
Hancock Co., Ky., 231
Hancock Co., Maine, 268
Hancock Co., Ohio, 636-637
Hancock Co., W. Va., 1386
Handley, J. O., 1385
Handy, H. P., 54
Hanover Co., Va., 1233, 1270-1274, 1291
Hanson, J., 827
Hanson Co., S. Dak., 854
Hardeman Co., Tex., 995-996
Hardin Co., Ohio, 638
Hardin Co., Tex., 997
Hardisty, H. H., 645, 673, 688
Hardy Co., W. Va., 1387-1388
Harford Co., Md., 294-295
Harkness, O., 827
Harley, David S., 143, 154, 321, 323-324, 326-327, 333, 336, 341, 343-344, 348, 352, 356, 364
Harley, J. P., 326
Harman, Amos R., 281
Harney, E. M., 1422, 1429, 1435, 1438, 1444, 1446
Harney, F. D., 1435, 1446
Harper Co., Kans., 216
Harris Co., Tex., 998
Harrison, H. H., 1385
Harrison, R. H., 172, 685, 690
Harrison & Warner, 191-192, 197, 206
Harrison Co., Ky., 232
Harrison Co., Ohio, 639
Harrison Co., Tex., 999
Harrison Co., W. Va., 1389-1390
Hart Co., Ga., 92
Hartford Co., Conn., 60-61
Hartley Co., Tex., 1000
Hartwell, J. G., 31
Harwood, C. E., 1183
Harwood & Watson, 150, 660
Haskell Co., Tex., 1001-1002
Hass, Albert, 345
Hatch, A. J., 40
Hauck, Jacob, 419
Hausmann, E. A., 965
Hawkins, Lee, 895, 903
Hawley, H. A., 581
Hawley, J. S., 792-793
Hayes, S. B., 148, 151, 165
Haynes, M. B., 188, 367, 377
Haynes & Woodard, 379
Hays Co., Tex., 1603
Hedick, ---, 1055
Heffer, J. C., 378, 385, 850, 861
Hein, J., 687
Heins, Gustavus, 656
Helton, James, 228
Hemphill Co., Tex., 1004
Henderson, D. E., 1203-1205, 1238, 1271
Henderson Co., Tex., 1005
Hendricks Co., Ind., 149
Hennepin Co., Minn., 381
Henning, J. S., 50
Henrico Co., Va., 1233, 1275-1282

Henry, M. S., 710
Henry Co., Ill., 116
Henry Co., Ind., 150
Henry Co., Ohio, 640
Herkimer Co., N. Y., 501
Herrick, L. W., 294
Herring, John R., 592
Herrmann, A. T., 39
Herrmann, Charles, 39
Hertford Co., N. C., 589
Hess, F., 350, 604
Heth, Stockton, 1339-1341
Hewitt, E. A., 225
Hewitt, G. W., 225
Hewson & FitzGerald, 386
Heydrick, C., 804
Heydrick, C. H., 804
Hickman, E. A., 399
Hickory Co., Mo., 398
Hidalgo Co., Tex., 1006
Hienton, Louise Joyner, 300
Higgins, J. Silliman, 137, 169, 172, 398, 403, 601, 603, 638, 658, 685
Higgins, Pattillo, 1028
Higgins, R. Thornton, 398, 403, 601, 603, 638, 658
Higginson, J. H., 504, 506, 551
Hilbush, J. R., 781
Hill, John, 607
Hill, John T., 497
Hill, S. W., 1307
Hill Co., Tex., 1007
Hills, Edward O., 134
Hills, I., See Hills, John
Hills, John, 455, 463, 737
Hills, V. G., 57
Hillsborough Co., Fla., 76
Hillsborough Co., N. H., 430
Hillsdale Co., Mich., 330-331
Hilthon, K. E., 852-853
Hilton, E. E., 416
Hindman, James, 722
Hixson, W. W., 179, 189, 1413, 1415, 1436
Hixson (W. W.) & Co., 180, 417, 1441
Hodge, A., 204
Hodgin, E. S., 844, 854
Hoeing, I. B., 231
Hoenck, Edward A. H., 371
Hoenck & Roosen, 371
Hoenscheidt, J., 215
Hoffmann, Jacob Paul, 1251, 1289, 1318
Holmes, Charles, 355
Holmes, J. W., 130
Holmes, P., 116
Holmes & Arnold, 115, 126, 129
Holmes Co., Ohio, 641, 681
Home Publishing Co., 325, 357
Hood Co., Tex., 1008-1010
Hoover, S., 682
Hopkins (G. M.) & Co., 71, 740
Hopkins, Griffith M., 62, 222, 270, 395, 438, 466, 469, 614, 697, 705, 730, 747a, 774, 779-782, 799, 819
Hopkins, Henry W., 705, 774
Hopkins Co., Tex., 1011
Hotchkiss, Jedediah, 1213-1214, 1223, 1235, 1249, 1256, 1268, 1284, 1290, 1295-1296, 1298-1299, 1311, 1335, 1344-1345
Hotchkiss Coll. no. 20, 1197
no. 21, 1227
no. 22, 1228
no. 23, 1234

Hotchkiss Coll.---Continued
no. 24, 1232
no. 25, 1233
no. 27, 1241
no. 28, 1247
no. 29, 1249
no. 30, 1251
no. 31, 1256
no. 32, 1254
no. 33, 1288
no. 34, 1255
no. 35, 1261
no. 36, 1266
no. 37, 1272
no. 38, 1273
no. 39, 1274
no. 40, 1280
no. 41, 1281
no. 42, 1284
no. 43, 1289
no. 45, 1291
no. 46, 1297
no. 47, 1307
no. 48, 1305
no. 49, 1206
no. 50, 1316
no. 51, 1317
no. 52, 1320
no. 54, 1331
no. 55, 1334
no. 56, 1337
no. 57, 1342
no. 58, 1353
no. 59, 1348
no. 60, 1349
no. 61, 1350
no. 62, 1351
no. 63, 1359
no. 64, 1367
no. 65, 1366
no. 175, 1332
no. 284, 1223
no. 289, 1235
no. 296, 1290
no. 298, 1295
no. 299, 1299
no. 301, 1311
Houston Co., Minn., 373
Houston Co., Tex., 1012
Howard Co., Md., 296
Howard Co., Tex., 1013
Howe, J., 312-313
Howell & Taylor, 1211
Hubbard, C., 1248
Hudson, Walter B., 706, 718, 720
Hudson Co., N. J., 450-452
Hughes, Henry, 671
Hughes, Matthew, 448
Hunnicutt, ---, 1036
Hunt, John P., 810, 1409
Hunt Co., Tex., 1014-1016
Hunter, B. J., 521, 540
Hunterdon Co., N. J., 453
Huntingdon Co., Pa., 755
Huntington Co., Ind., 151
Huron Co., Mich., 332, 353-354
Huron Co., Ohio, 642
Hutchinson, W., 1218, 1336, 1343
Hutchinson Co., Tex., 1017
Hyde & Co., 544
Hyde (Albert A.) & Co., 61

Iberville Parish, La., 254
Inch, Shelley, 17
Indiana Co., Pa., 756
Ingalls, George H., 1435

79

Ingham Co., Mich., 333
Ionia Co., Mich., 334
Iowa Co., Wis., 1421
Iowa Engraving Co., 203
Irion Co., Tex., 1018
Iroquois Co., Ill., 117
Irwin, ---, 749
Irwin, R., 804
Isanti Co., Minn., 374
Island City Abstract and Loan Co., 981
Isle of Wight Co., Va., 1283
Isler, John B., 286
Issaquena Co., Miss., 252, 388
Ivy, William, 1248
Izard, Walter, 1215-1216, 1218, 1221-1223, 1317, 1320-1321, 1336, 1338, 1343, 1367

Jack Co., Tex., 1019-1021
Jackson, A., 333-343
Jackson, M. L., 97
Jackson Co., Iowa, 190
Jackson Co., Mich., 335
Jackson Co., Mo., 399-400
Jackson Co., Tex., 1022-1023
Jackson Co., W. Va., 1391
Jacob, H., 1327
Jacobi, Arthur, 1412
James, S. A., 193
James City Co., Va., 1312
Janney, E., 647
Janney, J. D., 441-442, 647
Jarvis, Jacob, 639
Jasper Co., Iowa, 191
Jasper Co., Tex., 1024-1025
Jeff Davis Co., Tex., 1026
Jefferson Co., Colo., 53
Jefferson Co., Ga., 93
Jefferson Co., Ill., 118
Jefferson Co., Ind., 152
Jefferson Co., Iowa, 192
Jefferson Co., Ky., 233-234
Jefferson Co., Nebr., 420
Jefferson Co., N. Y., 502
Jefferson Co., Ohio, 643
Jefferson Co., Pa., 757
Jefferson Co., Tex., 1027-1028
Jefferson Co., W. Va., 1258, 1289, 1392-1395
Jefferson Co., Wis., 1422-1423
Jeffress, H. L., 1371
Jenkins, J. R., 338
Jenkins, Washington, 1180
Jenks, D. W., 27
Jennings & Herrick, 294
Jessamine Co., Ky., 225
Johnson, J. A., 849
Johnson, John, 264
Johnson, John F., 48, 693
Johnson, L., 587-588
Johnson, William P., 659
Johnson Co., Ind., 169
Johnson Co., Kans., 217
Johnson Co., Ky., 239
Johnson Co., Tex., 1029
Jonas, A. L., 228
Jones, S. L., 322, 324, 327-328, 330-331, 333, 335-336, 343-344, 348, 356, 364
Jones & Murphy, 1033
Jones Co., Tex., 1030-1031
Judson, C. H., 648
Juneau Co., Wis., 1424
Juniata Co., Pa., 782

Kaiser, A., 250
Kaiser, George, 285
Kalamazoo Co., Mich., 336
Kalkaska Co., Mich., 337-338
Kanawha Co., W. Va., 1396
Kane Co., Ill., 103, 119
Kankakee Co., Ill., 117
Karnes Co., Tex., 1032
Kashow, R. B., 452
Kaufman, Chas., 18
Kaufman Co., Tex., 1033-1034
Kearfott, J. Baker, 1381
Kearfott, John P., 1380
Keddie, Arthur W., 33
Keenan, F. W., 487
Keene, H. M., 844
Keeney, Collins G., 480, 490
Keily, James, 454, 456, 462, 464, 802, 1245, 1277-1278
Kellogg, Daniel, 330
Kellogg & Randall, 331, 663
Kelly, W. A., 594
Kelsey, D., 276
Kendall, S. D., 312-313
Kendall Co., Ill., 103
Kendall Co., Tex., 1035-1036
Kennebec Co., Maine, 269
Kennedy, D. H., 784
Kennedy, T. J., 724-725
Kennedy, Thomas G., 714
Kenosha Co., Wis., 1425, 1435
Kent Co., Del., 69
Kent Co., Md., 297
Kent Co., Mich., 339
Kent Co., Tex., 1037
Kentucky. Geological Survey, 231, 240
Keokuk Co., Iowa, 193
Ker, Sev. P., 1223
Kern Co., Calif., 18-20
Kern Co., Calif. Board of Supervisors, 18
Kern County Land Company, 20
Kerr Co., Tex., 1038
Kewaunee Co., Wis., 1426
Keyly, James, 643
Kimball, G. R., 857
Kimble Co., Tex., 1039-1040
King, George H., 396
King, Robert, 363
King, W. K., 770-771
King & Queen Co., Va., 1249
King Co., Wash., 1374-1375
King William Co., Va., 1249, 1284-1286
Kingman, E., Jr., 472
Kingman Co., Kans., 218
Kings Co., N. Y., 503-512
Kingsbury Co., S. Dak., 855
Kinney Co., Tex., 1041-1042
Kinter, J. A., 756
Kirker, J. W., 717
Kiser, Ellis, 176
Kizer, T., 606
Knell, William R., 1432
Knell (William R.) Publishing Co., 1432
Knight, J. Hamilton, 835
Knight, Jonathan, 815
Knopf, Herbert K., 624
Knox, John, 274
Knox Co., Ill., 120
Knox Co., Tenn., 873
Knox Co., Tex., 1043
Koons, David S., 140
Kornberg, G. A., 415
Kosciusko Co., Ind., 153

Krebs, Otto, 702-703
Kuhn, R. K., 441-442
Kyner, George E., 214
Kyzer, Paul B., 586, 837
Kyzer & Hellams, 838

Lacoe & Schooley, 768
La Crosse Co., Wis., 1427-1428
Lagrange Co., Ind., 155
Lake, D. J., 146, 149, 159, 164, 488, 525, 546, 601, 603, 636, 638, 645, 658, 673, 682, 688, 690, 821, 825
Lake, L. B., 445
Lake, Thomas M., 841
Lake, Ames & Davison, 713
Lake Co., Calif., 21
Lake Co., Ill., 122-123
Lake Co., Mich., 340
Lake Co., Ohio, 628
Lake Co., S. Dak., 856
Lamar Co., Tex., 1045
Lamb, Daniel W., 110
Lamb, O. J., 484
Lamoille Co., Vt., 1189
Lampasas Co., Tex., 1046
Lampen, M., 356
Lancaster Co., Pa., 758-763
Lane, F. M., 1372
Lapeer Co., Mich., 341, 353-354
La Porte Co., Ind., 154
La Prade, J. E., 1239
Larimer Co., Colo., 54
Larson, J. F., 860
Larson, Louis, 375
Larue Co., Ky., 235
La Salle Co., Ill., 121
La Salle Co., Tex., 1044
Lathrop, G. D., 523
Lathrop, J., Jr., 1425
Lathrop, James M., 1386
Lauderbrun, Fk., 789
Laurens Co., S. C., 838
Lavaca Co., Tex., 1047-1048
Law & Kirk, 834
Lawrence & Ogilbe, 695
Lawrence Co., Ind., 156
Lawrence Co., Pa., 764
Lawrence Co., S. Dak., 857
Leal, LaFayette, 482
Leamings, ---, 154
Leas, W. H., 176
Leavenworth Co., Kans., 219
Leavitt, Sheldon, 339
Lebanon Co., Pa., 734, 765
Le Baron, J. Francis, 73-75
Lee, Alexander Y., 702
Lee, Richard H., 475
Lee & Marsh, 268, 270, 272-273, 277, 643, 799
Lee Co., Tex., 1049-1050
Legg, ---, 970
Lehigh Co., Pa., 765a-767
Leisenring, ---, 1217
Leitch, Meredith, 1212
Lenawee Co., Mich., 342, 361
Leon Co., Fla., 77
Leon Co., Tex., 1051
Leonard, F. W., 378, 385, 850
Leonhardt, Th., 802
Levey, Morris, 502, 564, 573
Levy, M., See Levey, Morris
Lewis, A. C., 176
Lewis, Freeman, 745
Lewis, Hugh, 388

Lewis, S., 792-793
Lewis, T. J., 855
Lewis & Clark Co., Mont., 414
Lewis Co., Ky., 236
Lewis Co., N. Y., 513
Lewis Co., W. Va., 1397
Liberty Co., Tex., 1052-1053
Licking Co., Ohio, 644
Lightfoot, Jesse, 458, 460
Lightfoot & Geil, 539
Ligowsky, A., 484, 513, 1414
Lincoln Co., Maine, 270
Lincoln Co., Nebr., 421
Lincoln Co., Oreg., 693
Lincoln Co., S. Dak., 858-859
Linn Co., Iowa, 194-195
Litchfield Co., Conn., 62
Live Oak Co., Tex., 1054-1055
Livingston Co., Mich., 333, 343
Livingston Co., N. Y., 514-515
Livingston Parish, La., 255
Llano Co., Tex., 1056-1059
Lodge, Benjamin, 233
Loew, K., 255
Logan Co., Ill., 124
Logan Co., Ohio, 645
Long, George, 183
Loomis, Way & Palmer, 776
Loommis & Way, 1189
Lorain Co., Ohio, 646
Lorey, William, 559, 686-687
Los Angeles Co., Calif., 22-25
Lothrop, G. D., 479
Loudoun Co., Va., 1251, 1287-1289
Louisa Co., Iowa, 196
Louisa Co., Va., 1290-1293
Love, George, 1240
Lowden, H. L., 48
Lubbock Co., Tex., 1060
Lucas, A. L., 1014
Lucas Co., Ohio, 647-649
Ludlow, Andrew, 807
Lumsden, Charles L., 1339-1341
Lunenburg Co., Va., 1294-1296
Lutz, J. E., 1165
Luzerne Co., Pa., 768
Lycoming Co., Pa., 769
Lyman, Geo. C., 29
Lynch, John, 255
Lynch, John P., 1339-1341
Lynn Co., Tex., 1061
Lyon Co., Minn., 375
Lyttle, Dale C., 228

McAroy, Everard A., 547
McBride, George, 419
McCann, Charles A., 140
McCarty, D., 468
McCerren, Landry & Powell, 246-247, 249, 251, 253, 256, 258, 261-263
McChesney, J. B., 275
McChesny, U. B., 497
McClellan, C. A. O., 141, 148, 165, 171, 600, 676
McClellan (C.) & Co., 1192
McClellan, E. C., 422
McClellan, William, 616, 626, 640
McConnell, J. L., 753
McCook Co., S. Dak., 860
McCulloch Co., Tex., 1062
McDonald Co., Mo., 401
McDonnell, John, 596, 670
McDuffie, John, 583
McFarland, A., 252
McGann, James, 14-15

McGreevy, C. F., 138
McGreevy, O. A., 138
McHenry, Morris, 186
McHenry Co., Ill., 125
McKean Co., Pa., 770-773
McKee, Hugh, 717
McKee, L., 304
McKinnan, John, 84
McLaughlin, J. B., 756
McLaughlin & Kinter, 747
McLennan Co., Tex., 1063-1064
McLeod Co., Minn., 376
McLeran, Owen, 744, 1190
McMullen Co., Tex., 1065
McNabb, J. W., 295
McNair, ---, 768
McNiff, Patrick, 363
Macomb Co., Mich., 344, 365
McPherson Co., Kans., 220
McVicker, George A., 201
McWilliams & Thompson, 194
Madison Co., Ala., 4
Madison Co., Ill., 126-127
Madison Co., Ky., 237
Madison Co., Mo., 402
Madison Co., N. Y., 516-517
Madison Co., Ohio, 650
Madison Co., Tenn., 874
Madison Co., Tex., 1066
Madison Co., Va., 1241-1242, 1297-1298
Madison Parish, La., 256-257
Magee, William, 41
Magoffin Co., Ky., 240
Mahaska Co., Iowa, 197-199
Mahoning Co., Ohio, 651
Maierhofer & Briel, 121
Manchester, I. F., 1386
Manitowoc Co., Wis., 1429
Mann, Adin, 119
Mann, T. B., 312-313
Marble, R. R., 623
Marin Co., Calif., 26
Marion Co., Fla., 78-80
Marion Co., Ind., 157-158
Marion Co., Ky., 238
Marion Co., Ohio, 617, 638, 652
Marion Co., S. C., 839-840
Marion Co., Tex., 1067
Marsh, E. D., 567
Marshall, Thomas B., 89
Marshall, William Everard, 260
Marshall Co., Iowa, 200
Marshall Co., Tenn., 875
Marshall Co., W. Va., 1386
Marshall, Minn., Messenger, 375
Marshalltown, Iowa, Times-Republican, 200
Martenet, Simon J., 281, 287, 290, 295-297, 299, 301-302
Marti, J. M., 373
Martin Co., Ky., 240
Martin Co., Minn., 377
Martin Co., Tex., 1068
Mason Co., Tex., 1069
Mason Co., W. Va., 1398
Matagorda Co., Tex., 1070
Matheson & McMillan, 72
Matthews, S. H., 604, 614-615, 628, 654
Matthews & Taintor, 646, 653, 664, 668, 679
Matthews, Crane & Co., 119, 128
Maurhoff, E., 717
Maury Co., Tenn., 876
Maverick Co., Tex., 1071-1072
Maxcy, John W., 903, 1050, 1103, 1108

Maxey, John W., See Maxcy, John W.
Mayhew, ---, 1367
Mayhew, James H., 4
Mead, F. F., 1250
Mead, H. H., 214
Mecklenburg Co., Va., 1299-1303
Medina Co., Ohio, 653
Medina Co., Tex., 1073
Meigs Co., 627
Melish, John, 737, 783
Menard Co., Tex., 1074-1075
Menges & Ligowsky, 1414
Menominee Co., Mich., 345
Mercer, J. W., 390
Mercer & Fontaine, 390
Mercer Co., Ky., 226
Mercer Co., N. J., 454
Mercer Co., Pa., 774
Mergell, C. S., 868
Merrick, George A., 10
Merrimack Co., N. H., 431
Merry, Earl W., 689
Merry, F. C., 578
Meyer, Ernest L., 467
Miami Co., Ohio, 654
Michie, Peter S., 1214, 1268, 1298, 1335, 1344-1345
Michler, Nathaniel, 868, 1355
Middlesex Co., Conn., 63
Middlesex Co., Mass., 316
Middlesex Co., N. J., 455-457
Midland Co., Mich., 353-354
Mifflin Co., Pa., 775, 782
Milam Co., Tex., 1076
Mille Lacs Co., Minn., 374
Miller, A. B., 196
Miller, D. L., 1386
Mills Co., Tex., 1077
Milwaukee Co., Wis., 1430-1432
Miner Co., S. Dak., 861
Minnehaha Co., S. Dak., 862
Minto, George, 163
Mirick, W. A., 449
Missaukee Co., Mich., 346
Mississippi Co., Ark., 8
Mitchell, William L., 109
Mitchell Co., Tex., 1078-1079
Mobile Co., Ala., 5
Modoc Co., Calif., 27
Moessinger, George, 635
Moler, J. Douglass, 606
Monahon, Michael M., 775
Monmouth Co., N. J., 458-459
Monongalia Co., W. Va., 1399
Monroe Co., Mich., 347-348
Monroe Co., N. Y., 518-520
Monroe Co., Ohio, 655
Monroe Co., Pa., 776
Monroe Co., W. Va., 1400
Monroe Co., Wis., 1433
Montcalm Co., Mich., 349
Monterey Co., Calif., 28
Montgomery Co., Ind., 159
Montgomery Co., Ky., 239
Montgomery Co., Md., 298-299, 1289
Montgomery Co., N. Y., 521
Montgomery Co., Ohio, 656-658
Montgomery Co., Pa., 777
Montgomery Co., Tenn., 877
Montgomery Co., Tex., 1080
Montgomery Co., Va., 1304-1307
Montour Co., Pa., 730
Moody Co., S. Dak., 863
Moore, I. B., 473
Moore, Isaac W., 744, 1190
Moore, P. N., 231
Mora Co., N. Mex., 470
Morehouse Parish, La., 258-259

Morehouse, Sisson & Co., 404
Morgan, Benjamin, 463
Morgan, F. A., 1435, 1446
Morgan, F. B., 1424, 1446
Morgan Co., Ky., 239
Morgan Co., Mo., 403
Morgan Co., Ohio, 659
Morgan Co., W. Va., 1401
Morris, J. W., 956, 1159
Morris, William E., 715, 777
Morris Co., N. J., 460
Morris Co., Tex., 1081
Morrison, John, 706, 718, 720
Morrison, Samuel, 631
Morrow Co., Ohio, 617, 660
Morse, G. W., 162
Morton, ---, 1360
Morton, L., 627
Mortson, O. C., 413
Moses, J. R., 846
Moss, James E., 280
Moss, Thomas B., 94
Motley Co., Tex., 1082
Mowry, Andrew S., 312-313, 621, 650, 683, 1442
Multnomah Co., Oreg., 694
Murphy, E. J., 524, 629
Murphy & Bolanz, 945
Murray Co., Minn., 378
Muskegon Co., Mich., 352
Muskingum Co., Ohio, 661

Nabers, J. A., 1164-1165
Nacogdoches Co., Tex., 1083
Nansemond Co., Va., 1283, 1308-1310
Nantucket Co., Mass., 306
Napa Co., Calif., 29-30
Nash, G. V., 1424, 1435, 1446
Nash, Joseph D., 143, 154, 326-328, 333, 343
Nash, W. F., 1435
Navarro Co., Tex., 1084
Neal, William, 147
Neff, James, 700
Nelson Co., Va., 1206-1208, 1311
Nevada Co., Calif., 31
New Castle Co., Del., 70-71
New Haven Co., Conn., 64-65
New Kent Co., Va., 1312
New London Co., Conn., 66
New York & Texas Land Co., 1042
Newberry Co., S. C., 841
Newman, N., 97
Newport Co., R. I., 827-829
Newton, John C., 1009, 1095, 1108
Niagara Co., N. Y., 522-523
Nicholas Co., W. Va., 1402
Nichols, B., 483
Nichols, George, 1386
Nichols & Gorman, 591
Nicollet Co., Minn., 379
Niederheiser, F. L., 598
Noble Co., Ind., 161
Nodaway Co., Mo., 404
Nohl, W. S., 1411
Nolan Co., Tex., 1085-1086
Noll (E. P.) & Co., 394, 592, 1381
Noll, John B., 655
Norfolk, L. H., 700
Norfolk Co., Mass., 317-318
Norfolk Co., Va., 1309, 1313, 1333
Norfolk Co., Va. Board of Supervisors, 1313
Norman, Okla., Democrat-Topic, 691
Northampton Co., N. C., 589, 1269

Northampton Co., Pa., 778-780
Nottoway Co., Va., 1314-1315
Nueces Co., Tex., 1087
Nugent, F. J., 47
Nunan, Philip, 597, 618, 642

Oakland Co., Mich., 350, 365
O'Beirne, P., 644, 668, 684
O'Beirne (P.) & Co., 144
O'Beirne & Boell, 644
O'Byrne, P., See O'Beirne, P.
Ocean Co., N. J., 461
Oceana Co., Mich., 351
O'Conner, James, 1292
O'Connor, R. F., 501, 543, 555
Oglethorpe Co., Ga., 94
O'Hea, Richard A., 389
Ohio Co., Ind., 162
Ohio Co., Ky., 231
Ohio Co., W. Va., 1386, 1403
Oldham Co., Tex., 1088
Oltmanns, C. W., 1311
Oneida Co., N. Y., 524-525
Onondaga Co., N. Y., 526-530
Ontario Co., N. Y., 531-534
Opperman, J., 773
Orange Co., Calif., 25, 32
Orange Co., Fla., 81
Orange Co., N. Y., 535-538
Orange Co., N. C., 590
Orange Co., Tex., 1089-1090
Orange Co., Vt., 1188
Orange Co., Va., 1316-1321
Orleans Co., N. Y., 523, 539
Orleans Co., Vt., 1189
Osborn, D. S., 68
Osborn, H. C., 67-68
Oskaloosa, Iowa, Weekly Herald, 198
Ostness, A. M., 844
Oswego Co., N. Y., 540
Otero Co., N. Mex., 471
Otey, W. N. P., See Otey, William Newton Mercer
Otey, William Newton Mercer, 1339-1341
Otley, J. W., 440, 454, 456, 464, 487, 498
Otley, Van Derveer & Keily, 465
Otsego Co., N. Y., 541-542
Ottawa Co., Mich., 352
Ottawa Co., Ohio, 618, 648
Ouachita Parish, La., 260-261
Ouellette, L. P., 1378
Overman, A. C., 147
Oxford Co., Maine, 271

Page, J. L., 275
Page, J. O., 497
Page, J. Q., 265
Page, W. B., 231
Page Co., Va., 1345
Painter, S. M., 723-724
Palmer, C., 1438, 1445
Palo Pinto Co., Tex., 1091-1093
Panhandle Abstract Co., 1031
Panola Co., Tex., 1094
Parker Co., Tex., 1095-1096
Parry, William, 441-442
Paschall, Thomas H., 802
Passaic Co., N. J., 438
Patrick Co., Va., 1322
Pattengill, G. Delevan, 1419
Pattison, H. A., 741-742
Pattison, Thomas, 142

Patton, J. Houston, 1329
Paul, Hosea, 679
Paulding Co., Ga., 95
Payne, Byron S., 848, 860
Peck, A. Y., 479, 519, 523, 529, 534, 576, 645, 673, 688
Peck, I. D., 479, 519, 523, 529, 534, 576
Peck, John S., 1217
Peckham, S. C. B., 1183
Peckham, William C., 174
Pecos Co., Tex., 1097
Peelor, David, 756
Peet, Anne Olmstead, See Peet, Annie Olmstead
Peet, Annie Olmstead, 536, 541
Pegg, S.M., 832
Pendleton, S. T., 1353
Pendleton Co., W. Va., 1404
Pennington, J. T., 45
Penobscot Co., Maine, 272
Peoria Co., Ill., 128
Perris, William, 504
Perry, C. N., 24
Perry Co., Ind., 163
Perry Co., Ohio, 662
Perry Co., Pa., 782
Peterson, E. Frank, 378, 385, 843-850, 852-853, 855-856, 858, 860-861, 863-865, 867
Peterson, William A., 370
Pettibone, D. A., 353-354
Pettis Co., Mo., 405
Peyton, G., 1200
Philadelphia Co., Pa., 783-784
Phillips, William, 91
Pickaway Co., Ohio, 663
Pierce Co., Wash., 1376
Pierce Co., Wis., 381
Pike Co., Ill., 129
Pike Co., Pa., 785-786, 818
Pima Co., Ariz., 6
Pima Co., Ariz. Board of Supervisors, 6
Pioneer Press Co., 382
Piscataquis Co., Maine, 273
Pitkin Co., Colo., 55
Pittman, Daniel, 91
Platen, Charles G., 85-86
Plumas Co., Calif., 33
Plumb, H. S., 597
Plummer, Frederic G., 1376
Plymouth Co., Mass., 319
Pocahontas Co., W. Va., 1405
Pointe Coupee Parish, La., 254
Polk Co., Fla., 82
Polk Co., Iowa, 201-203
Polk Co., Tex., 1098-1099
Pollock, T. H., 416
Pomeroy, A., 445, 483, 519, 525, 576, 705, 719, 726, 728, 732, 736, 774, 817
Pomeroy (A.) & Co., 752, 798
Poorman, Daniel, 208
Portage Co., Ohio, 664
Potter Co., Pa., 787-788
Potts, H. S., 380
Powel, R. M., 101
Powhatan Co., Va., 1323-1324
Poyner, Digges, 1339-1341
Prairie Co., Ark., 9
Preble Co., Ohio, 665-666
Presidio Co., Tex., 1026, 1100
Pressler, Charles W., 920, 970, 977, 982, 1014, 1016, 1048, 1114, 1143, 1154, 1174
Pressler, Herman, 932, 949, 1064, 1093, 1095, 1113, 1149, 1159, 1167, 1172

Preston Co., W. Va., 1406
Price, Jacob, 70
Prince Edward Co., Va., 1325-1327
Prince Edward Co., Va., Board of
    Supervisors, 1327
Prince George Co., Va., 1328-1332
Prince Georges Co., Md., 300-302
Prince William Co., Va., 1251, 1255
Princess Anne Co., Va., 1333
Prindle, A. B., 581, 701
Providence Co., R. I., 830
Prowers Co., Colo., 56
Pueblo Co., Colo., 57
Pulaski Co., Ark., 10
Pulaski Co., Va., 1368
Punnett Bros., 17, 30, 46
Purdy, C. T., 1447
Putnam Co., Ind., 164
Putnam Co., N. Y., 543
Putnam Co., Ohio, 667

Queens Co., N. Y., 505-506, 510,
    512, 544

Racine Co., Wis., 1434-1435
Rainey, Charles T., 704, 754
Rains Co., Tex., 1101-1103
Rakestraw, Joseph, 818
Ramsey, Henry J., 855
Ramsey Co., Minn., 380-381
Rand, J. B. G., 229
Randall, G. A., 1438, 1445
Randolph, J. Innes, 1221, 1247,
    1294, 1306
Randolph Co., Ind., 165
Randolph Co., W. Va., 1407
Rapides Parish, La., 244
Rappahannock Co., Va., 1242, 1255,
    1334-1335
Ratcliffe, John G., 177
Rauch, J. D., 138
Raynolds, W. F., 285
Rea, Samuel M., 70, 462, 480-481,
    498, 700
Rea & Otley, 514
Red River Co., Tex., 1104-1105
Redd, James T., 1282
Redding, T. B., 1434, 1440
Redwood Co., Minn., 382
Rees, Hugh, 1352
Rees, James H., 103
Refugio Co., Tex., 1106
Reily & Co., 393
Remington, T. J. L., 136
Rensselaer Co., N. Y., 545-546
Reynolds, Thomas, 1287
Reynolds & Darling, 218
Rice, E., 1183
Rice, S. H., 21
Richards, Henry M., 708-709
Richie, W. W., 160
Richland Co., Ohio, 668
Richland Co., S. C., 842
Richland Parish, La., 251
Richmond Co., N. Y., 547-554
Rickey, Joseph M., 643
Ricksecker, L. E., 44
Riddle, James N., 1380
Riecker, Paul, 38
Riecker, Huber & Mench, 38
Riley & Hoffman, 751
Riniker, Henry, 127
Roanoke Co., Va., 1223, 1336-1338
Roberts, W. M., 652

Roberts Co., Tex., 1107
Robertson, C. G., 304
Robertson, S. B., 245
Robertson Co., Tex., 1108
Robins, James B., 305
Robinson, ---, 1311
Robinson, F. B., 666
Rock Co., Wis., 1436
Rockbridge Co., Va., 1339-1343
Rockingham Co., N. H., 432-434
Rockingham Co., Va., 1344
Rockland Co., N. Y., 538, 555
Rockwall Co., Tex., 1033, 1109-1110
Roe, F. B., 719, 728
Roessler, A. R., 910, 933, 994,
    1001, 1019, 1056, 1122
Rogers, D. D., 83
Rogerson, A. E., 524, 545, 556,
    629
Rollandet, Edward, 470
Rooney, W. T., 1426
Roskruge, George J., 6
Ross, S., 787
Ross Co., Ohio, 669
Rowan, V. J., 23
Rowe, S. J., 1124, 1152-1153
Rowland, H. A., 220
Rowley & Peterson, 844, 854, 858,
    866
Rullmann, John D., 897-899
Rumbough, G. P. C., 10
Rummerfield, B. F., 391
Rumsey, William D., 414
Runnels Co., Tex., 1111-1113
Rush Co., Ind., 166-167
Rusk Co., Tex., 1114
Russell, F. D., 1055
Russell, R. R., 808
Rutherford Co., Tenn., 878
Rutland Co., Vt., 1190

Sabine Co., Tex., 1115-1116
Sacramento Co., Calif., 34
Sagadahoc Co., Maine, 274
Saginaw Co., Mich., 353-355
St. Clair Co., Ill., 130-131
St. Clair Co., Mich., 344
St. Croix Co., Wis., 381
St. Joseph Co., Ind., 168
St. Joseph Co., Mich., 356-357
St. Landry Parish, La., 262
St. Lawrence Co., N. Y., 556
St. Louis Co., Mo., 406-407
St. Martin Parish, La., 254, 262
Salem Co., N. J., 462
Saline Co., Mo., 408
Salt Lake Co., Utah, 1179
San Diego Co., Calif., 35
San Jacinto Co., Tex., 1117-1119
San Joaquin Co., Calif., 36
San Mateo Co., Calif., 37
San Patricio Co., Tex., 1120-1121
San Saba Co., Tex., 1122-1123
Sanborn Co., S. Dak., 864
Sandow, George, 11
Sandusky Co., Ohio, 648, 670-671
Sanford, G. P., 169, 172, 682, 685
Sanilac Co., Mich., 358
Santa Barbara Co., Calif., 38
Santa Clara Co., Calif., 39
Santa Clara Co., Calif. Board of
    Supervisors, 39
Santa Cruz Co., Calif., 40
Santa Fe Co., N. Mex., 472
Saratoga Co., N. Y., 557
Sargent Co., N. Dak., 592

Sauk Co., Wis., 1437
Saunders, J. G., 593
Schaeffer, J. S., 449
Schaerff & Bro., 406
Schenectady Co., N.Y., 558
Schleicher Co., Tex., 1124
Schleis, A. M., 1426
Schofield, John, 296
Schoharie Co., N. Y., 559
Schooley, David, 768
Schütze, E., 882, 886, 927, 1018,
    1145
Schultz, William P., 98
Schuyler, James D., 35
Schuyler Co., N. Y., 560
Schuylkill Co., Pa., 789-793
Scioto Co., Ohio, 672
Scott, David, 717
Scott, James D., 573, 763, 792-793,
    1190, 1245
Scott, Joshua, 758, 760-761, 763
Scott, Mark D., 859
Scott, Walter, 792-793
Scott Co., Iowa, 204
Scott Co., Ky., 241
Searles, James M., 388
Sedgwick Brothers & Stilson, 178
Seevers, Byron V., 198
Semple, E. A., 1248
Seneca Co., N. Y., 479, 561-563
Seneca Co., Ohio, 673-675
Shackelford, H. B., 47
Shackelford Co., Tex., 1125
Shapard, Stevens & Co., 906
Shasta Co., Calif., 41
Shaw, William R., 269, 274
Shaw & Cunningham, 620
Shawassee Co., Mich., 328
Sheafer, P. W., 791
Shearer, W. O., 288, 572, 825
Sheboygan Co., Wis., 1438
Shelby Co., Ind., 169
Shelby Co., Ohio, 676
Shelby Co., Tenn., 879
Shelby Co., Tex., 1126-1127
Shenandoah Co., Va., 1345
Shepherd, Fred. A., 34
Sherburne Co., Minn., 374
Sherman, James M., 816
Sherman, R. M., 169, 172
Shields, J. B., 458, 460, 489, 502,
    556
Shipman, Abraham, 781
Shoemaker, A., 148
Short, Harold C., 219
Short, William, 312-313
Shütze, E., See Schütze, E.
Sidney, J. C., 283, 446, 491, 537,
    549, 700
Sidney & Neff, 526-527, 577, 699
Silver Bow Co., Mont., 415
Simmons, H. H., 645, 673, 688
Sims, B., 1209
Sisemore, Willis, 228
Siskiyou Co., Calif., 42
Siverd, Eli F., 323-324, 327, 333,
    343-344, 348, 356, 364
Skene, Frederick, 547
Skinner, J. L., 69
Skinner, R. J., 175, 657
Skinner & Kenyon, 625
Small, Daniel, 722, 758, 775, 824
Smith, A. A., 27
Smith, A. M., 1307
Smith, Charles T., 60, 65, 568
Smith (D. R.) & Co., 306, 319
Smith (E. W.) & Co., 178, 1248
Smith, Eneas, 489

Smith, George, 739
Smith, George M., 145
Smith (H. & C. T.) & Co., 63, 315
Smith, Horace, 60, 65, 568
Smith, J. A., 188
Smith, J. L., 83, 91, 749, 812-813, 836, 1363, 1368, 1395
Smith (J. L.) & Co., 278
Smith (John L.) & Co., 309
Smith, Magill, 1367
Smith, Robert Pearsall, 493, 521, 568, 573, 599, 715, 738, 1277-1278, 1287
Smith, Roscoe W., 536
Smith, Thomas, 734, 801, 823
Smith, W. A., 1339-1341
Smith, W. B., 953, 1094
Smith, William P., 1288
Smith & Bartlett, 435
Smith & Bumstead, 316, 318
Smith & Coffin, 432-433
Smith & Gillett, 514
Smith & Ingraham, 311
Smith & Morley, 310, 426-427, 436
Smith & Peavey, 423-425, 431
Smith & Stroup, 98, 401
Smith & Wistar, 70, 440, 462, 777
Smith Co., Tex., 1128
Smith, Gallup & Co., 225, 307, 457, 469, 546, 779
Smith, Gallup & Hewitt, 701, 782
Smith, Gallup & Holt, 459
Smith, Mason & Co., 428-430
Smyth Co., Va., 1346
Snedecor, V. Gayle, 2-3
Snyder, F. M., 108
Snyder, L. M., 101
Snyder (L. M.) & Co., 107
Snyder Brothers, 101
Solano Co., Calif., 43
Somerset Co., Maine, 275
Somerset Co., N. J., 463-465
Somerset Co., Pa., 794-797
Somervell Co., Tex., 1129
Sommers, S. L., 1246-1247, 1328-1329, 1331
Sonoma Co., Calif., 44
Soule, G. G., 822
Southampton Co., Va., 1330, 1332
Southgate, W. B., 871
Southgate (W. W.) & son, 871
Southwestern Map Co., 216
Southwick, Joseph, 269, 274, 735
Spafford, O., 731
Spicer, Wells, 182
Spink Co., S. Dak., 865
Spoon, William L., 582
Spotsylvania Co., Va., 1318-1319, 1347-1355
Stackhouse, J. W., 527
Stafford Co., Va., 1356-1361
Stahlberg, A. J., 22
Stairs, W. H., 156
Stakemann, M., 905, 960, 963, 987, 1013, 1026, 1068, 1079, 1086, 1100, 1141
Stanford's Geographical Establishment, 1352
Stansbie, Alexander C., 462
Stark Co., N. Dak., 593
Stark Co., Ohio, 677-678
Starke Co., Ind., 170
Starr Co., Tex., 1130
Steele Co., Minn., 383
Steinson, J. A., 385, 845
Stephens, James M., 283
Stephens Co., Tex., 1131-1132
Stephenson Co., Ill., 132

Sterling Co., Tex., 1133
Steuben Co., Ind., 171
Steuben Co., N. Y., 564
Stevens, E. M., 854, 858
Stevens, F. W., 906
Stevens, Frank B., 845, 852-854
Stevens, Homer W., 845, 849, 854
Stevens Co., Wash., 1377
Stickney, J. K., 858
Stinson, D. S., 275
Stoddart & Everett, 613
Stokes, M. W., 168
Stoll & Thayer Co., 25
Stone, C. K., 519, 576
Stone, Cyrus, 673
Stone & Stewart, 581
Stone & Titus, 146, 149, 645, 688
Stonewall Co., Tex., 1134
Story Co., Iowa, 205
Stout, J. W., 328
Strafford Co., N. H., 435
Strahan, Charles Morton, 88
Stratton, David, 388
Street, Sam, Dallas, Tex., 946
Street, Sam, Dalton, Ga., 96
Street, Samuel M., 98
Strickland, Thomas C., 411-412
Stringfellow, U. K., 637
Strong, J. M., 945
Strother, D. H., 1380
Strum, G. P., 1211
Sturdevant, W. H., 768
Suffolk Co., N. Y., 565
Sullivan Co., N. H., 435
Sullivan Co., N. Y., 566
Sullivan Co., Pa., 798
Summit Co., Ohio, 679
Sumner Co., Tenn., 880
Sundy, C. F., 846, 848, 852-853
Surry Co., Va., 1330, 1332
Surveyor General's Office, Santa Fe, N. Mex., 471
Susquehanna Co., Pa., 799
Sussex Co., N. J., 466
Sussex Co., Va., 1330, 1332
Sutter Co., Calif., 45-46
Sutton Co., Tex., 1135-1136
Sweeney, Frank R., 1157
Sweet, Homer D. L., 529-530
Swensson, J. A., 250
Swisher, James, 605
Sykes, George, 441-442
Sykes & Gwathmey, 1313

Taber, A., 308
Taber, C., 308
Tackabury, Rowley & Co., 867
Taggart, Thomas, 304
Taintor (S. & R. S., Jr.) & Co., 513
Taintor, Dawson & Co., 496, 571
Talbot Co., Md., 303
Tanner, Henry S., 790, 795
Tarrance, James, 173
Tarrant Co., Tex., 1137-1139
Tate, George W., 590
Tatham, William, 363
Tator, W. J., 523, 529
Taylor, Robert, 284
Taylor, Yardley, 1287
Taylor Co., Tex., 1140-1141
Tehama Co., Calif., 47
Tensas Parish, La., 263-264
Terrell, O. O., 932, 967, 985, 1016, 1119, 1143, 1154, 1172

Texas. General Land Office, 881-896, 900-904, 907-909, 911-913, 915, 917-927, 929-932, 934-936, 938-944, 947-950, 952-956, 958-959, 961-962, 964-968, 970-971, 973-980, 982-986, 988-993, 995-1000, 1002-1004, 1006-1012, 1014-1018, 1020-1025, 1027, 1029-1030, 1032, 1034-1041, 1043-1044, 1046-1055, 1057-1067, 1069-1078, 1080-1085, 1087-1091, 1093-1096, 1098-1099, 1102-1103, 1105-1111, 1113-1116, 1118-1121, 1123-1130, 1132-1136, 1138, 1140, 1142-1147, 1149-1163, 1166-1169, 1171-1178
Texas & Pacific Land Office, 1100
Texas & Pacific Railway Co., 916, 951, 957, 960, 969, 972, 1045, 1092, 1101, 1104, 1131, 1137, 1170
Texas Land & Immigration Co. of New York, 910, 933, 994, 1001, 1019, 1122
Thielepape, George J., 1011, 1129
Thomas, B. F., 397
Thomas, J. C., 1382
Thompson, M. H., 120
Thompson (M. H.) & Brother, 125, 184
Thompson & Everts, 100, 187, 190, 195
Throckmorton, S. R., Jr., 29
Throckmorton Co., Tex., 1142-1143
Thweatt, J. G., 9
Tiffany, J. M., 477
Tilden, S. D., 721, 769
Tillson, Oliver J., 569-570
Tioga Co., N. Y., 567
Tioga Co., Pa., 800
Tippecanoe Co., Ind., 172
Titus, C. O., 158, 167, 169, 172, 479, 519, 523, 525, 529, 534, 576, 601, 603, 638, 658
Titus, Clarence, 673
Titus Co., Tex., 1144
Todd Co., Minn., 384
Tolland Co., Conn., 67
Tom Green Co., Tex., 1145-1147
Tompkins Co., N. Y., 568
Torrey, Hiram J., 475
Torrey, Jason, 818
Tower, L. L., 1377
Towson, James W., 619
Tracy & Rutt, 392
Traill Co., N. Dak., 594
Travd [i.e., Izard], Walter, 1223
Travis Co., Tex., 1148-1149
Trcziyulny, Charles, 727
Treat, S. Willard, 479, 483, 523, 529, 534, 705, 732, 774, 817
Tremble, A. V., 481
Trempealeau Co., Wis., 1439
Treveres, J. J., 76, 82
Trimble, A. V., 480
Trine, Z. V., 57
Trinity Co., Calif., 48
Trinity Co., Tex., 1150
Trommlitz, George, 56
Truesdell, J. M., 122
Trumbull Co., Ohio, 680
Trumpbour, Jacob, Jr., 499
Tucker, M. G., 1435, 1439, 1446
Tucker, T. B., 148
Tucker, Thomas, 1409
Tulare Co., Calif., 49
Tulare Co., Calif. Board of Supervisors, 49
Turner Co., S. Dak., 866

Tuscarawas Co., Ohio, 681-682
Tuscola Co., Mich., 353-354, 359
Tuttle & Co., 753
Tyler, M. H., 1430, 1442
Tyler Co., Tex., 1151-1153
Tyler Co., W. Va., 1408

Ufford, E. A., 844
Ulster Co., N. Y., 569-571
Underwood, Eugene, 231
Union Co., N. J., 467
Union Co., Ohio, 683
Union Co., Pa., 801-802
Union Co., S. Dak., 867
U.S. Army. Arkansas Dept. Topographical Bureau, 7
U.S. Army. Bureau of Topographical Engineers, 298, 1394
U.S. Army. 8th Corps, 285
U.S. Army. Middle Dept., 285
U.S. Army. Office of the Chief of Engineers, 1214, 1268, 1298, 1335, 1344-1345
U.S. Army of the Potomac, 1355
Upshur Co., Tex., 1154

Vail, Lewis, 609
Van Buren Co., Mich., 324
Van Campen & Johnson, 228
Vance, Coffee & Pill, 873
Van Derveer, Lloyd, 443, 453-454, 456, 464-465, 539
Van Steenburg, B. B., 188
Van Vechten, James, 104-106, 135
Van Zandt Co., Tex., 1101, 1155
Varlé, Charles, 291, 1258
Vaughan, David, 486
Venango Co., Pa., 803-805
Ventura Co., Calif., 25
Vermillion Co., Ind., 173
Vernon Co., Mo., 409
Vickery, G. C., 55
Vignoles & Ravenel, 834
Vigo Co., Ind., 174
Vinten, Charles, 785
Vogel, L. G., 368
Volusia Co., Fla., 83
Von Erdmannsdorff, H., 401
Von Hasseln, J. H., 832-833
Von Leicht, Ferd., 18
Von Mittendorfer, M., 1056
Von Rosenberg, E., 889, 895, 936, 967
Vose (J. W.) & Co., 788

Waagner, Gustavus, 406
Wabash Co., Ind., 175
Wagner, M. C., 326
Wagner, Theodore, 11
Wagner, William, 759, 824
Wahkiakum Co., Wash., 1378
Waite, F. C., 219
Wake Co., N. C., 591
Wakefield, G. D., 274
Waldo Co., Maine, 276
Walker, Addison, 882
Walker, Edward L., 707, 797
Walker, Virgil L., 394
Walker Co., Ga., 96
Walker Co., Tex., 1156-1157
Walkup, W. B., 44
Waller Co., Tex., 1158-1159

Walling, Henry F., 63, 66, 132, 136, 174, 267-268, 271-273, 277, 306-320, 425, 428-429, 431, 436, 447, 457, 459, 469, 505, 533, 550, 574-575, 608, 621, 641, 650, 662, 669, 721, 729, 768-769, 776, 800, 826-827, 830, 1181-1185, 1187-1189, 1191, 1425, 1430, 1442
Walling, Henry F., Jr., 621
Walling & Gray, 3
Walling & Rice, 662
Walling, Rice & Moon, 608
Wallis, W. R., 230
Walpole & Smith, 180
Walworth Co., Wis., 1440-1441
Wapello Co., Iowa, 206-207
Ward, A. J., 828-829
Warner, A., 137, 146, 149, 158-159, 164, 167, 169, 172, 483, 636, 645, 673, 685, 688
Warner, C. S., 148, 151, 153, 165, 171, 445, 483, 600, 636, 645, 673, 676, 688, 701
Warner, George E., 191-192, 197, 206
Warner, L. C., 148, 151, 165, 676
Warner & Foote, 185, 202, 205, 209, 211, 366, 369, 372, 376, 383, 405, 1433
Warner & Higgins, 111
Warren, W. H., 1075
Warren Co., Ind., 146
Warren Co., Iowa, 208
Warren Co., Ky., 242
Warren Co., N. J., 468-469
Warren Co., N. Y., 572
Warren Co., Ohio, 684-685
Warren Co., Pa., 806-814
Warren Co., Va., 1240, 1345
Warwick Co., Va., 1369
Washburn, A. E., 259
Washburn, W. M., 257
Washington & Lee University. Board of Survey, 1213, 1296
Washington College, Va., See Washington & Lee University
Washington Co., Ga., 97
Washington Co., Ky., 238
Washington Co., Maine, 277
Washington Co., Md., 291, 304
Washington Co., Minn., 381
Washington Co., Miss., 389
Washington Co., N. Y., 573
Washington Co., Ohio, 686
Washington Co., Pa., 703, 815-817
Washington Co., Tex., 1160
Washington Co., Vt., 1191
Washington Co., Va., 1362-1364
Washtenaw Co., Mich., 360-362
Watonwan Co., Minn., 385
Watson, J. J., 1434, 1440
Watson, J. V. B., 612
Watson, M. H., 612
Waukesha Co., Wis., 1442-1443
Waukesha, Wis., Weekly Press, 1443
Waupaca Co., Wis., 1444
Way, Palmer & Co., 729, 800
Wayne Co., Mich., 347, 363-365
Wayne Co., Mo., 410
Wayne Co., N. Y., 574-576
Wayne Co., Ohio, 687
Wayne Co., Pa., 818-819
Webb Co., Tex., 1161
Weber Co., Utah, 1180
Webster Co., Mo., 411-412
Wells, John, 794-795
Wenig, Emile, 342, 360-361, 476, 559

Wertman & Niederheiser, 598
West, M. D., 95
West Baton Rouge Parish, La., 254
West Carroll Parish, La., 251
West Point, Nebr., Republican-Advertiser, 417
Westbrook, J. B., 133
Westchester Co., N. Y., 577-578
Westmoreland Co., Pa., 703, 820-821
Weston, George F., 374
Wetzel Co., W. Va., 1409
Weyss, John E., 868
Wharton Co., Tex., 1162-1163
Wheelock, D. F. A., 813
White Co., Ill., 133
Whiteford, R., 64, 440
Whiteside, John E., 698, 706, 714, 716, 718, 727, 737, 743, 745, 789, 794, 815, 820
Whiteside Co., Ill., 134
Whitfield Co., Ga., 98
Whiting, H. A., 855
Whitley Co., Ind., 176
Whittekin, F. F., 750
Wigram, John, 486
Wilbarger Co., Tex., 1164-1165
Wilbur, N. R., 523, 529
Wildy, J. H., 22
Will Co., Ill., 103, 135
Willard, Jacob, 148, 616, 626, 640
Willard, Kingman & McConahy, 176
Williams, A. T., 78-79
Williams (C. S.) & son, 632
Williams, Charles, 235
Williams, D. G., 765a
Williams, Jesse, 631
Williams & Dorr, 607
Williams Co., Ohio, 688
Williams, Dorr & Co., 677-678
Williamson, M. T., 879
Williamson, William, 855-856
Williamson Co., Tex., 1166-1167
Williard, J. G., 609
Willis, Robert H., 418
Willits, W. C., 53
Wilson, C., 328, 333, 343
Wilson, George W., 334
Wilson, J. A., 1332
Wilson, James, Jr., 1418
Wilson, John, 117
Wilson, T. B., 928
Wilson Co., Tex., 1168
Windham Co., Conn., 68
Windham Co., Vt., 1192
Windsor Co., Vt., 1193-1195
Winkler Co., Tex., 1169
Winnebago Co., Ill., 136
Winnebago Co., Wis., 1445-1446
Winters (J. N.) & Co., 1112
Wise, ---, 1055
Wise Co., Tex., 1170-1172
Wislocki, S., 39
Witzel, P., 467
Wolfe, G. F., 753
Wolfe, John N., 620
Wood, John, 1196, 1224, 1259-1261, 1275-1276, 1304, 1310, 1322, 1362, 1365, 1379, 1383-1384, 1387-1390, 1392, 1396, 1398-1404, 1406-1408, 1410
Wood, William E., 538
Wood, William H., 452
Wood Co., Ohio, 648, 689
Wood Co., Tex., 1173-1174
Wood Co., W. Va., 1410
Wood Co., Wis., 1447
Woodbury Co., Iowa, 209
Woodford, E. M., 60, 68, 423-424

Woodford & Bartlett, 67, 660
Woodford Co., Ky., 225, 243
Woodland, James L., 884, 927, 979, 982, 1129
Woods, James, 674-675
Worcester Co., Md., 305
Worcester Co., Mass., 320
Worth Co., Iowa, 210
Wrigglesworth, E. T., 1421
Wrigglesworth, W. J., 1421
Wright, E. T., 24
Wright Co., Iowa, 211

Wyandot Co., Ohio, 690
Wyandotte Co., Kans., 221-222
Wynne, Amos, 977, 1050
Wyoming Co., N. Y., 579
Wyoming Co., Pa., 822
Wythe Co., Va., 1365-1368

Yamhill Co., Oreg., 695
Yandes, S. L., 148
Yates Co., N. Y., 580-581

Yazoo Co., Miss., 390
Yoder, R. A., 585
Yolo Co., Calif., 50-51
York Co., Maine, 278
York Co., Pa., 823-825
York Co., Va., 1312, 1369
Young Co., Tex., 1175-1177
Yuba Co., Calif., 52

Zavala Co., Tex., 1178